מבורכה

ArtScroll Judaica Classics®

Rabbi Nosson Scherman / Rabbi Meir Zlotowitz
General Editors

Reb Michel's

Published by

Mesorah Publications, ltd

Shmuessen

The inspiring ethical lectures of a patriarch of Mussar,
the Mashgiach of Mesivtha Tifereth Jerusalem,
RABBI MICHEL BARENBAUM

FIRST EDITION
First Impression . . . March 1996

Published and Distributed by
MESORAH PUBLICATIONS, Ltd.
4401 Second Avenue
Brooklyn, New York 11232

Distributed in Europe by	*Distributed in Israel by*
J. LEHMANN HEBREW BOOKSELLERS	**SIFRIATI / A. GITLER — BOOKS**
20 Cambridge Terrace	4 Bilu Street
Gateshead, Tyne and Wear	P.O.B. 14075
England NE8 1RP	Tel Aviv 61140
Distributed in Australia & New Zealand by	*Distributed in South Africa by*
GOLDS BOOK & GIFT CO.	**KOLLEL BOOKSHOP**
36 William Street	22 Muller Street
Balaclava 3183, Vic., Australia	Yeoville 2198, Johannesburg, South Africa

---

ARTSCROLL JUDAICA CLASSICS ®
Reb Michel's Shmuessen
© *Copyright 1996, by MESORAH PUBLICATIONS, Ltd.*
4401 Second Avenue / Brooklyn, N.Y. 11232 / (718) 921-9000

Typography by CompuScribe at ArtScroll Studios, Ltd.
4401 Second Avenue / Brooklyn, N.Y. 11232 / (718) 921-9000

Printed in the United States of America by Noble Book Press Corp.
Bound by Sefercraft Inc., Quality Bookbinders, Brooklyn, N.Y.

Dedicated to the memory
of our beloved father

ר׳ שלום יעקב ב״ר צבי ז״ל

נפטר א׳ טבת, תשי״ט

תנצב״ה

He came to these shores as a young man
in the early part of this century
and fought the battle for Torah and *Yiddishkeit*
against the overwhelming assimilationist trends
of his day.

His *tzedakah,* kindness and *chesed*
towards family and community
were his hallmark.

May the *tzedakah* given
to enable publication and distribution
of this important volume
be an uplifting for his *neshamah*.

יחיאל מיכל ועטרה דזייקאב ומשפחתם
Marvin and Atara Jacob and Family

מצבת זכרון

ר׳ אליהו ב״ר אליעזר ז״ל

נפטר כ״ח שבט

וזוגתו יעטע בת ר׳ משה הכהן ע״ה

נפטרה י׳ כסלו

❧❧

ר׳ יוסף ב״ר שמעון ז״ל

נפטר י״ג מנחם אב

וזוגתו בילא בת ר׳ גדליה ע״ה

נפטרה ח׳ אדר

❧❧

הילד אליהו ב״ר יוסף שמעון ע״ה

נפטר י״ב מנחם אב

תנצב״ה

הסכמת מרן הגאון רבי משה פיינשטיין זצוק"ל
לספר שיחות מוסר חלק א'

RABBI MOSES FEINSTEIN
455 F D R DRIVE
NEW YORK, N. Y. 10002
ORegon 7.1222

משה פיינשטיין
ר"מ תפארת ירושלים
בנוא יארק

בע"ה

[מכתב בכתב יד]

הנה ידידי ואהובי באהבת נפש עזה הרב הגאון המפורסם מוהר"ר מיכל בירענבוים שליט"א, אשר יחד אנחנו עוסקים במתיבתא תפארת ירושלים בתכלית ותועלת התלמידים בתורה ובראת ה' טהורה זה שלשים שנה, וכבר במשך השנים יצאו הרבה תלמידים גדולים בתורה ובראת שמים באופן גדול וגם שעוסקים בהרבצת תורה והרבה תלמידים שעוסקים בדרך ארץ אבל גדולים בתורה ובראת שמים והם לתפארת בישראל ומקדשים שם שמים בהנהגתם הנכונה ובמדותיהם הטובות, וכמעט כל התלמידים שלמדו במשך זמן הזה בכל אופן שנמצאים עתה ובכל מקום שנמצאים הם לתפארת הם ומשפחותיהם, וכן מקום אנחנו ומתפללים להשי"ת שער ביאת גואל צדק במהרה נזכה להרביץ תורה ובראת שמים לתלמידים חשובים, ובכח גדול מאד השפיע הגר"מ בירענבוים שליט"א במאמריו המוסרים לאמונה טהורה ולאהבת התורה והמצוות ומדות הישרות, וכל התלמידים שהיו במשך הימים והושפעו מהדברים והמוסרים לאמונה ולראת ואהבת השי"ת והתורה ומדות הטובות ומדות הישרות הפצירו בידידי הגר"מ שליט"א שידפיס מה שאפשר לפניו ממאמריו לזכות הרבים, ובודאי ענין גדול וחשוב הוא שיזכה הרבים בזה שידפיס וייצאם לאור עולם, וידוע ומפורסם אשר ידידנו הגר"מ בירענבוים שליט"א הוא אדם גדול וגאון בתורה ויש לו חד"ת בעניני הלכה הראוין לצאת לאור עולם, אבל לעת עתה הוא מדפיס מאמריו להתעוררות לאהבת התורה ולראת ה' אשר נחוץ מאד, ואני בברכה לידידי שיזכה להדפיס כל מאמריו וכל חדושיו לזכות הרבים ועי"ז באתי עה"ח בט"ו תמוז תשל"ז

נאום משה פיינשטיין

Author's Preface

מה אשיב לה׳ כל תגמולוהי עלי

How can I repay HASHEM
for all his kindness to me?
(*Psalms* 116:12)

It is now half a century that I have been privileged to serve as
Mashgiach at Mesivtha Tifereth Jerusalem. Of that time, 40 years
were spent working with the *talmidim* together with the Rosh
HaYeshiva, HaGaon HaRav Moshe Feinstein זצוק״ל.

I am truly honored that the Yeshiva's administration has
decided to publish an English translation of my Hebrew work,
Sichos Mussar, to make it more accessible to a broader reading
public.

It is my sincere wish that this *sefer* finds favor in the eyes of
the populace and that they study it, so that I may partake of
the communal merit, which is so important, particularly as I grow
older.

I appreciate the many efforts of the Yeshiva administration and
of my dear friend Rabbi Meir Zlotowitz, who spared no time
and effort to insure that this volume is beautifully produced. I
would also like to express my thanks to Rabbi Yaakov Blinder
and Rabbi Moshe Schapiro who translated the material from the
Hebrew.

Rabbi Michel Barenbaum

Rosh Chodesh Adar, 5756

Preface

The Yeshiva takes great pleasure in publishing this volume to commemorate the Mashgiach's fifty years — a *yovel* — of service to the yeshiva and its *talmidim*. The *shmuessen* in this volume, which are taken from his Hebrew *Sichos Mussar*, are examples of his combination of heart and mind. With such *shmuessen*, he molded our *talmidim* into the sort of people worthy to be regarded as students of my father זצ״ל. As a man who is great in both Torah and *mussar*, the Mashgiach has been able to convey the message of *gadlus* he not only espouses but embodies.

My father זצ״ל described him as "a great man and *gaon* in Torah whose *Chiddushei Torah* are worthy of publication"; and he spoke of the yeshivah's talmidim as people "who were influenced by the Mashgiach's words and his *mussar* toward *emunah*, fear and love of Hashem, the Torah and good character traits." Surely there can be no greater testimony to the Mashgiach's caliber as a *talmid chacham* and molder of talmidim.

As the Talmud (*Yoma* 86a) teaches: וְאָהַבְתָּ אֵת ה׳, *You shall love Hashem*; this means that you shall cause G-d's name to be loved through your behavior; that you should study Torah and Mishnah, serve Torah scholars, and deal pleasantly in personal relations. Then, what will people say about you? "Praiseworthy is his father who taught him Torah! Praiseworthy is his teacher who taught him Torah! Woe to those who did not study Torah! That person who studied Torah — see how beautiful are his ways, how proper are his deeds. Of him Scripture says, '[Hashem] said to me: You are my servant, O' Israel, for in you do I take pride.' "

Because the Mashgiach demonstrated this to our *talmidim*, my father זצ״ל always felt grateful to him. We cannot thank him enough.

We bless him with many long and healthy years to continue his work to make the Name of Hashem beloved and to inspire *talmidim* to follow in his footsteps.

To the *gaon* and *tzaddik*, our Mashgiach, we say, "Thank you!"

Rabbi Dovid Feinstein

In the week of שֶׁמֶן זַיִת זָךְ,
pure olive oil to light the lamp of Torah, 5756

◄§ Table of Contents

בראשית
Bereishis

The Mystery of Creation

As one begins learning *Parashas Bereishis*, one immediately realizes that the human mind cannot fully grasp the manner in which Hashem created the universe. For example, a corporeal being cannot possibly fathom how Hashem created matter from an empty void (יֵשׁ מֵאַיִן), and to the majority of people the profound kabbalistic principles contained in this *parashah* remain a complete mystery.

Nevertheless, it is our obligation to contemplate upon these passages, for they contain the foundation stones of the Torah. As the verse says, "The end of a matter is better [understood] from its beginning" (*Ecclesiastes* 7:8) — in order to gain greater understanding about ourselves and the world in which we live, we must delve deeply into "its beginning."

Let us begin by taking a closer look at the first *Rashi* on the *parashah*, which cites the well-known *Midrash*:

> "R' Yitzchak said: 'The Torah should have begun from the verse, "This month shall be for you the beginning of the months ..." (*Exodus* 12:2), since this is the first *mitzvah* that Israel was commanded to fulfill. Why, then, did the Torah begin with *Genesis*? Because He wished to "declare to His people the power of His works in order to give them the heritage of the nations" (*Psalms* 111:6): If the nations would one day say to Israel, "You are thieves, for you have occupied the homeland of seven nations," [Israel] would say to them, "The entire universe belongs to God. He created it, and He granted it to whomever He deemed fit. It was His desire to give it to them [the seven nations], and then it was His desire to take it from them and give it to us [Israel]!" ' " (*Bereishis Rabbah* 1:2).

Ramban finds this *Midrash* difficult to understand, since there seems to be a much more simple and straightforward reason why the Torah begins with *Genesis*: in order to establish the most fundamental tenet of faith, namely, that the universe did not always exist, but was created by Hashem. If a Jew does not believe in this principle, he is considered as though he had renounced the entire Torah. If so, *Ramban* wonders, how could R' Yitzchak have even entertained the possibility of omitting these *parashios*?

Ramban explains that R' Yitzchak certainly recognized the importance of this *parashah* and the fundamentals of faith contained therein. Nevertheless, since the Torah's description of how the universe came into being is so profound that it cannot be fully grasped by any mortal, R' Yitzchak could not understand why the Torah describes it in such great detail.

We do see, though, that the universe's genesis *is* explicitly mentioned in the Ten Commandments: "Remember the Sabbath day to sanctify it . . . *For in six days* HASHEM *made the heavens and the earth, the sea and all that is in them, and He rested on the seventh day"* (*Exodus* 20:8-11). This clearly proves that a Jew is expected to contemplate the universe's genesis despite all its unsolved enigmas, for otherwise, why would the Torah explain the reason for Shabbos in terms of the Six Days of Creation? The answer must be that *Parashas Bereishis* conveys a clear message that is accessible to all: It unequivocally declares to both Jew and gentile that Hashem is the Creator.

Similarly, the accounts of the Garden of Eden (*Gan Eden*) and the Flood, although shrouded in mystery, also contain important lessons that are accessible to all: namely, that sin incurs punishment. Adam and Eve sinned, and they were banished from the Garden of Eden; the inhabitants of the world sinned, and they were utterly destroyed. This serves as a warning to all nations that should they sin, Hashem will surely cast them into exile and give their homelands to another people.

But now, let us see what else can be learned from the universe's genesis. Let us begin by analyzing the Sages' following statement:

> "Six hundred and thirteen *mitzvos* were said to Moses . . . [King] David came and stood them upon eleven *mitzvos* . . . Habakkuk came and stood them upon one

— 'Through his faith, a righteous person shall live' "
(*Habakkuk* 2:4) (*Makkos* 23b).

Apparently, Habakkuk believed that the basis of the entire Torah is true "faith." Why?

Because when one truly believes that Hashem created the entire universe, one reaches certain logical conclusions: If Hashem created the entire universe, He must have had a reason; if He had a reason, existence must have a purpose; if existence has a purpose, it stands to reason that humanity is expected to play a major role in attaining it; if so, what is *my* role? What is expected of *me*? What is *my* purpose in life?

It was through a similar line of reasoning that Abraham discovered Hashem. The Sages say that Abraham pondered upon Creation, until he saw a palace going up in flames. Abraham thought, "If there is a palace, it must have an owner!" At that point, Hashem revealed Himself to Abraham.

Similarly, we learn from a *Midrash* that when Onkelos was deliberating whether to convert to Judaism, he went to consult Andrianus, who asked him, "What do you see in [Israel], the lowliest nation of all?" Onkelos replied, "Even the most undistinguished Jew believes in Creation and knows what is expected of him in this world."

Belief in Creation is also the underlying theme of the blessings we recite prior to eating or drinking. In order to instill into the depths of our being that "The earth and its fullness is HASHEM's" (*Psalms* 24:1), we recite a blessing to Hashem for every benefit we derive from the world He created. The Sages attributed so much importance to these blessings that they said, "Whoever derives pleasure from this world without reciting a blessing has robbed Hashem, for he does not recognize that the earth is His" (*Berachos* 35).

On a similar note, Isaiah rebuked Israel by saying, "The ox knows its owner, the ass, its master's trough. [But] Israel does not know, my nation does not reflect" (*Isaiah* 1:3). Implicit in the prophet's reproof is that a person would never sin were he to reflect upon the fact that Hashem created the universe, including life, mankind, and all its needs.

In the end of tractate *Makkos*, the Sages teach that whenever the *Beis Din* would lash transgressors, a lash made from donkey hide would be used. The Sages said, "[In essence,] Hashem said, 'Let the one who knows its master's trough [the donkey] come and collect from he who *does not* know his Master's trough [the transgressor]!' " What a degrading experience that must have been — to be lashed by a donkey! But this is exactly how a person who commits sin should feel, even nowadays when lashings are no longer administered. The principle conveyed by the prophet's words remains unchanged.

As we have said above, "The end of a matter is better [understood] from its beginning" (*Ecclesiastes* 7:8). So consider, ponder, reflect upon the purpose of the universe, the purpose of mankind, the purpose of *your own life*. Remember that all of Creation is renewed each day, as we say in the Morning Prayer Service (*Shacharis*), "In His goodness, He renews daily, perpetually, the world of Creation. As it is said: '[Give thanks] to Him Who makes the great luminaries, for His kindness endures forever.' " Do not forget that it is He Who sustains all of Creation at every moment.

With this understanding, we may clarify a difficult Talmudic passage:

> "R' Yochanan said: 'Whoever recites the blessing of the [New] Month in its appropriate time, it is considered as though he had welcomed the countenance of the Divine Presence. [For] here the verse says, "*This* month shall be for you the beginning of the months . . ." (*Exodus* 12:2), and there the verse says, "*This* is my God, and I will build Him a sanctuary" (ibid., 15:2). [Just as in the latter verse Israel merited to see the Divine Presence so clearly that they were able to point at it with their finger, so too, one who blesses the month shall merit to this degree of Divine revelation]' " (*Sanhedrin* 42a).

The obvious question to be asked at this point is why such a great reward is given to one who fulfills the *mitzvah* of sanctifying the new moon. Regarding no other *mitzvah* do the Sages say, "It is considered as though he had welcomed the countenance of the Divine Presence." Furthermore, the Sages went on to say:

> "The academy of Rabbi Yishmael taught: Had Israel not been privileged to greet the countenance of their Father in Heaven except for once a month, it would

have sufficed them" (ibid.). *Rashi* paraphrases as follows: "Had Israel not been commanded any other *mitzvah* but this one, which merits them to welcome the countenance of the Divine Presence once a month, it would have sufficed them."

Again, what is it about this *mitzvah* that gives it so much importance?

The answer is that when one acknowledges that Hashem is the Creator, and that He recreates all of existence each day, one has constructed the philosophical platform upon which the entire Torah stands. In order to enable the Jewish people to maintain this awareness, Hashem programmed into the laws of nature that the moon disappear and reappear once a month. This simulated act of matter-from-nothingness Creation puts a Jew's view of the world back into perspective and reaffirms his belief in Hashem's omnipotence. In this heightened spiritual state, he welcomes the countenance of the Divine Presence and merits the entire Torah.

In tractate *Sanhedrin* (38), the Sages explain that man was created last of all the creatures so that he should not falsely claim that he helped Hashem create the universe, and therefore fail to acknowledge that "there is none other than Him." Every creature in the universe must acknowledge that "there was no other than Him" in the universe's genesis, that the world's continuing existence is not due to any laws of nature or chance, but only because Hashem wills it to continue existing. One who truly grasps the concept "there is no other than Him" realizes that even moving one's little finger would not be possible were it not that Hashem had decreed it.

It is this absolute faith that is the foundation stone of the entire Torah.

Encountering Our Heavenly Father

It is customary to say the prayer *Aleinu Leshabei'ach* after reciting the Sanctification of the Moon (*Kiddush Levanah*). The *Biur*

Halachah (§426) suggests that this is done in order to dispel any notion that we are showing honor to the moon in its own right. We recite *Aleinu*, which reaffirms our belief in Hashem as the Creator and Master of all the forces of nature; our praise upon witnessing the marvels of nature are only a vehicle through which we arrive at a fuller appreciation of *Hashem's* role in controlling nature - as it says (*Isaiah* 40:26), "Lift your eyes on high and look [into the heavens]; Who created all these things?"

Perhaps we could offer another explanation for this custom. The Talmud (*Sanhedrin* 42a) says, "It was taught in the academy of R' Yishmael: Had Israel not been privileged to greet the countenance of their Father in Heaven except for once a month (at the Sanctification of the Moon) it would have sufficed them." Why is this considered to be such an awesome experience of "encountering our Heavenly Father"? Mankind, having been created at the end of Creation, never witnessed the phenomenon of Hashem creating something *ex nihilo* — creating matter from a void. In nature we tend to see new objects or living things as being "born" from some preexisting item or elements. The one phenomenon in nature which can be viewed as suggesting (in its outward appearance) the emergence of a completely new object where there was previously nothing at all is the appearance of the moon after it had *completely* disappeared from our sight for a time. This is the closest thing a human being can witness to the concept of Creation *ex nihilo*. This is why the Talmud considers the Sanctification of the Moon to be such a profound experience of confronting the glory of the Divine Presence (*Shechinah*). Perhaps, then, this is the reason why we close the ceremony with *Aleinu Leshabei'ach*, which stresses Hashem's role as the Creator of the Universe.

The Sin of Cain

Cain and Abel both brought offerings before Hashem — Abel, the shepherd, from his flock, and Cain, the farmer, from his crops. Hashem accepted Abel's offering, but was not pleased with that of Cain. We are not told why it was that Hashem rejected Cain's offering. *Rashi* explains that it was of inferior quality. *Chizkuni*, however, offers a different explanation — that Cain brought the offering after he had first partaken of the food himself, while Abel brought "of the *firstborn* of his flock." This is a significant difference. We find that the Torah obligates us to give over to Hashem the first fruits of the field (*bikkurim*) (see *Exodus* 23:19). Dedicating the very first fruits that emerge at the beginning of the season brings us to a more concrete realization that *everything* that grows in the field is by the grace of Hashem. If someone would dedicate a different portion of his crop to Hashem, it would allow for the feeling that "it is my strength and the power of my own hand that have acquired me this wealth" (*Deuteronomy* 8:17). Although Cain actually preceded his brother in bringing his offering to Hashem, he was nevertheless held accountable for his lack of sensitivity regarding this concept.

After Cain saw that Abel's offering was pleasing and his own was not, he became despondent with bitterness, and Hashem asked him, "Why has your countenance fallen?" (*Genesis* 4:6). *Sforno* explains that Hashem meant to impart a lesson to Cain. It was unreasonable for him to be jealous of his brother's favorable treatment, Hashem told him, for there was good reason why Cain's own offering had been rejected. The error Cain had made could still be easily rectified; there is always an opportunity to bring other offerings to Hashem, this time with the proper frame of mind. Whenever an oversight has been committed, it is not proper to dwell on one's mistake and become depressed by it; one should concentrate instead on how to go about righting the wrong. "If you improve yourself, you will be able to raise yourself up" (ibid., v. 7). Cain was told to ponder the causes of Hashem's reactions to both offerings and to draw the necessary conclusions about his own self-improvement. *Ramban* adds that Hashem actually told Cain that he was capable of "rising up" *above* his brother, for Cain was the older of the two, and was entitled to the birthright of the firstborn. "You can overcome [the urge to sin]," though it is constantly "crouched at the doorway" (ibid.) of your heart to tempt you to act improperly.

Hashem's communication to Cain proved to be of no avail, however, and Cain's jealousy only festered within him until he was driven to commit fratricide. From this episode we can see just how potent the power of jealousy is — "it can remove someone from the world" (*Avos* 2:11). The jealous heart blinds man to his own best interests and deafens him to the voice of reason, even when it comes from the mouth of Hashem Himself! A person's actions are, in a sense, determined by his strength of character. If he allows himself to be ruled by his passions and emotions, there is no limit to the depths to which he may descend. If, however, it is his intellect which gains prominence over his emotions, he will be able to follow the right course of action at all times. Thus, a person must be on constant guard to subordinate his emotions to his intellect.

We can also learn from the story of Cain and Abel the extent to which Hashem wants man to repent. After Cain's ruthless murder of his brother, Hashem asked him, "Where is Abel your brother?" *Rashi* explains that Hashem wished to supply him with an opportunity to admit his guilt and thus mitigate the harsh punishment that awaited him. Nevertheless, Cain merely responded with his famous retort, "Am I my brother's keeper?" trying, as it were, to "fool" Hashem into believing that nothing had happened. His trait of jealousy once again blinded Cain into deluding himself that he could escape Hashem's wrath with a lame excuse rather than through heartfelt contrition!

Adam's Environment

The *Midrash* says: " 'This is the account of the descendants of Adam — on the day that God created man, He made him in the likeness of God' (*Genesis* 5:1). An important Torah precept is: Do not say, 'Since I have suffered humiliation, let my companion suffer humiliation as well.' Know Whom you humiliate [when you commit transgressions] — as the verse says, 'on the day that God created man, He made him *in the likeness of God*'!'"

We tend to forget that mankind is in a fallen state. This is a terrible tragedy, for if we would only grasp what Adam was like prior to the sin of the Tree of Knowledge and compare this lofty image with our own lowly condition, we would keep well away from sin. We will now explain this concept in greater detail.

Hashem said, "Let us make man in Our image, after Our likeness" (ibid., 1:26). We are very fortunate for having been created in the likeness of God, and even *more* fortunate that we were informed of this fact. For had the Torah not revealed this information to us, it is very likely that we would never have discovered it by ourselves. And as *Ibn Ezra* said, "If a person does not know himself, how can he know his God?" The Sages confirm the importance of knowing one's spiritual roots in their explanation of how the Patriarchs managed to perceive the entire Torah before the revelation at Mount Sinai. According to the Sages, the Patriarchs deduced the entire Torah by looking inwards into their own beings and recognizing the Divine origins of their soul. Let us, then, also look inwards and recognize the Divine origins of our souls.

The Torah says, "And HASHEM God (יְ־ה־וֹ־ה אֱלֹהִים) formed the man of dust from the ground, *and He blew into his nostrils the soul of life*" (ibid., 2:7). In reference to this verse, *Ramban* writes, "By using the full Divine Name (יְ־ה־וֹ־ה אֱלֹהִים), the verse hints at the exalted nature of man's soul ... It did not originate from the elements ... but rather, it is the breath of the Almighty, from His own mouth ..."

Ramban affords us another glimpse at Adam's exalted spiritual roots in his commentary on *Genesis* 2:9. He insinuates that Adam was as compelled to fulfill Hashem's will as the angelic beings, which perceive Hashem so clearly that they cannot even *entertain the concept* of free will. Similarly, on verse 2:17, *Ramban* cites the Sages' statement, "Had Adam not sinned, he would never have died." He explains as follows: "The lofty soul provides eternal life, since the Divine essence which it contained at the time of Creation remains adhered to it forever ... However, when [Adam] committed the sin of the Tree of Knowledge, he became a mortal being. At the reception of the Torah [at Mount Sinai], the venom of the sin of the Tree of Knowledge ... ceased, and [Israel] merited to [regain] the spiritual stature of Adam prior to the sin."

Midrash Koheles depicts Adam's spiritual grandeur as follows: "When Hashem created Adam, he took him [and showed him] all the trees in the Garden of Eden. He said to him, 'See how beautiful and perfect are My deeds. Everything I created, I created for you. Make sure that you do not ruin and destroy My world!' "

And yet, despite Adam's lofty spiritual stature and his closeness to Hashem, somehow, he sinned. And what disastrous repercussions to himself and to the entire Creation!

> "To Adam He said: 'Because you listened to the voice of your wife and ate of the tree ... accursed is the ground because of you; through suffering shall you eat of it all the days of your life. Thorns and thistles shall it sprout for you, and you shall eat the herb of the field. By the sweat of your brow shall you eat bread until you return to the ground, from which you were taken: For you are dust, and to dust shall you return ...' So Hashem banished him from the Garden of Eden, to work the soil from which he was taken" (ibid., 3:17-23).

We cannot fathom what this must have meant to the angelic being called Adam. To be banished from Hashem's presence and see His perfect world ruined as a consequence of his own sin must have been harder for Adam to bear than a hundred deaths. To make matters worse, the aftereffects of his sin tarnished the spiritual purity of his own offspring, engendering the Generation of the Flood.

Nefesh HaChaim discusses the idea of realizing the horrific consequences of one's own sins: "The *Tanna* says, 'Know what is above you' — even though you do not see with your own eyes the awesome repercussions of your deeds, know for certain that everything that takes place in the Divine realms is due to you, and in accordance with your deeds. A person's heart should tremble within him! What great ruin and destruction he can cause through his wrongdoings!"

To illustrate the disastrous repercussions of sin, let us compare the present state of nature with that of the past: According to the *Midrash*, Cain and Abel were born on the very same day that Adam and Eve were created: Compare this swift birth with the discomfort experienced by women today during the nine months of pregnancy, a phenomenon which we take for granted. Similarly, the Sages teach that in the days of Shimon ben Shetach, so much rain fell that the grains of wheat grew as large as kidneys, and the grains of barley grew as large as olive pits. Shimon ben Shetach's generation preserved samples of this grain in order to show future generations the detrimental effects of sin. As the verse says, *"Your transgressions have diverted these things, your sins have withheld the good from you"* (*Jeremiah* 5:25; see *Taanis* 23). What great curses man brings upon himself through sin!

Similarly, in reference to the verse, "They heard the sound of HASHEM God manifesting itself in the garden toward evening; and the man and his wife hid from HASHEM God among the trees of the garden" (*Genesis* 3:8), the *Midrash* says: "[At first,] the essence of the Divine Presence dwelled in the lower world. When Adam sinned, it withdrew. When Cain sinned, it withdrew even more."

The Sages also teach that during Noah's generation, mankind's sins caused nature itself to become corrupted. In reference to the verse, "God saw the earth and behold it was corrupted, for all flesh had corrupted its way upon the earth" (ibid., 6:12), *Rashi* explains that humanity's immoral sexual conduct influenced the animals, until they, too, cohabited with other species. The *Midrash* adds that even the land "committed adultery" — the people would sow one type of seed, but the land would produce another.

What emerges from all this is that we, today, are living in a fallen reality. We tend to forget this fact. Time and again, we confuse our fallen state for the majestic environment which existed in the first days of Creation. However, *Parashas Bereishis* serves to remind us of our mistake. On a yearly basis, we are reminded of the damage we have inflicted upon ourselves and the entire universe through our transgressions. It is our responsibility to bear this in mind, and to rectify our deeds.

With this heightened awareness of the pristine state of the universe prior to the emergence of sin, we can well understand why scientists have found plant and mineral evidence which "proves" that the world is several million years old. Who can imagine the size of the plants which grew in the first days of Creation, the types of reptiles which roamed the earth, or the composition of the atmosphere during that era? Obviously, if we would measure the fossils of that exalted age with scientific instruments calibrated for our fallen reality, the results would not be very meaningful. Indeed, we might even come up with the preposterous theory that the world has been in existence for several million years!

The Importance of Honesty

The Torah says, "The earth had become corrupt before God; and the earth had become filled with robbery ... God said to Noah, 'The end of all flesh has come before Me, for the earth is filled with robbery through them; and behold, I am about to destroy the earth' " (*Genesis* 6:11-13).

In reference to this verse, the Sages said, "[In] a box full of sins, for which is one prosecuted first? Robbery. For even though [Noah's generation] committed numerous grave transgressions, 'the end of all flesh' came about as a consequence of robbery and theft" (*Sanhedrin* 108).

Ramban explains that the sin of robbery carries a harsher punishment than other transgressions because man instinctively knows that it is wrong. As the Sages said, "Had the Torah not [prohibited robbery], we would have learned [the prohibition] from the ant" (*Eiruvin* 100). Here, the Sages refer to the verse, "Lazy one, go to the ant, see its ways and become wise. It has no overseer, yet it lays stores of food throughout the summer" (*Proverbs* 6:6). The *Midrash* explains that once an ant has carried a particular piece of food, no other ant will touch it even though it has "no overseer" enforcing law and order. King Solomon's message is that mankind should learn from the ant and desist from committing theft.

From the severity of the punishment that befell Noah's generation, one would think that they committed gross acts of robbery. However, the *Midrash* teaches that they stole *less than the worth of a perutah* from one another, a crime so petty that it was not even subject to the authority of the courts. In answer to the question, "But why were the *victims* of theft also punished?" the *Midrash* explains that they, too, committed חמס, or iniquity — they berated too vociferously those who stole from them. For this crime, the entire world was destroyed!

Does this severe definition of חמס still apply today? Well, let us see how *halachah* defines חמס. In *Bava Metzia* (48) we learn that if a person conveys money to someone through an act of possession on a movable object, he may retract, since money is only acquired by physical possession. Even so, a person who retracts under such circumstances "will be punished by the One Who punished the Generation of the Flood." At first glance, it is difficult to understand why such an individual deserves to be punished, since according to the strict letter of the law, he did nothing wrong. Evidently, however, the answer is that the Torah's definition of justice is much more demanding than our own notions on the matter.

The Torah's strict definition of justice is also evident in *Parashas Lech Lecha*. Following Abram's victory over Chedorlaomer, the king who had captured the inhabitants of Sodom and seized their possessions, the king of Sodom said to Abram, "Give me the people and take the possessions for yourself" (*Genesis* 14:21). Even though the people and the possessions were rightfully his, Abram declined this offer by saying, "I lift up my hand to HASHEM, God, the Most High, Maker of heaven and earth, if so much as a thread to a shoestrap; or if I shall take from anything of yours!" (ibid., v. 22). Abram, however, appended his refusal by adding, "Only what the young men have eaten, and the share of the men who accompanied me: Aner, Eshcol, and Mamre — they will take their portion" (ibid., v. 24). The Sages say that Abram was held liable for this last clause, since, for a person of his spiritual stature, it was tantamount to robbery (*Chullin* 89).

Similarly, the Sages say that if a person does not return the greeting of someone whom he commonly greets in return, he has in effect committed an act of robbery. Who can claim to be innocent of these sins? As the Sages say, "Most people [are held accountable] for robbery" (*Bava Basra* 165).

The following account illustrates this point vividly:

> On one of his numerous trips, R' Israel Salanter decided to pay an unexpected visit to a former student. At the sight of the venerable Rabbi approaching his store, the

former student scrambled into an adjacent room in order to change into his Sabbath finery. In his haste, he neglected to close the money drawer . . .

R' Israel noticed the open money drawer as soon as he walked in. With mounting concern, he looked around and saw that he was all alone in the store. R' Israel thought to himself: "The Sages said that the majority of people are guilty of robbery and only a minority commit sexual transgressions. Nevertheless, out of concern for this small minority, they instituted the prohibition of *yichud*, or being alone with someone else's wife. How much more so must it be prohibited to stay alone in the same room with someone else's *money!*" Without a second thought, he jumped through the window.

How careful we must be in order to avoid committing robbery!

An employee's responsibility to his employer is also defined by the Torah in Jacob's address to Laban: "This is how I was: By day scorching heat consumed me, and frost by night; my sleep drifted from my eyes" (*Genesis* 31:40). If an employee falls short of these standards, it is very possible that he has committed an act of robbery. It is for this reason that the *Shulchan Aruch* rules that a day laborer may not tire himself by working extra hours at night, nor weaken his body by practicing self-denial.

The Sages attached so much importance to employees' responsibilities that they exempted them from the obligation to recite the first blessing over bread ("Blessed are You . . . Who brings forth bread from the earth") and the last blessing of Grace After Meals. Furthermore, the Sages ruled that if an employee is at work when it is time to recite the *Shema*, he may only interrupt his work to recite the first verse, but then proceed to recite the rest of the *Shema* while working.

It is a sad fact that robbery is a common occurrence in our daily lives, especially in our dealings with others. According to *Rambam*, the Torah prohibits stealing anything at all, even from a gentile — one who robbed a gentile must return the stolen object to its rightful owner. The *Haga'os Maimonios* cites a *Tosefta* that says, "A person who has robbed a gentile is obligated to return [the stolen object], for robbing a gentile is *a more severe sin* than robbing a Jew, since [one who robs a gentile] also desecrates the Name of Heaven."

The Torah is so strict regarding robbery that it even holds a person responsible for *the mere thought* of committing this sin. As *Ramban* explains, the verse, "And you shall not covet your fellow's wife, you shall not desire your fellow's house, his field, his slave, his maidservant, his ox, his donkey, *or anything that belongs to your fellow*" (*Deuteronomy* 5:18), prohibits entertaining certain thoughts and limits the range of a person's very emotions. Hence, we see that it is possible to commit robbery through mere thought. No wonder the Sages said, "The majority of people are guilty of robbery"!

The Sages teach that a person who deceives another through his speech, or in monetary matters, is also considered to have committed an act of robbery — by bringing anguish upon his victim he has effectively "stolen" his peace of mind. The prohibition against deceiving another person applies *even if it pleases the deceived party* . To illustrate, the Talmud recounts that R' Nachman once met R' Safra and Rava on the outskirts of town. R' Nachman evidently thought they had come to honor and welcome him, but R' Safra and Rava made a point of telling him that they had come for a different reason. Had they not corrected R' Nachman, they would have committed the transgression of גניבת הדעת (lit., "theft of the mind"), for as *Rashi* explains, R' Nachman would have felt indebted to them. From this we learn that merely causing someone to feel indebted to us is tantamount to an act of robbery.

The inherent difficulty in avoiding the sin of robbery and its prevalence among the Jewish people is evident in the phrasing of *Ne'ilah*, the prayer we utter at the close of Yom Kippur: "That Yom Kippur has been given to us, an end, a forgiveness, that we may desist from the robbery of our hands." Many of us unwittingly commit this sin simply because we remain ignorant of the Torah's definition of it. We continually make the mistake of using our own sense of judgment to determine what constitutes robbery. For this reason, we dismiss petty acts of theft as insignificant. The Talmud, however, says "He who robs even a *perutah*'s worth is regarded as though he had robbed [his victim's] soul." The only answer to the problem is to subjugate our frequently misguided ethical conceptions to the Torah's pristine codes of conduct.

The transgression of robbery is not restricted to interpersonal relationships. In various Talmudic passages, the Sages discuss the concept of "robbing" Hashem. For example, they said, "He who draws pleasure from this world without [reciting] a blessing robs Hashem and the Congregation of Israel." *Rashi* explains: "By committing transgressions, they [cause the] produce to be stricken, thereby impeding Hashem's benevolence to mankind."

Parashas Noah teaches the importance of preventing ourselves from committing robbery, and the dire consequences of committing this transgression. Let us become proficient in the Torah's definition of this sin, and take the necessary steps to prevent ourselves from unwittingly violating it.

The Merit of the Righteous

In reference to the verse, "For in seven more days' time I will send rain upon the earth . . ." (*Genesis* 7:4), the Sages ask, "What was the significance of these seven days? Rav said: They were the seven days of mourning over Methuselah — to teach you that the eulogies of the righteous delay the arrival of affliction" (*Sanhedrin* 108).

Ostensibly, the Sages meant that just as the merit of the righteous delays the arrival of affliction while they are alive, so too, the eulogies said in their honor delay the arrival of affliction after their death. The concept of the righteous' merit delaying impending destruction is implicit in the dialogue between Hashem and Abraham regarding the fate of Sodom, for Hashem conceded, "I will not destroy [Sodom and Gomorrah] *on account of the ten*" (*Genesis* 18:32).

Alternatively, the Sages' statement may be interpreted as follows:

Hashem does not desire to punish the wicked, but only that they repent. Hence, when there are righteous individuals in any given generation, the possibility always exists that the wicked will follow the righteous' example and return to the ways of the Torah. Hashem, therefore, withholds punishment and waits for the generation to repent. This reprieve continues even after the righteous have passed away, for the Sages said that also the *death* of the righteous atones for a generation's sins. How does the death of the righteous atone? By causing the rest of the generation to think, "If he, who was so righteous, was taken, Hashem's judgment must be truly awesome. It is time to repent for my sins!"

Hashem delayed the flood as long as Methuselah was still alive, and waited an additional seven days, until the end of the mourning period. Since the world still had not repented for their sins after this reprieve, it became clear to Hashem that they never would. Therefore, He unleashed the torrential waters upon the world.

On the other hand, some people's faith can actually be *weakened* by the death of righteous individuals. Just as hardship is said to remove the sins of an individual by bringing him closer to repentance, hardship may also drive a transgressor even further away from the ways of Hashem. A prime example of this was Elisha son of Avuyah, who renounced his faith when he saw the tongue of R' Chutzpis HaMeturgaman being dragged along the ground. Instead of concluding, "If such a righteous person was taken, Hashem's judgment must be truly awesome. I must repent for my sins," he concluded that "there is no judgment nor Judge in this world."

The Sages teach us that Esau was a victim of this pitfall. They infer this from the following verses:

> "Jacob simmered a stew, and Esau came in from the field, and he was exhausted.
> "Esau said to Jacob, 'Pour into me, now, some of that red stuff, for I am exhausted.'
> "Jacob said, 'Sell, as this day, your birthright to me.'
> "Esau responded, 'Look, I am going to die, so of what use to me is a birthright?' " (ibid., 25:30).

What prompted Esau to sell his invaluable birthright for a measly portion of red lentil stew? The Sages explain that as soon as Esau returned from the field, he noticed that Jacob was cooking lentil stew, a food that was then customarily served to mourners. Jacob informed Esau that their grandfather, Abraham the Patriarch, had passed away while Esau had been out in the field. Esau's faith in Hashem was shattered beyond repair by this news. He asked himself, "[How unjust!] The forces of retribution struck down *this* sage?" At that very moment, Esau renounced his belief in Divine reward and punishment, and proceeded to commit five severe transgressions (see *Bava Basra* 16).

From this we learn two crucial lessons: How important it is to continually fortify our faith in Heaven, and the extent to which we depend on Hashem's Divine assistance to guide us in the ways of holiness. Just as good fortune and prosperity can threaten one's faith in Hashem, so can hardship and destitution undermine one's system of belief.

The Importance of Peace

In reference to *Genesis* 11:9, *Rashi* asks:

> "Whose sin was greater — the Generation of the Flood, which *did not* plan a rebellion against God, or the Generation of the Dispersion, which *did?*
>
> "[The answer is that] the former, who committed robbery and contended with one another, [deserved] to be utterly destroyed in the Flood. In contrast, the latter, who dwelt amicably in brotherly love with one another, [were spared despite their blasphemies]. This demonstrates how hateful is strife and how great is peace!"

Regarding the importance of peace, the Sages said, "The Holy One, Blessed is He, found no vessel other than peace to contain blessing for Israel, as the verse says, 'Hashem will give might to His nation, HASHEM will bless His nation *with peace*'" (*Psalms* 29:11) (*Uktzin*).

Similarly, the *Midrash* says, "Great is peace! For even when the Jewish people worship idols, as long as they live peacefully with each other, Hashem, as it were, says, 'Because they are at peace with each other, I do not have control over them. As the verse says, "Ephraim has attached himself to idols — let him be" ' " (*Hosea* 4:17).

Tiferes Yisrael, on tractate *Uktzin*, cites the following passage from the Talmud as conclusive proof that peaceful coexistence does indeed restrain the forces of retribution from exacting punishment from idol worshipers:

> "Ahab did not leave a single mountain or hill in the Land of Israel upon which he did not erect an idol. Even so, they would go out to war and be victorious. The reason is that there was peace between them. For Obadiah had hidden 100 prophets [in a cave], yet when Elijah the Prophet stood on Mount Carmel and proclaimed, 'I alone remain a prophet to HASHEM,' not one person in the crowd informed on [Obadiah] by saying [to Elijah], 'You are a liar! [Obadiah has hidden 100 prophets in a cave!]' " (*Talmud Yerushalmi*, *Pe'ah*).

If this principle applies to transgressors, how much more does it apply to those who fulfill Hashem's will!

In contrast, the Talmud illustrates the negative consequences of strife, even when it is "for the sake of Heaven":

> "Once, the following incident took place in a synagogue in Tiberias: R' Elazar and R' Yossi differed in opinion with each other concerning the law of *muktzeh* on Shabbos. In their agitated state, they ripped the Torah scroll [they were learning from]. R' Yossi ben Kasma, who was there, declared, 'I will be very surprised if this synagogue does not become [a temple of] idol worship' " (*Yevamos* 96).

Indeed, we later learn that it did. This incident clearly illustrates the catastrophic repercussions of strife. Let us all internalize this lesson; let us pursue peace and avoid quarrel at all cost.

The Patriarchs —
Spiritual Role Models for All Time

The Torah is very effusive in its account of the Patriarchs' lives, to the degree that the Sages concluded, "The conversations of the Patriarchs' servants were more pleasing than the Torah [study] of [the Patriarchs'] descendants." One of the reasons why the Torah goes to such great lengths is because these narratives illustrate the awesome spiritual potential of each and every Jew.

It is therefore our duty to contemplate upon the deeds of the Patriarchs, perceive their greatness, and emulate them by striving to fulfill our own potential. *Tanna DeVei Eliyahu* (Ch. 25) expresses this principle as follows: "A person must say to himself, 'When will my deeds reach the deeds of my forefathers, Abraham, Isaac, and Jacob?' " Let us now fulfill this mandate by carefully analyzing the Torah's account of the Patriarchs' lives. Only in this manner will we gain a true understanding of the difficult tests of faith which they faced.

We learn that Hashem told Abraham, "Go for yourself from your land, from your relatives, and from your father's house to the land that I will show you. And I will make you a great nation; I will bless you, and make your name great, and you shall be a blessing" (*Genesis* 12:1-2). *Ramban* points out that even though the Torah does not inform us of the events which led up to this commandment, we must draw upon the historical information provided by the *Midrash* in order to view Abraham's spiritual achievements in the proper perspective. The facts are as follows:

While living in Ur Kasdim, Abraham had been constantly harassed for his belief in monotheism, a theology regarded as sacrilegious by the idol-worshiping masses. Opposition to Abraham's set of beliefs steadily grew, finally reaching its apex when Abraham was punished for his "heresy" by being cast into a blazing furnace. Abraham miraculously survived, and was commanded by Hashem to flee to the city of Haran, where he settled down. Hashem then spoke to Abraham again and commanded him to continue his journey to an unknown destination, "to the land that I shall show you."

One reason why we do not fully appreciate the inherent difficulty of this trial is that, nowadays, moving from one city to another has become almost routine. However, we must remember that in ancient times, leaving one's family circle and homeland was totally unthinkable; it was something which was just not done.

Yet we find that Abraham heeded Hashem's command and left his homeland. And why was he forced to leave? Only because of his belief that the Master of the universe was One. In order to gain the freedom to practice his unconventional religion and worship the One God, Abraham chose to wander from place to place like a nomad for an unspecified period of time, until the day Hashem would signal him that he had reached his destination. Can you imagine suddenly having to leave all your loved ones behind and embarking on a difficult journey for an unknown number of years, bound for an unknown destination? How great was Abraham's love for Hashem!

In recognition of Abraham's devotion to Hashem, the Sages said, "[The verse says,] 'We have a small sister [אָחוֹת לָנוּ קְטַנָּה] (Song of Songs 8:8) — this is a reference to Abraham the Patriarch, who rectified (אִיחָה) all the inhabitants of the world [by teaching them that] the world has One Father, and that He created the entire Creation. Bar Kapara says: [It refers to Abraham,] who mended (אִיחָה) the tear."

The explanation to Bar Kapara's cryptic statement is as follows: Man, when Hashem created him, was a righteous being who constantly adhered to the Divine Presence, and, as a consequence, was able to reside in the lower worlds. Due to the transgressions of later generations, however, the Divine Presence abandoned the corporeal realms. This catastrophic development marked the onset of the era of הַסְתָּרַת פָּנִים , in which Hashem, as it were, "averts His countenance from man" — this chasm is what Bar Kapara called "the tear."

At this stage, an ominous shroud of spiritual darkness enveloped the world. From its midst emerged pure evil, which was embodied by such wicked individuals as the Generation of Enosh, Nimrod, and Terah. Then came Abraham the Patriarch and rectified "the tear," or deep chasm, that had formed between man and God. Abraham proclaimed to all the inhabitants of earth that God is One. After pondering upon Creation, he had finally concluded, "The palace must have an owner!" Abraham, like the other Patriarchs, attained this exalted level of spiritual awareness independently, without any instruction. Courageously, Abraham disseminated his revolutionary theology among the masses despite the staunch — and sometimes violent — opposition he faced. According to the Sages, this is why he was called Abraham the Ivri (אַבְרָהָם הָעִבְרִי) — the entire world stood on one side (in Hebrew, עֵבֶר), while he stood on the other.

Abraham succeeded in persuading many members of his generation that the Almighty was the Creator of the universe, and that there was a purpose to Creation. For Abraham recognized the magnificence of mankind and its "likeness" to God. He perceived that Hashem created mankind for a very lofty purpose, and not just to eke out an existence. By disseminating these beliefs among the world's inhabitants, Abraham managed to efface the theological chasm dividing humanity from God.

By reflecting upon the lives of the Patriarchs, we not only gain new insight into man's unlimited spiritual potential, but also attain a deeper awareness of Hashem. This concept can be better understood in light of the following incident, as recounted in the Talmud (*Yerushalmi Bava Metzia* 2:5): R' Shimon ben Shetach once purchased a donkey from a gentile, upon which he found a precious stone. R' Shimon immediately returned the precious stone to the gentile, which prompted the gentile to exclaim, "Blessed is the God of the Jews!" Similarly, by closely analyzing the deeds of the Patriarchs — Hashem's servants — we also gain a deeper comprehension of their Master — the Almighty, or "God of Abraham."

The Patriarchs are the very foundations of our spiritual essence, as the Sages said, "The [deeds of the] forefathers determine [the deeds] of their descendants." This is why the Sages said that if we should fail to emulate the Patriarchs' righteous ways, we temporarily cease to be regarded as their descendants: "Whoever does not show mercy towards others, it is certain that he is not of the seed of Abraham" (*Beitzah* 32).

Thus, if we wish to define our own purpose in life, we must see ourselves within the larger context of the Patriarchs' life-roles. Only by superimposing the two images will we see a true representation of our own spiritual essence. This principle is evident in the Sages' statement, " 'My faith is firm as a wall, my breasts are as towers' (*Song of Songs* 8:10) — 'my faith is firm as a wall' refers to Abraham; 'my breasts are as towers' refers to Chananya, Mishael and Azariah." The implication is that Chananya, Mishael and Azariah drew — or "suckled" — spiritual nourishment from Abraham, the wellspring of faith, and that this infused them with the courage and strength of will to voluntarily sacrifice their lives for the sake of sanctifying Hashem's Name. Through this metaphor, the Sages convey that Abraham ingrained his intense devotion to God into the genes of his future spiritual descendants.

Many of the *mitzvos* that we perform on a daily basis are actually derivatives of the Patriarchs' greatest attributes. For example, *Ramban* writes in reference to the *mitzvah* "cleave to Him" (*Deuteronomy* 11:22): "This means that a person should continuously remember his love for Hashem. It should not slip his mind even 'when you walk on the way, when you retire, and when you arise' ... *this was the spiritual level of the Patriarchs*, who were the repositories of the Divine Presence." Similarly, in reference to the *mitzvah* "Him shall you serve" (ibid., 6:13), *Ramban* writes: "Before Hashem, a person should act like a slave who is at the constant bidding of his master, and who considers the work he does for his master more important than his own. He should fulfill the edict 'Let all your deeds be for the sake of Heaven' — and even when taking care of his own physical needs he should do everything for the sake of Heaven. Thus, he should eat, sleep, relieve himself, all for the sake of Heaven. *For even though the Patriarchs occupied themselves with their herds and other mundane tasks, their minds were constantly focused on Hashem.*"

Furthermore, Jewish history itself was largely predetermined by the Patriarchs. In explanation of the Torah's lengthy account of Abraham's sojourns (see *Genesis* 12), *Ramban* writes: "The Sages said, 'The [deeds of the] forefathers determine [the deeds] of their descendants' — the Torah describes [Abraham's sojourns] at length because *they all reveal what will transpire [to his descendants] in the future.*"

The Sages say that Hillel's perseverance in Torah study despite his severe poverty obligates all poor men to study Torah diligently. Similarly, the Patriarchs' righteous deeds obligate us to reach our own spiritual potential to the same degree as they. We cannot exempt ourselves from this responsibility with the facile excuse, "It's too difficult, I can't," for the Patriarchs bequeathed their greatest attributes to us, their spiritual legacy. Instead, we have an obligation to find within us the necessary strength of will to emulate the ways of the Patriarchs to the best of our abilities.

Abraham's Flight to Egypt

The Torah tells us that after Abraham followed Hashem's command to move away from Haran to the land of Canaan, "there was a famine in the land, and Abraham went down to Egypt" (*Genesis* 12:10). *Ramban* comments on this: "This was a great sin that Abraham did, albeit unwittingly, bringing his righteous wife Sarah into the risk of sin (by pretending she was not married to him) because he was afraid of being killed by the Egyptians (who would want to steal his wife); instead he should have trusted in Hashem that He would protect both of them from harm. Furthermore, the very fact that he left the Land of Israel (*Eretz Yisrael*) — where Hashem had explicitly commanded him to dwell — because of a famine was itself a sin, for Hashem would surely have saved him from starving in His chosen land. It was in retribution for this sin that Hashem decreed that Abraham's descendants be exiled to Egypt and subjugated to Pharaoh." By the severity of the punishment, we may infer the gravity of Abraham's sin, though it was committed unintentionally.

Maharal (in *Gevuros Hashem*) rejects *Ramban's* comment out of hand. If leaving the Land of Israel and lying about Sarah's identity were such terrible sins and incurred such stern punishment, he asks, how is it that Abraham repeated these same actions several years later when he went to the land of the Philistines and claimed Sarah was his wife? Furthermore, how could Isaac not have learned from his father's "mistake," using the very same ruse about his wife (*Genesis* 26:7)? Nevertheless, the *Zohar* indeed makes a similar observation concerning the verse, "Please say you are my sister, so that it may go well with me (i.e. they will bestow gifts upon me — *Rashi*) for your sake" (ibid., 12:13): "How could Abraham, who was fearful of sin, say this about his wife just so that they [the Egyptians] would bestow favors upon him?" This comment of the *Zohar* is apparently the source for *Ramban*'s statement.

Sforno explains Abraham's request to Sarah as follows: If we tell them you are my wife, they will surely kill me; but if they think you are my sister, instead of killing me they will offer me huge amounts of money for your hand in marriage — which I will, of course, reject. I will then have enough time to escape from that land before anything adverse actually happens.

The commentator *Divrei Shaul* (cited in the Chavel edition of *Ramban*) offers an answer to *Maharal*'s question, on behalf of *Ramban*. Abraham believed himself to be unworthy of miraculous intervention on the part of Hashem. He thought that if he put himself in danger, he might very well be killed, and people would think, "See how the servant of Hashem was deserted by Him in his time of need!" In order to prevent such a desecration of Hashem's name (*chillul Hashem*) from occurring, Abraham decided — for Hashem's sake — that he had to avoid being killed by the Egyptians at all costs. This miscalculation is what *Ramban* says was his sin. We find a similar idea in *Sanhedrin* 107a, where the Talmud tells us that David, when he was fleeing from his mutinous son Absalom, considered worshiping idolatry (only outwardly, of course) so that people should not say, "Such a righteous king is being killed by his son!" which would be a desecration of Hashem's Name. Since David, in his humility, believed that Absalom might indeed succeed in his wicked plans to kill him, he reasoned that it would be in the interest of Hashem's glory for him to worship idols rather than to lead people to believe that Hashem had abandoned His anointed king.

Incidentally, it would seem that *Ramban*'s contention is contradicted by the words of a *Midrash* which *Ramban* himself quotes: "Hashem said to Abraham, 'Go out and blaze the trail for your descendants (who will one day also descend to Egypt because of a famine) ...' You find that everything that happened to Abraham happened to his descendants ..." The *Midrash* clearly considers all these events to be commands of Hashem ("*Hashem said* to Abraham..."), which seems to disagree with *Ramban's* assertion that he descended to Egypt against God's will.

The Covenant of Circumcision

The *Gemara* tells us that the commandment of circumcision (*bris*) is a great one, for "if not for this commandment, the very heavens and earth would not stay in existence, as it says, 'If not for my covenant by day and by night, I would not have set the laws of the heavens and the earth' " (*Jeremiah* 33:25). The *Gemara* interprets the "covenant (*bris*) by day and by night" to be a reference to circumcision (*bris milah*). There is a difficulty in this interpretation, however, because the verse refers to a covenant which is "by day and by night," while circumcision may only be performed during the day. (R' Akiva Eiger poses this question in his *Teshuvos* as well.)

The answer to this problem lies in a comment made by *Sforno* in his commentary on the verse, "And it shall be a sign of a covenant between me and you" (*Genesis* 17:11): "[The mark of circumcision] is to be a constant reminder for us to follow His ways, as a seal that a master makes on the body of his slave." The purpose of the mark of circumcision is thus to serve as an ongoing reminder that we are Hashem's servants. In this sense, circumcision is indeed a covenant that exists "by day and by night."

The *Gemara* (*Menachos* 43b) tells how King David was once in a bathhouse and was shocked when he realized that he was bereft of commandments at that moment — there is no Torah, no *tzitzis*, no *tefillin*, etc. in a bathhouse. He was relieved when he realized that the mark of circumcision was one thing which could never be taken away from him, and that it could serve as his link to spirituality even when all else is taken away. It was on that occasion, the *Gemara* says, that he composed the psalm, "For the conductor on the *Sheminis*, concerning the eighth" (*Psalms* 12) — the "eighth" being interpreted as a reference to circumcision, which is performed on the eighth day of one's life. The question arises: What solace could David derive from considering this commandment, which had been performed so many years earlier? According to *Sforno's* comment cited above, this question is easily answered. It was not the *act* of circumcision that brought David solace, but rather the permanent *sign* of the circumcision — the constant reminder of our servitude to Hashem. It was the symbol of our total subservience to Hashem's will at *all* times, even when we are not actively involved in performing commandments, that made David realize that the Jew is never severed from his attachment to the Divine will.

The Chessed of Abraham

Abraham's love for performing acts of *chessed* (lovingkindness) was one of his greatest attributes. In this *parashah*, the Torah devotes a significant number of verses to illustrate this trait, and thereby clarifies why Abraham merited to become the spiritual father of all mankind.

The *parashah* begins with Abraham "sitting by the entrance of the tent in the heat of the day" (*Genesis* 18:1). The Sages tell us that this episode occurred on the third day after his circumcision, when the wound is extremely painful and the patient is feeling most weak. In fact, the pain and physical weakness that is felt on the third day after circumcision is so great that the *Shulchan Aruch* lists a number of legal exemptions and leniencies which apply only under these circumstances.

To make matters worse, Abraham was 99 years old at the time, an infirm age by any standards. Knowing that Abraham would never turn away guests despite his frail physical condition, Hashem decided to spare him the strain of accommodating guests by bringing a heat wave that would dissuade wayfarers from venturing out into the road. Abraham, however, could find no solace. He tossed and turned in bed, not trusting his servant to carefully scan all four directions for signs of potential guests, nor of informing him if he would find any. Forlornly, Abraham sat "by the entrance of the tent in the heat of the day," squinting his eyes against the sun in an effort to detect a human figure on the horizon. Perceiving Abraham's profound unease and discomfort, Hashem relented and sent three angels in the guise of men.

We all know the story, but have we ever stopped to think of its implications? Do the principles conveyed therein coincide with our preconceived notions of what it means to do *chessed*? Just think: Since no one asked Abraham for assistance, why was he so bothered? Why didn't he simply conclude, "It seems that no one needs my help today"?

Obviously, the answer is that Abraham did not view *chessed* as a mode of behavior to be adopted when and if the need arises, but as a way of life, a spiritual need emanating from the depths of his being. Unlike us, he did not exempt himself from the obligation to do *chessed* due to his physical discomfort. Just as an ill person does not deny himself food or water, so Abraham could not fathom forgoing the spiritual need to do *chessed* because of his pain.

This urge to do *chessed* is something we must all strive to attain, as is evident in the prophet's words: "Mortal! He told you what is good and what HASHEM demands of you — nothing more than to act justly, *love kindness*, and walk in modesty with your God" (*Micah* 6:8). To "*love* kindness" means to feel an intense desire to perform acts of *chessed*. It is a mindset where *chessed* becomes an integral component of one's life, where a lack of opportunity to help another human being makes one feel as though one were missing a limb, and where one does not live only for oneself.

When R' Akiva was asked, "If your God loves the poor, why does He not provide them with a livelihood?" he answered, "In order that we be spared the affliction of *Gehinnom*" (*Bava Basra*). R' Akiva's concept of *chessed* was a complete reversal of our own: He viewed *chessed* as a God-sent opportunity through which to perfect his soul, as opposed to us, who view *chessed* as an obligation to help those in need. According to R' Akiva, the poor do not benefit from us, but rather, we benefit from them. The poor provide us with the opportunity to feel the pain of another human being and respond with generosity, thereby purifying our soul.

The Sages said, "From beginning to end, the Torah is [essentially about] performing acts of *chessed*" (*Sotah* 14). In other words, *chessed* is the foundation stone of Torah. Significantly, the Sages derived this principle from the verse, "HASHEM God made for Adam and his wife garments of skin, and He clothed them" (*Genesis* 3:21) — Hashem showed compassion even after Adam and Eve transgressed His commandment. It is our obligation to emulate this Divine attribute, as the Sages explicitly stated: "[The verse says,] 'HASHEM will confirm you for Himself as a holy people, as He swore to you if you observe the commandments of HASHEM, your God, *and you go in His ways'* (*Deuteronomy* 28:9) — just as He is kind and compassionate, so must you be kind and compassionate."

Let us pay close attention to the "small details" that the Torah deemed fit to include in this *parashah*: Abraham left Hashem's presence in order to welcome his guests. Despite his advanced age and severe physical discomfort, Abraham *ran* to them because he perceived that they did not wish to inconvenience him. Although he suspected them of being Arabic idol worshipers, he continued to serve them in a manner befitting the greatest righteous men of the generation. Abraham humbly offered to fetch them "some water" and "a morsel of bread," but then the verse says: "So Abraham hastened to the tent to Sarah and said, 'Hurry! Three *se'ahs* of meal, fine flour! Knead and make cakes!' Then Abraham *ran* to the cattle, took a calf, tender and good, and gave it to the youth who hurried to prepare it. He took cream and milk and the calf which he had prepared, and placed these before them; he stood over them beneath the tree and they ate" (*Genesis* 18:6-8).

Afterwards, Abraham beseeched Hashem in a most insistent manner — bordering on impertinence — to spare Sodom and Gomorrah, the cities which represented the very antithesis of Abraham's ethical beliefs. Why? Because Abraham simply could not bear the pain of seeing Hashem's creatures dissociating themselves from their Maker. In a similar vein, when the *Saba miKelm* was informed of the death of one of the most influential apostates of his generation, he let out a sigh and said, "What a pity that he died without repentance!" His instinctive response came from the depths of his heart, for he truly cared about every Jew. Hence, he did not just say, "Blessed is the Almighty for having killed him!"

In *Parashas Chayei Sarah*, the Torah again devotes a significant number of verses to illustrate the attribute of *chessed*, this time, that of Rebecca:

> "The servant [Eliezer] ran towards [Rebecca] and said, 'Let me sip, if you please, a little water from your jug.' She said, 'Drink, my lord,' and quickly she lowered her jug to her hand and gave him drink. When she finished

giving him drink, she said, 'I will draw water even for your camels until they have finished drinking.' So she hurried and emptied her jug into the trough and kept running to the well to draw water; and she drew for all his camels. The man was astonished at her, reflecting silently to know whether HASHEM had made his journey successful or not" (ibid., 24:17-21).

According to *Sforno*, "the man was astonished at her" means that Eliezer was astounded at the alacrity and enthusiasm with which Rebecca performed *chessed* (10 camels drink approximately 140 gallons of water). "Reflecting silently" means that Eliezer held his tongue and did not chivalrously protest her excessive generosity, for he wished to see whether her *chessed* was sincere, or whether in the end she would demand payment for her labor. Only when the last camel finished drinking and she turned to go on her way did Eliezer become convinced that he had found a suitable wife for Isaac: "When the camels *had finished drinking*, the man took a golden nose ring . . . and two bracelets on her arms" (ibid., v. 22).

Part of our obligation to do *chessed* includes noticing the manner in which Hashem does *chessed* with the Creation. As the Sages said, "[The verse says] 'HASHEM will confirm you for Himself as a holy people, as He swore to you if you observe the commandments of HASHEM, your God, *and you go in His ways*' (*Deuteronomy* 28:9) — just as He is kind and compassionate, so must you be kind and compassionate" (*Sotah* 14).

The *Tomer Devorah* expounds on this point and delineates the 13 Divine Attributes that we are bound to emulate. Regarding the Attribute of Lovingkindness, the *Tomer Devorah* explains that Hashem continually provides life to every living thing. Were He to withhold life from a man for even a moment, he would immediately cease to exist. Further, in His great kindness, Hashem provides *all* men with life, including the wicked. How difficult it is for us to emulate this attribute!

Our obligation to perform acts of *chessed* on behalf of others is so great that the Sages said, "Whoever has the capability to pray for his fellow but refrains from doing so is considered a sinner. If he is a *talmid chacham*, he must make himself sick for his sake, as King

David said, 'And I, when they fall ill, wear sackcloth [and] afflict myself through fasting' " (Berachos 12).

The Talmud recounts that when R' Gamliel (the Nassi, head of the Sanhedrin) invited the Sages to his house for a celebration, he personally served them food and drink. His guests felt extremely uncomfortable being waited upon by the greatest Torah sage of the generation, but then R' Eliezer spoke. He said, "We find another eminent person who served others: Abraham was the most eminent person of his generation, yet he personally stood over them [and attended to their every need]. This, despite the fact that he took them for Arabs." R' Tzaduk said to them, "Until when will you ignore the honor of the Almighty? He makes the wind blow and prepares a table for every single individual!" (Kiddushin 32). What R' Tzaduk meant is that Abraham's generosity stemmed from his desire to emulate Hashem's generosity towards every living creature. Just as Abraham recognized Hashem's chessed and did his best to emulate it, so must we take note of the kindness with which Hashem sustains the world and try to act accordingly. R' Gamliel was simply fulfilling this obligation, and therefore, the Sages had no reason to feel uncomfortable at being served by the Nassi.

At first glance, it would seem that no one performed more acts of chessed than Noah and his sons. The Sages describe in great detail how Noah's family would work around the clock to feed the animals in the ark. R' Levi said, "Throughout those 12 months, Noah and his sons did not taste sleep" (Midrash Tanchuma). The Sages say that a certain species of bird felt so sorry for Noah that it abstained from eating in order to lighten Noah's workload (see Sanhedrin 108). Nevertheless, despite Noah's great acts of chessed, he fell short of what Hashem expected of him, and he was duly punished. Although this might seem unfair at first, we must keep in mind that man has an obligation to perfectly emulate Hashem's chessed towards His Creation. Thus, even though the extent of Noah's chessed towards the animals in the ark surpassed by far that of most men, he was judged in accord with his own potential to do chessed, which apparently he did not fulfill. So too, each one of us has an obligation to emulate the Creator's attribute of chessed in accordance with his own potential, and not necessarily in accordance with socially accepted norms.

In order to emphasize the importance of performing acts of *chessed*, the Sages said, "[The *mitzvah*] of accommodating guests is greater than welcoming the countenance of the Divine Presence. From where [do we learn this]? From Abraham, who asked the Holy One, Blessed is He, 'My Lord, if I find favor in Your eyes, please pass not away from Your servant' (*Genesis* 18:3), and then proceeded to accommodate his guests" (*Shabbos* 127). It would seem that a person who fulfills the *mitzvah* of accommodating guests also merits to welcome the countenance of the Divine Presence, for through this *mitzvah* he emulates the Almighty and shows care and concern for His creations. In fact, this very act inherently contains elements of welcoming the countenance of the Divine Presence.

Even though performing acts of *chessed* is of utmost importance, we must also take great care to carry out these deeds with sensitivity. For example, the Sages said, "He who gives a *perutah* to a poor person is blessed with six blessings, but he who says words of solace to him is blessed with 11 blessings" (*Bava Basra* 9). This implies that the *mitzvah* of giving charity includes empathizing with the needy individual, as well as encouraging and caring for him on a personal level.

The Sages said, "R' Yannai once saw a certain individual giving money to a poor person in public. He said to him, 'Better that you had not given it to him, for you have embarrassed him' " (*Chagigah* 5). From here we learn that charity must be given tactfully, in order to spare the needy individual from feeling shame. In fact, it should be given in such a manner that the poor individual does not even feel he is a recipient of someone else's generosity. This principle is also what the Sages had in mind in the following statement: "[The verse says,] 'The dove came back to [Noah] in the evening, and behold, it had plucked an olive leaf with its bill' (*Genesis* 8:10). R' Elazar said: The dove said before the Holy One, Blessed is He, 'Master of the Universe! Let my food be as bitter as olives as long as it is provided by You, and not sweet as honey and provided by flesh and blood!" (*Sanhedrin* 108). In other words, a needy person's dignity is as important to him as his physical needs. Therefore, it is the duty of one who gives charity to respect the feelings of the needy.

Indeed, the *Shulchan Aruch* rules, "One must give charity with a pleasing countenance, with joy and good spirit. One must empathize with the needy person's sorrow and speak comforting words to him. If charity is given with an annoyed and resentful look, [the bestower] loses the merit [of the *mitzvah*]" (*Yoreh De'ah* 259). The *Shach* adds, "Even if the [annoyed] person gives a large sum, he is regarded as having transgressed the prohibition, 'let your heart not feel bad when you give him' (*Deuteronomy* 15:10)."

The immense obligation incumbent upon us to perform acts of *chessed* clarifies the well-known *Midrash* that Jacob was held accountable for withholding his daughter Dinah from Esau. According to the *Midrash*, Jacob suspected that if Dinah would marry Esau, she would stand a good chance of persuading him to repent for his sins. However, out of fear that the opposite would occur — that Esau would corrupt Dinah — Jacob decided to conceal her from his brother. As a consequence, Jacob was punished and an even worse fate befell Dinah — she was violated by Shechem son of Hamor, a Hivvite (see *Genesis* 34:2). In reference to this *Midrash*, the *Saba miKelm* points out that Jacob was well within his rights in refusing to marry his daughter to a profoundly wicked man such as Esau. According to the strict letter of the law, he certainly had no obligation to do so. Nevertheless, Jacob was judged harshly for withholding from Esau the chance to repent for his sins.

The Sages said that if someone's tree should shed its leaves out of season, he should paint the tree with *sikra*, a red dye. This way, passersby will notice the tree and beseech Hashem to have mercy upon it. The *Saba miKelm* would cite this ruling to illustrate the immense obligation incumbent upon us to show concern for our fellow Jews — the Sages assumed that any Jew who would see the afflicted tree would naturally stop and pray to Hashem on behalf of the tree's owner. How great is our obligation to care for the welfare of our fellow Jews!

Rambam writes: "It is a rabbinically ordained positive commandment to visit the sick, comfort mourners, take out the dead, provide a bride with the means to marry, escort one's guests, make burial arrangements, carry [the body] with one's shoulder, walk before it, eulogize the deceased, and bury him ... These are physical acts of *chessed* [which earn a person] untold reward. Although all these *mitzvos* are rabbinically ordained, they are included in the *mitzvah* of 'Love your fellow like yourself' " (*Hilchos Aveilus* 14:1). He adds,

"The reward for escorting [one's guests] is greatest. It is a directive instituted by our father Abraham, a way of the *chessed* that he followed: He fed, gave drink, and escorted travelers. Accommodating guests is even greater than welcoming the countenance of the Divine Presence ... Escorting them is even greater than accommodating them, as the Sages said, 'Whoever does not escort them, it is as if he spills blood" (ibid., 14:2).

From *Rambam's* words, it is clear that Abraham's attainment of the attribute of *chessed* obligates us to follow in his footsteps and fulfill our own potential in this regard. As mentioned earlier, every person must say to himself, "When will my deeds reach the deeds of my forefathers?"

It is important to remember that *everyone* is obligated to perform acts of *chessed*, even people who spend most of their days learning Torah. As the Sages said, "He who occupies himself only with Torah study, it is as though he has no God" (*Avodah Zarah* 17). *Rashi* explains, "he has no God *to protect him.*" Here, the Sages mean that if a person who learns Torah does not perform acts of *chessed*, he is evidently lacking an awareness of Hashem's *chessed* with the world. Thus, in a sense, it is "as though he has no God," and consequently, Hashem will not protect such an individual. This principle can be better understood through the simple analogy of an impertinent youth — all who encounter him assume that he is an orphan, attributing his rude behavior to his lack of a suitable role-model. So too, a Torah scholar who does not perform *chessed* is likened to a spiritual orphan, for he lacks an awareness of Hashem's attributes.

With this idea, we may gain greater insight into the words of the prophet: "So says HASHEM, 'Let not the wise man laud himself with his wisdom, and let not the strong man laud himself with his strength, and let not the rich man laud himself with his wealth. Only with this may one laud himself — discernment in knowing Me, for I am HASHEM Who does kindness, justice, and righteousness in the land, for in these is My desire,' the words of HASHEM" (*Jeremiah* 9:22-23). The prophet teaches that it would be wrong for a man to "laud himself" for his natural attributes or his wealth, for all these are granted to him by Hashem. The only thing that a person can claim to have earned in this world is "knowledge of Hashem." After attaining this level of awareness, he must then use it to perceive the manner in which Hashem bestows of His goodness onto the entire Creation. Ultimately, he must come to the realization that, "I am HASHEM Who does kindness," and, "in *these* is My desire."

Perhaps the importance of *chessed* can best be summarized by the following Talmudic passages:

> "Whoever disregards his character traits [and forgives others], all his sins shall be disregarded" (*Rosh Hashanah* 17). *Rashi* explains, "the Attribute of Justice will not examine his sins closely, for whoever is merciful towards people, he shall be shown mercy from Heaven."
>
> "When R' Elazar ben Parta and R' Chanina ben Tradion were arrested, R' Chanina said to R' Elazar, 'How fortunate you are! You were arrested for five things, and you shall survive. Woe to me! I was arrested for one thing, and I shall not survive. For you occupied yourself with Torah study *as well as acts of chessed*, while I only occupied myself with Torah study'" (*Avodah Zarah* 17).

Why Hashem Loved Abraham

The verse says, "And HASHEM said, 'Shall I conceal from Abraham what I do, now that Abraham is surely to become a great and mighty nation, and all the nations of the earth shall bless themselves by him? For I have loved him *because he commands his children and his household after him, that they keep the way of HASHEM, doing charity and justice ...'*" (*Genesis* 18:18-19). In reference to this verse, the Sages said, "This nation has three identifying traits: the compassionate, the humble, and those who perform kind deeds ... Those who perform kind deeds [is derived] from the verse, 'For I have loved him because he commands his children and his household ... *doing charity* and justice'" (ibid.) (*Yevamos* 79). As *Rashi* explains, the Sages' statement conveys that Hashem loved

Abraham primarily because he would instruct his children and the members of his household to observe Hashem's ways.

When we take into account the many courageous and selfless acts that Abraham performed throughout his lifetime, the Sages' statement is ostensibly difficult to understand. Why would the ostensibly unremarkable act of educating his children overshadow Abraham's more conspicuous expressions of devotion to Hashem? What about the ten trials that Abraham successfully underwent? What about Abraham's courageous efforts to disseminate monotheism among a rabidly paganistic society?

The reason we find the Sages' statement difficult is that our premises are all wrong. We tend to think that a person is judged solely on the basis of his own achievements. Thus, when a person devotes himself to observing the laws of the Torah and achieves a high level of faith in Hashem, we conclude that he has come close to reaching spiritual perfection.

The Torah, however, teaches us otherwise — unless a person perpetuates his love for Hashem by imparting his principles of faith to his descendants, he remains far from having attained his full potential. This is what the Sages meant when they said, "Who is a boor? He who does not raise up his children in Torah." In other words, if a person — even an erudite Torah scholar — fails to instruct his children to follow the ways of the Torah, this is a sign that he himself lacks awareness of the true value and importance of Torah.

Hence, despite Abraham's many selfless acts for the sake of sanctifying the Name of Heaven, Hashem would not have said, "For I have loved him," had Abraham not imparted his set of beliefs to his descendants.

The Binding of Isaac upon the Altar

The verse says, "And it happened after these things that God tested Abraham and said to him, 'Abraham,' and he replied, 'Here I am.' And He said, 'Please take your son, your only one, whom you love — Isaac — and go to the land of Moriah; bring him up there as an offering upon one of the mountains which I shall tell you" (*Genesis* 22:1-2).

Rashi explains that "after these things" refers to the following dialogue between Satan and the Almighty, which transpired immediately after Isaac's circumcision:

The Satan said, "From the great feast Abraham prepared [in honor of Isaac's circumcision], he did not offer You a single bullock or ram!"

Hashem answered, "Did he indeed do all this only for his son [and not in My honor]? Why, if I were to tell him, 'Sacrifice [your son] before Me,' he would not hesitate!"

Regarding Hashem's statement, "Please take your son," *Rashi* writes, "God pleaded with Abraham to withstand this test, for otherwise people would say that his earlier tests were without substance."

Rashi's interpretation is difficult to understand. Why would Abraham's previous nine tests have been invalidated had he failed to fulfill this astonishingly difficult commandment? Let us remember that for no other reason than his belief in Hashem, Abraham hid from Nimrod for 13 years, was flung into a burning furnace, and was forced to leave his family and homeland. When he finally arrived in Canaan, he was forced to leave due to famine. Even so, his faith in Hashem did not waver. In Egypt, Sarah was promptly kidnaped and taken to Pharaoh, who planned to take her for a wife. Nevertheless, Abraham kept his faith in Hashem. Afterwards, his nephew Lot was captured by hostile kings, and Abraham was forced to confront them in battle and rescue him. Nevertheless, Abraham's faith did not waver. God then told Abraham that his offspring would suffer under four monarchies. At an advanced age, he was commanded to circumcise himself and his son; despite the infirmities of old age, Abraham fulfilled this commandment on the very same day he received it. When Hashem commanded Abraham to drive away Ishmael and Hagar, he overcame his overwhelming compassion for his son and wife and heeded the words of the Almighty. Finally, Hashem gave Abraham his last and most difficult test — to sacrifice Isaac upon an altar. Why, then, does *Rashi* imply that the previous nine tests would have been invalidated had Abraham failed to fulfill the tenth?

Furthermore, if the previous nine tests had not sufficiently proven Abraham's complete devotion to Hashem, why would the tenth test have proven it any more conclusively? One could theoretically argue that Abraham's willingness to sacrifice his entire being to Hashem was nothing out of the ordinary. As we have seen throughout history, millions of individuals have given up their lives for what they considered "a just cause." Perhaps Abraham was just another example of an individual who attributed so much importance to his beliefs that he was willing to die for them. If so, why was Abraham's last test considered so momentous? In order to understand, we must delve deeper into the mystery of *Akeidas Yitzchak*.

Notice that the verse says, "Please take *your son, your only one, whom you love* — Isaac — and go . . ." (ibid., v. 2). In explanation of this seemingly redundant usage, *Rashi* says, "Why did God not say directly, 'Take Isaac'? First, He wanted to avoid startling Abraham and thereby causing him to lose his mind. Second, He wanted to make the commandment more precious to Abraham, and to give him merit for complying with every single word."

On a deeper level, it is possible that Hashem conveyed to Abraham through these apparently repetitious words the difficulties this test would present to him. Hashem in essence said to Abraham, "I am asking you to take your son, whom you miraculously bore when you were 100 years old, your only one, whom you love. Realize what a difficult thing I am asking you to do! Yes, I am asking you to sacrifice Isaac, your progeny, whom you hoped would perpetuate your faith in Me to future generations. Nevertheless, please do this for Me!"

In addition to Abraham's sentiments for his only son, there were other reasons why this test presented almost insurmountable difficulties: Abraham knew the true value of human life. He prayed fervently to Hashem to spare the wicked inhabitants of Sodom and Gomorrah because he was full of compassion for all living beings, even if they were the most impenitent of sinners. Now, he was being asked to do what was utter anathema to him — to perform a cruel act and snuff out the life of another human being; furthermore, that of his own son!

Essentially, Hashem's commandment shattered Abraham's entire belief system to the core. Since that very first day when he had discovered Hashem's existence, Abraham had believed in a compassionate God who loathed human sacrifice (a practice prevalent in Abraham's day). Abraham relentlessly fought for this ideal throughout his entire life. It was for this belief that he had endured untold humiliation, hardship, and persecution. But now, he had finally been proven wrong — evidently, he had been championing a false ideal all those years. Who can imagine the pain, the humiliation, the dejection Abraham must have felt at this moment? How could he bear it?

Hashem's commandment was all the more perplexing due to its location. Abraham could not understand how sacrificing Isaac upon a desolate mountain would further the cause of monotheism among the world's inhabitants or strengthen their faith in the Almighty. How could it, if no one would know about it? The entire affair seemed so senseless!

The *Midrash* teaches that immediately after the commandment was given, Satan appeared to Abraham. Satan said, "Grandfather, have you lost your mind? You're not going to slit the throat of the son born to you at 100 years of age, are you? Tomorrow, God will accuse you of murder!" But Abraham replied, "Even so, [I shall do it]."

Despite all his nagging doubts, his emotional pain, his profound disappointment, Abraham heeded Hashem's words. The verse tells us, "So Abraham woke up early in the morning and saddled his donkey; he took his two young men with him and Isaac, his son; he split the wood for the offering, and stood up and went to the place of which God had spoken to him" (ibid., v. 3).

Even though he was not commanded to, Abraham woke up early the next morning to set out on the fateful journey. He personally hitched the saddle onto his mount, wanting to fulfill every detail of Hashem's commandment with his own hands.

Abraham also made sure to take firewood just in case he would not find any near the mountain where Isaac was to be sacrificed. Once again, he was not commanded to do so. Why, then, did Abraham go to the trouble of carrying the bundle of firewood during the three-day journey? Why did he not leave the firewood behind and hope against hope that he would not find any near the mountain? Perhaps in such an eventuality he would be exempted from having to fulfill the *mitzvah*.

The answer is that we cannot imagine the intensity of Abraham's love for Hashem. Abraham could simply not feel at ease until he had taken care of the last detail necessary to fulfill His commandment. Regarding Abraham's firewood, the *Midrash* says, "[The verse] says, 'he split the wood for the offering' — the significance of this deed was very great, for on the merit of Abraham splitting the wood for the offering, Hashem split the Red Sea on behalf of the Israelites."

After gaining this new insight into *Akeidas Yitzchak*, the answer to the two questions introduced earlier is self-evident: True, the nine tests Abraham underwent before *Akeidas Yitzchak* were extremely difficult. However, because they coincided with — and were sometimes a consequence of — his theological tenets, they were only indicators that Abraham was indeed very committed to his set of beliefs. As yet, no proof had been provided to show that Abraham's level of devotion to Hashem transcended beyond the natural human willingness to sacrifice one's life for an ideal. Many men had died on battlefields for the sake of noble causes — perhaps Abraham had been willing to endure so many years of hardship for the "noble idea" called monotheism.

Akeidas Yitzchak, however, proved that Abraham's devotion to Hashem transcended the barriers of intellectual understanding and moral perception. For even though every fibre of his being recoiled at the prospect of sacrificing Isaac upon the altar, Abraham's burning love for Hashem drove him on towards Mount Moriah. In this tenth and final test, Abraham proved that he was willing to sacrifice to Hashem not only his son, not only his own life, but also that which was most precious to him: *his ideals, his principles, his intellect, his very psyche.* This is why *Akeidas Yitzchak* surpassed all the other nine trials.

The following *Midrash* further illustrates this point: "Master of the Universe! When You said to me, 'Please take your son . . .,' I could have responded as follows: 'Yesterday You said to me, "Through Isaac will offspring be considered yours" (ibid., 21:12), and now You tell me, "Please take your son. . ."!?' However, I did not. Instead, I restrained my lovingkindness in order to do Your will."

We, too, must follow in the footsteps of the Patriarchs. As the Sages said, "One is obligated to recite a blessing over adversity in the same manner as one recites a blessing over good fortune" (*Berachos* 60). Just as Abraham performed Hashem's commandment to sacrifice his son with enthusiasm, love, and joy, so must we humbly accept all of Hashem's decrees even when they are painful.

King Saul exemplified this trait. Even though the prophet Samuel had warned him that he and his three sons would perish in battle against the Phillistines (see *I Samuel* 28:19), King Saul nevertheless took his three sons and fought in the battle. As expected, he and his three sons died (ibid., 31:2-5). In reference to this event, the *Midrash* says, "At that time, the Holy One, Blessed is He, said to the ministering angels, 'Look at the beings that I created in My world! He goes to war knowing that he will be killed, and he takes his sons along with him! He rejoices at being struck by the forces of Divine Judgment!' "

Similarly, Moses was told, "Take vengeance for the Children of Israel against the Midianites, *[and] afterwards you will pass away*" (*Numbers* 31:2), yet the very next verse says, "Moses spoke to the people, saying, 'Arm men from among yourselves for the legion that they may be against Midian ...' " *Rashi* points out that "although God had told Moses that he would die after this war, Moses did not delay, but proceeded with alacrity to carry out the *mitzvah*." The *Midrash* adds, "Had Moses wished, he could have lived a good many more years [by simply delaying] the war."

Jacob's Humility

We must do some reading between the lines to really appreciate Jacob's lofty spiritual level. For instance, the Torah makes no mention of his 14-year stay at Shem and Eber's yeshivah. Instead, we are left to derive this fact on our own from the chronology of the period. Why indeed is the Torah so cryptic about such an important period of Jacob's life?

The answer is that the Torah relates the events of Jacob's life in the self-effacing tone that Jacob himself would have assumed. Jacob was called "a wholesome man abiding in tents" (*Genesis* 25:27). His achievements were internal; they were purely for the sake of Heaven, and not means by which to gain the honor of men. Jacob saw nothing extraordinary in devoting 14 years of his life to Torah study. It is as if Jacob had said to himself, "This is the minimum I can do to strengthen my faith in Hashem before I leave *Eretz Yisrael* and go to live side by side with idol worshipers such as Laban." Had Jacob himself been telling us the story of his life, he too would not have bothered to mention the "unextraordinary" fact that he spent 14 years of his life learning in Shem and Eber's yeshivah.

Jacob exemplified the Sages' maxim, "If you have learned much Torah, do not think too highly of yourself, for that is why you were created!" This is evident from *Rashi's* interpretation of the verse, "[Jacob] lay down in that place" (ibid., 28:11) — "in *this* place he lay down, but he *did not* lie down throughout the 14 years he served in the house of Eber, for he was studying Torah." Apparently, Jacob also took this astounding achievement for granted. We can almost envision him shrugging at our amazement and saying, "How else does one learn the holy Torah?"

The *Chafetz Chaim's* explanation of the verse "I rejoice over your words like one who has found a great treasure" (*Psalms* 119:162) illustrates this point further: "King David rejoiced over Torah study as a person would rejoice over finding a great treasure. What is the analogy? That King David related to Torah study in the same manner as a person would react if he would be shown into a vast treasure house and given a limited time in which to collect valuables — he would neither sleep nor slumber, but expend his last ounce of energy in gathering as much of the treasure as humanly possible." Similarly, the Sages said, "Better one moment of *mitzvos* and kind deeds in this world than an entire existence in the World to Come."

Jacob's exalted level of spiritual purification can also be inferred from the verse, "Jacob awoke from his sleep and said, 'Surely HASHEM is present in this place *and I did not know!*'" (*Genesis* 28:16) — as *Rashi* explains, Jacob in essence said, "Had I known, I would not have slept in such a holy place!" From this we see that in order not to defile the sanctity of Mount Moriah, Jacob would have willingly forgone the prophetic visions and immeasurable blessings that he gained by virtue of having slept there.

Similarly, Jacob's humility is evident from the verse, "Then Jacob sent angels ahead of him to Esau ... He charged them, saying: 'Thus shall you say, "To my lord, to Esau ... I have lodged with Laban (עִם לָבָן גַּרְתִּי) and lingered until now"'" (ibid., 32:5). As *Rashi* explains, the numerical value of the word גַּרְתִּי (lodged) is תרי"ג, an allusion to the 613 *mitzvos*. Thus, Jacob in essence warned Esau, "Though I have lodged with Laban, I have observed the 613 Divine Commandments, and have not learned from his evil ways" — even under the threat of death, Jacob could not get himself to boast of his achievements outright, but only hint at them.

The Sale of the Birthright

The Torah says, "Jacob simmered a stew, and Esau came in from the field, and he was exhausted. Esau said to Jacob, 'Pour into me, now, some of that very red stuff, for I am exhausted.' He therefore called his name Edom" (*Genesis* 25:29-30). The Sages explain that since Abraham had passed away on that day, Jacob was preparing Isaac a red-lentil stew, the traditional mourner's meal (*Bava Basra* 16b). *Rashi* explains that the round shape of lentils resembles a wheel, a symbol of the recurrence of death. Apparently, this symbolism brought comfort to mourners. Why?

One answer may be that when a mourner is reminded that he is not alone in his sorrow, that death is a curse endured by all of mankind, his pain is somehow alleviated. The knowledge that others have, and will, suffer the same sorrow as he makes the mourner feel less forlorn, for he knows that he is not alone in his anguish.

On a deeper level, it is possible that thinking about the recurrence of death makes the mourner realize that he himself will not live forever. As the Sages explain, Hashem introduced death into the world in order to strike fear of the Divine into the hearts of men. Thus, after reflecting upon the death of his loved one and the recurrence of death, the mourner gains a greater understanding of the transient nature of this world. Realizing that he, too, will one day be taken by death, he repents for his sins and resolves to dedicate more energy towards achieving his spiritual potential.

Esau, however, saw the lentils and completely missed the message. Paying no attention to the lentils, the mourners sitting on the ground, or Abraham's death, Esau focused on only one thing — satisfying his physical desires. He barged into the house of mourning and callously demanded, "Pour into me, now, some of that very red stuff, for I am exhausted." *Sforno* explains that onlookers gave Esau the derogatory name "Edom" (in Hebrew, "red"), as if to say, "You are so lacking in human values, so consumed with your hunting and plunder, that you look at the stew and notice only its color! You too shall be called 'Red'!"

The fact is that Esau's failure to comprehend the symbolism of the lentils was an accurate reflection of his personality. He was a superficial person — just as he exerted all of his energy towards attaining the superficial and ephemeral rewards of this world, so too, his mind could not see past the exterior appearance of the lentils. How could he have recognized profundity when his every moment was devoted to superficiality? It is not surprising that all he saw was some red stew.

At this point, Esau's unsuitability to inherit Abraham's spiritual heritage became blatantly clear to Jacob. This prompted Jacob to persuade Esau to sell him the birthright. Appropriately, Esau sold the birthright — including the rights of exclusive privilege to Abraham's spiritual legacy — for a bowl of "some red stuff." Once again, Esau failed to see the deeper significance of things. He reasoned, "What have I gotten out of this birthright? Nothing! On the other hand, that bowl of red stew will at least give me some energy!"

The following verse says, "Jacob gave Esau bread and lentil stew, and he ate and drank, got up and left; thus, Esau spurned the birthright" (*Genesis* 25:34). As *Ramban* explains, Esau spurned the birthright by getting up and returning to his hunting. He adds, "The only desire of fools is to eat, drink, and fulfill their desires as they come. They show no concern for tomorrow." We learn from this that had Esau not "gotten up and left," his callous demand for food could have been overlooked — perhaps he was ravenous. Rather, it was his impudent departure that was inexcusable. By leaving so abruptly, Esau demonstrated that he did not feel the slightest remorse for having sold the right of exclusive privilege to serve Hashem for a measly bowl of stew. In fact, he did not think he had done anything wrong.

There is a lesson here for all of us. Like Esau, people naturally think that they are always right, that their actions are always justified. Had Esau stopped for a moment and reflected upon his behavior, he might well have realized the inherent absurdity of selling an invaluable birthright for a bowl of stew. He might have caught himself in time and begged Jacob to annul the sale. However, this was not to be. Esau did not give his behavior a fleeting thought, and, as a result, he caused eternal and irrevocable damage to himself and all his future descendants. So too, if instead of always justifying our behavior to ourselves we would once in a while try to evaluate our deeds objectively, we might just catch ourselves in time. As the Sages said, "If you see a Torah scholar who committed a transgression at night, do not harbor criticism against him [the following] day, lest he has repented. *Lest* he has repented? Rather, *surely* he has repented" (*Berachos* 19a). In other words, although a Torah scholar may sometimes unwittingly sin, he must discipline himself to constantly reevaluate his deeds. The same obligation applies to us — no one likes to admit his mistakes, but it is our duty to try.

Isaac and His Father's Merits

Hashem appeared to Isaac and told him that He would be with him and bless him "because Abraham listened to My voice, and observed My safeguard, My commandments, My statutes and My teachings" (*Genesis* 26:5). *Sforno* explains this as follows. Abraham "observed Hashem's safeguard" means that he always practiced the virtues of kindness to others. This he did whenever he "called in the Name of Hashem." The "commandments, statutes and teachings" refer to the seven Noahide laws that Abraham would teach others, while he served as an example to them by strictly observing them. The Sages (in *Bereishis Rabbah*), however, derive from this verse that Abraham observed *all* the laws of the Torah — not just the seven Noahide laws.

It is interesting to note that Hashem did not tell Isaac that he was deserving of His blessing on his own merit, but only by the merit of his father. The same sort of expression is repeated in v. 24: "I will bless you and multiply your seed *because of My servant Abraham*." We do not find such a phenomenon with Jacob, and certainly not with Abraham. The explanation is that, at this point, Isaac had not yet aroused himself to "call out in the Name of HASHEM" (v. 25). Once he did so, however, the Torah says, "Avimelech went to him from Gerar ... and said to him ..., 'HASHEM has been with you ... Now you are the blessed one of HASHEM.' " After that point we do not find that Isaac had any more unpleasant episodes or quarrels with any of his neighbors, for at that time he began to merit the protection of Hashem "firsthand," without recourse to the merits of his father. Jacob, on the other hand, was from youth a "dweller of tents" (ibid., 25:27), someone who involved himself with the study, and undoubtedly the dissemination, of Hashem's Torah in the yeshivah of Shem and Ever.

In reference to the Midrashic interpretation of this verse cited above — that Abraham and his descendants kept all the commandments (*mitzvos*) of the Torah, although they had not yet been commanded — *Ramban* asks, how is it that Jacob built a pillar (ibid., 28:18) and married two sisters (ibid., 29:23,28), since both acts are prohibited by the Torah (see *Leviticus* 26:1; ibid., 18:18)? Similarly, how could Amram marry his aunt (*Exodus* 6:20), which the Torah forbids in *Leviticus* 18:14? *Ramban* answers that the forefathers only kept the Torah's laws on a voluntary basis, and only in the Land of Israel; Jacob and Amram's "unlawful" marriages both took place outside of the Land of Israel, in Aram and in Egypt. It was for this reason, *Ramban* explains in *Leviticus* 18:25, that Rachel died immediately upon Jacob's reentrance into the Land of Israel.

Another opinion holds that only the Torah's laws dealing with "righteousness and justice" (*Genesis* 18:19) were kept by the forefathers, and not all 613 commandments. This explains all the discrepancies mentioned by *Ramban*. *Chizkuni* offers yet another explanation for the seemingly forbidden marriages of Jacob and Amram. He suggests that the forefathers, not having been born as full-fledged Jews, had the status of "converts." According to *halachah*, a convert is considered to be "born again" when he converts, and is not halachically "related" to any of his biological family. He is thus permitted (theoretically, although the Rabbis forbade it) to marry his own sister, mother, daughter, aunt, etc. This explains how Jacob married two sisters — technically they were not sisters. Another explanation given by the commentators is that Leah and Rachel were only half-sisters; that is, they had different mothers. *Halachah* states that, for non-Jews, half-siblings are only considered siblings if they share a common mother; a common father is not enough to establish fraternity. Thus, Leah and Rachel were not technically considered sisters.

Missed Opportunities

The verse says, "Jacob departed from Beer-sheba and went toward Haran. He encountered the place and spent the night there ..." (*Genesis* 28:10-11). *Rashi*, quoting the Sages, explains that as Jacob approached Haran, the thought suddenly occurred to him, "How could I have passed by the place [Mount Moriah] where my forefathers prayed and not have offered a prayer myself?" Jacob then wished to retrace his steps, and miraculously, he was suddenly transported back to Mount Moriah. This explains why the next verse begins "He encountered the place ..."

Two questions immediately come to mind: Why didn't Jacob pray on Mount Moriah when he passed by it, and why didn't he realize his oversight before arriving at Haran, a city hundreds of kilometers away?

One possible answer is that Jacob initially thought that no more blessings could be evinced from Hashem by praying on Mount Moriah. He thought that the all-inclusive blessing given to Abraham — "I shall surely bless you and greatly increase your offspring like the stars of the heavens and like the sand on the seashore, and your offspring shall inherit the gate of its enemy" (ibid., 22:17) — had "depleted" the spiritual treasure-house atop Mount Moriah. Alternatively, Jacob thought he had no need to pray to Hashem for his own welfare, since Abraham and Isaac had already been promised that their offspring — namely, Jacob — would multiply and flourish.

However, after passing by Mount Moriah and refraining from praying there, Jacob proceeded to the yeshivah of Shem and Eber, where he spent the next 14 years studying Torah with utmost diligence. The more Torah he learned, the more Jacob came to the realization that a *tzaddik* should not rely solely on the promises

Hashem made to his forefathers. Instead, a *tzaddik* must make the effort to earn his own merit. This conclusion did not crystallize in Jacob's mind until he reached the outskirts of Haran. At that point, he wished to return to Mount Moriah, and miraculously, he was suddenly transported there.

An important lesson emerges from this interpretation: We must be very careful not to miss golden opportunities for spiritual growth. For even Jacob, the greatest of the Patriarchs, almost overlooked the opportunity to pray on Mount Moriah. Had he not realized his error before entering the gates of Haran, it stands to reason that he would have missed the prophetic visions which he merited on Mount Moriah. Consequently, the Evening Prayer Service (*Maariv*) would not have been attributed to him, and he would not have merited the prophetic vision of the heavenly ladder. Further, he would not have received the eternal blessing: "The ground upon which you are lying, to you will I give it and to your descendants. Your offspring shall be as the dust of the earth, and you shall spread out powerfully westward, eastward, northward and southward; and all the families of the earth shall bless themselves by you and your offspring ... I will not forsake you until I will have done what I have spoken about you" (ibid., 28:14-15). Certainly, the same can be said of us — Hashem presents us with countless opportunities to grow spiritually every single day, yet sadly, we overlook the majority of them.

Joseph's brothers also missed valuable opportunities for spiritual growth. Upon their return from Egypt, they discovered to their utter dismay that their money had been returned to their satchels. The verse says, "Their hearts sank, and they turned trembling one to another, saying, 'What is this that God has done to us?' " (ibid., 42:28). Had they reflected upon this incident and made a greater effort to truly understand why God had done this to them, they would have concluded that Joseph was still alive in Egypt. Unfortunately, they squandered this golden opportunity to rectify their sin. The Sages criticized the brothers' response, citing the verse, "The folly of a man corrupts his ways, and [then] his heart grows angry at God!" (*Proverbs* 19:3).

How many times have we responded in this manner to seemingly unfavorable events? Not only do we squander God-given opportunities for spiritual growth by failing to perceive the message contained within the occurrence, but we also feel anger towards "the powers that be" for subjecting us to such discomfort!

Undoubtedly, we must contemplate the events in our lives more carefully and make a greater effort to perceive the messages contained therein. If we would yearn to take advantage of all the opportunities which Hashem presents to us, we would surely merit Divine assistance in the same manner as Jacob merited to be miraculously transported back to Mount Moriah.

There Are No Guarantees
for the Righteous in This World

In the fourth verse of *Parashas Vayishlach*, we learn that "Jacob became very frightened" (*Genesis* 32:8). This verse seems difficult to understand, since Hashem had explicitly promised Jacob, "Behold, I am with you; I will guard you wherever you go, and I will return you to this soil; for I will not forsake you until I will have done what I have spoken about you" (ibid., 28:15). Why, then, did he become frightened? Surely Jacob did not doubt Hashem's word.

Similarly, the *Midrash* says, "Two human beings were given guarantees by Hashem, yet they both became afraid. [Who were they?] The greatest of the Patriarchs, and the greatest of the Prophets. The greatest of the Patriarchs — Jacob — was told by Hashem, 'Behold, I am with you ...,' but in the end he became fearful. The greatest of the Prophets — Moses — was told by Hashem, 'For I shall be with you,' yet he, too, became afraid."

In order to answer the question, we must first note that the Sages stopped short of actually criticizing Jacob for feeling afraid. In fact, nowhere in Talmudic literature do we find that it is inherently wrong for a person not to rely completely on a Divine promise. The Jewish people's attitude in the days of Mordechai and Esther is poignant proof: According to the Sages, the Jewish people said, "If the Patriarch Jacob became frightened despite having heard Hashem's assurances, how much more do *we* have reason to be frightened!"

Clearly, then, Jacob was not blamed for becoming frightened in the face of danger. On the contrary, the Sages inferred from this an eternal lesson: "From here we learn that there are no guarantees for the righteous in this world."

As to why Jacob became frightened, the Sages explain, "Jacob thought, '[Unlike me,] [Esau] has been accumulating merit for living in *Eretz Yisrael* and honoring his parents.'"

We find that the manner in which Jacob conducted himself in his encounter with Esau serves as a model for all generations. Even though the Sages *did* criticize Jacob for behaving too submissively towards Esau — he should not have sent Esau so many gifts, or referred to himself as "Jacob your servant" — they faithfully followed his example throughout the ages. The Talmud relates that Rebbi once instructed R' Effes to compose a letter to Emperor Antoninus. He wrote, "From Yehudah the Prince to Emperor Antoninus." As soon as Rebbi read the salutation, he tore the letter in pieces.

"Now write, 'From your servant Yehudah to our master, Emperor Antoninus,'" Rebbi ordered.

R' Effes asked, "But why do you demean your honor so?"

Rebbi replied, "Am I better than my ancestor? Did Jacob not say, 'Thus says Jacob your servant'?"

Now that we have established the principle, "There are no guarantees for the righteous in this world," we must learn how and under what circumstances it applies. For example, we find various instances in Scripture where even individuals who *did not* receive Divine assurances are accused of lacking faith in Hashem and making independent efforts to extricate themselves from danger. The classic example is Joseph — the Sages say that his efforts to have the Chamberlain of the Cupbearers release him (see ibid., 40:14) reflected a lack of faith in Hashem, and thus, it was decreed that Joseph spend an additional two years in prison. At first glance, however, we see nothing wrong in Joseph's conduct, since we have established that "There are no guarantees for the righteous in this world."

The difficulty is made even stronger by the *Ramban's* commentary on the first verses of *Parashas Vayishlach*: "This *parashah* was written in order to teach us that the Holy One, Blessed is He, saved [Jacob] His servant and delivered him from the hand of [an enemy] who was stronger ... It also teaches us that [Jacob] did not trust in his own righteousness, and made great efforts to save himself. The *parashah* contains eternal lessons, for everything that happened to [Jacob] our forefather during his encounter with Esau shall continually occur to us [in our encounters] with the descendants of Esau. It would be in our best interest to adhere to the ways of [Jacob], and adopt the three strategies that he adopted — prayer, appeasement of the enemy, and warfare."

The *Ramban's* words quite clearly advocate taking positive action when the need arises, in congruence with the principle established above, "There are no guarantees for the righteous in this world." If so, why was Joseph punished for asking the Chamberlain of the Cupbearers to have him released? How did Joseph's behavior differ from Jacob's?

As with all resolutions, the answer to this difficulty lies in achieving a synthesis between two opposites: While it is true that a person must have faith in Hashem, it is also true that he must take positive action to extricate himself from danger. The only variable is a person's "faith threshold." In other words, when a person is capable of having complete faith in Hashem, he is expected to do just that. Were he to make independent efforts to extricate himself from discomfort, he would be held accountable for lacking sufficient faith. On the other hand, in situations which demand more faith than a person is capable of having, he *has an obligation* to take independent action to extricate himself from danger, for "there are no guarantees for the righteous in this world."

So too, Jacob was not held accountable for taking matters into his own hand because, as the verse explicitly tells us, *he had become frightened*. The commentaries offer numerous explanations why Jacob grew frightened, but all agree that his fear was justified. In contrast, Joseph should not have become frightened, for the verse explicitly says, "HASHEM was with Joseph" (ibid., 39:21). He was therefore punished for making independent efforts to extricate himself from danger unnecessarily. Obviously, Joseph's "shortcoming" is almost imperceptible to us, and it is only because he was such an extraordinary *tzaddik* that he was judged by a hairsbreadth and found culpable.

The Selling of Joseph

These two *parashios* — *Vayeishev* and *Mikeitz* — are extremely difficult to understand. Taken at face value, they portray Joseph's brothers as a group of jealous and violent men eager to spill the blood of their own brother, regardless of the unbearable pain this would cause their father.

Even Judah, who saved Joseph's life by persuading the brothers to take him out of the pit and sell him to a caravan of Ishmaelites, did not exonerate himself from guilt. How could he have sold his own brother to slavery? Why did he not worry that the sudden transition from being Jacob's favorite son to becoming the lowly slave of idol worshipers would prove too difficult for Joseph to bear? Furthermore, how could Judah have cast him into the pit? True, the verse says, "the pit was empty, no water was in it" (*Genesis* 37:24), but the Sages infer from this, "there was no *water* in it, but there *were* snakes and scorpions in it" (*Rashi, Shabbos* 22a). According to this interpretation, casting Joseph into the pit was tantamount to murdering him with their own hands!

Ramban provides part of the answer. He explains that the brothers were unaware that the pit contained snakes and scorpions when they cast Joseph in. Even when they lifted him out, they did not notice the contents of the pit. Had they seen the snakes and scorpions when they pulled him out, they would have realized that a great miracle had transpired for Joseph's sake. This would have proved beyond a doubt that he must be a great *tzaddik*, and they surely would not have sold him. Unfortunately, they did not notice the contents of the pit.

Ohr HaChaim offers a different explanation. Reuben *did* see the snakes and scorpions, yet he did not consider them a threat to

Joseph's welfare. Reuben knew that unlike human beings, animals do not have the power to kill a person who has not been inscribed for death by the Heavenly Court. Thus, by throwing Joseph into the pit swarming with deadly animals, Reuben actually *ensured* Joseph's safety, as the verse says, "Reuben heard, and he rescued him from their hand" (*Genesis* 37:21). This seems a very unique interpretation, but it is firmly based on the *Zohar*.

Still, it is difficult to understand how the brothers could have deliberately inflicted such intense suffering upon their father Jacob. True, Joseph spoke slanderously of his brothers before Jacob, claiming that he had seen them eating a limb from a live animal, and that Leah's sons frequently slighted the sons of "the maidservants," Bilhah and Zilpah (*Rashi*, ibid., v. 2). And true, the brothers considered Joseph's dreams to be nothing but the nocturnal reflections of his waking fantasies, and hated him all the more as someone who thought only about selfishly dominating his peers. But still, to *kill* their own brother, to sell him as a slave to gentiles? It is so difficult to understand!

Even more perplexing is the fact that nowhere does the Torah condemn the brothers for their cruel deed. On the contrary, we see that Aaron the *Kohen* carried the names of *all* the Tribes upon the breastplate, including those that actively participated in selling Joseph. As the verse says, "Aaron shall bear the names of the sons of Israel on the Breastplate of Judgment when he enters the Sanctuary, as a constant remembrance *before* HASHEM" (*Exodus* 28:29). And the Sages have stated, "Whoever says that King David sinned is simply mistaken, for the verse says, 'David was successful in all his undertakings, *for God was with him*' (*I Samuel* 18:14) — is it possible that he committed a sin and yet 'God was with him'?" (*Shabbos* 55). Thus, we are forced to say that the brothers were not held liable for selling Joseph, for had they been, their names would not have merited to be "a constant remembrance *before* HASHEM."

Similarly, in explanation as to why Hashem did not reveal to Jacob what truly had happened to Joseph, *Rashi* says, "The brothers made a pact that whoever would reveal the truth to Jacob would be ac-cursed, and they gained Hashem's cooperation." Now, if the brothers had committed a crime, how could they have obtained Hashem's con-sent? It would appear that Hashem actually *approved* of their deed!

With so much evidence suggesting the brothers' innocence, we must conclude that there is more to the selling of Joseph than meets the eye. This is actually true of *all* the apparent transgressions committed by Jacob's sons. For example, in reference to the verse, "Reuben went and lay with Bilhah, his father's concubine" (*Genesis* 35:22), the Sages said, "Whoever says that Reuben sinned is simply mistaken, for the Torah itself testifies in that very verse, 'The sons of Jacob were twelve' " (*Shabbos* 56). *Rashi* explains, "This teaches that they were all equivalent and *all righteous*." From the fact that the Torah explicitly mentions the sins of Jacob's sons without holding them liable, it is obvious that these deeds are not meant to be taken at face value.

Ironically, the only brother who *was* held accountable for his actions was Judah, even though it was he who persuaded the brothers to sell Joseph instead of killing him. The reason: "He who begins a *mitzvah* has an obligation to complete it." As *Rashi* explains in reference to the Sages' statement, "Whoever blesses Judah is guilty of blasphemy" (*Sanhedrin* 10), Judah did not "complete the *mitzvah*" — he should have instructed his brothers to return [Joseph] to their father, instead of merely convincing them to throw him into the pit. How bizarre! The brothers who intended to kill Joseph and sold him as a slave were not held liable, but Judah, who made an effort to save him, was!

Sforno offers the following explanation: The reason why the brothers "conspired against [Joseph] to kill him" is because they thought his real intention was to spy on them and then bring back an unfavorable report to Jacob. They suspected Joseph of employing such underhanded methods to alienate Jacob from the rest of the brothers and ultimately earn them a curse or punishment. This explains how such righteous individuals, whose names were "a constant remembrance before HASHEM," could have entertained the thought of killing or selling their own brother — they thought it was a *mitzvah* to do so.

As proof for this contention, *Sforno* points out that the brothers never actually felt remorse for selling Joseph. Even in the most difficult moments of Joseph's staged melodrama in Egypt, the brothers only said, "Indeed, we are guilty concerning our brother *inasmuch as we saw his heartfelt anguish when he pleaded with us*

and we paid no heed; that is why this anguish has come upon us"
(Genesis 42:21). They only felt remorse for their cruelty, and thought
they were now being punished in kind. However, they did *not* regret
selling Joseph, since they felt that they had full justification — does
the Torah not say, "If someone is coming to slay you, rise early and
slay him first"? This also explains how the brothers could have so
calmly sat down to eat after casting Joseph into the pit (ibid., 37:25) —
they saw no other method by which to protect themselves from
Joseph's damaging campaign of defamation.

Reuben was the only exception. As the verse says, "Reuben spoke
to them, saying, 'Did I not speak to you saying, "Do not sin against
the boy," but you would not listen! Behold, his blood as well is being
avenged' " (ibid., v. 22). He alone among the brothers recognized that
they had made a fatal mistake in assessing Joseph's intentions,
misinterpreting his youthful impetuousness for scheming malicious-
ness.

Still, it is difficult to understand how the spiritually exalted
progenitors of Israel could have failed to perceive that Joseph's
dreams were not fantasy, but Hashem's will. In reference to the verse
"Then we shall see what will become of his dreams" (ibid., v. 20),
Rashi quotes a *Midrash* that says, "The [brothers] said, 'Let us kill
him,' but the verse concludes for them, 'Let us see whose words shall
prove true — yours, or Mine!' " How could the forebearers of the
prophets have remained oblivious to Hashem's designs?

The answer lies in *Rashi's* commentary on the verse, "So he sent
him from the depth of Hebron [מֵעֵמֶק חֶבְרוֹן]" (ibid., v. 14): "But
Hebron is situated on a *mountain*! Rather, the term מֵעֵמֶק חֶבְרוֹן is to
be understood figuratively — Jacob's decision to send Joseph to his
brothers who sold him into slavery was in fulfillment of the עֵצָה
עֲמוּקָה, 'the profound, deep design' that had been confided to
Abraham, who was buried in Hebron. The sense of this 'design' was
that Joseph's trip would initiate the fulfillment of Hashem's prophecy
to Abraham, 'Your offspring shall be aliens in a land not their own'
(ibid., 15:13)."

The *Zohar* sheds light on the role that Providence played in
bringing about Joseph's sale: Logically, Jacob should not have sent
Joseph, who was so intensely disliked by the brothers, to inquire after
their well-being. Instead, Jacob should have sent one of his servants

to Shechem. That he sent his favorite son is proof that Hashem intervened in order to fulfill His prophecy to Abraham.

Furthermore, the Torah explicitly mentions that Joseph was unable to find his brothers until the serendipitous meeting with "a man" in the wilderness who happened to know exactly where the brothers were encamped (see ibid., 37:15). As the *Ramban* explains, this "man" was none other than the angel Gabriel, whom God sent to lead Joseph to his brothers in order to fulfill the prophecy to Abraham. Similarly, the Sages add, "It would have been fitting that Jacob be taken down to Egypt in metal chains in order to fulfill the decree [made to Abraham], but his merits had an influence" (*Shabbos* 89).

Clearly, then, we see that the selling of Joseph was an act of Providence. Because it had to happen, the prophetic powers of Joseph's brothers were deliberately obscured by Hashem, and they remained oblivious to the fact that his dreams were not mere fantasies, but an accurate prediction of their destiny. This phenomenon is alluded to by the verse, "I . . . turn wise men back and cancel their plans" (*Isaiah* 45:25).

This also explains why, despite all the obvious hints, the brothers never suspected for a moment that Pharaoh's viceroy was actually Joseph. Even when Joseph, still under disguise, seated the brothers according to age, the verse merely says, "The [brothers] looked at one another in astonishment" (*Genesis* 43:33). According to *Midrash Tanchuma*, Joseph assigned the seating at the banquet by tapping his goblet and calling out, "Reuben, Simeon, Levi, and so on, sons of one mother, be seated in that order!" He did the same with the sons of Bilhah and Zilpah, but when he came to Benjamin he said, "He has no mother, *and I have no mother, so let him sit nearest to me.*" And still, the brothers did not recognize him!

Jacob's prophetic powers were also obscured at this time. When the brothers returned from Egypt the first time and informed their father that Pharaoh's viceroy demanded to see Benjamin, Jacob complained, "Why did you treat me so ill by telling the man that you had another brother?" (ibid., 43:6). In reference to this statement, the Sages said, "Jacob had never spoken such senseless words before. Hashem said, 'Here I am busy appointing his son to the throne, and all he can say is, "Why did you treat me so ill?" ' "

Joseph was the only one whose prophetic vision remained unimpaired. As *Ramban* explains, the reason why Joseph did not alleviate Jacob's pain by sending him a message with the news that he was still alive is because Joseph knew that Providence had decreed that his dreams must come true. This is why Joseph demanded that the brothers bring Benjamin to him: He had dreamt that he and his brothers "were binding sheaves in the middle of the field, when, behold! — my sheaf arose and remained standing; then behold! — your sheaves gathered around and bowed down to my sheaf" (ibid., 37:7). In this dream, *all* of Joseph's brothers had bowed down to him, including Benjamin. Since every last detail of the dream was of crucial importance, Joseph persisted in concealing his identity, and he demanded that the brothers bring Benjamin from Canaan. Although he knew that his demand would cause his beloved father untold pain and emotional turmoil, Joseph saw this as a necessary step towards fulfilling Hashem's decree.

The strongest proof that Joseph was fully aware of the Hand of Providence are his own words: "Then Joseph said to his brothers, 'I am Joseph your brother! It is me, whom you sold into Egypt. And now, do not be distressed nor reproach yourselves for having sold me here, *for it was to be a provider that God sent me ahead of you ... Thus God has sent me* ahead of you to insure your survival in the land, and to sustain you for a momentous deliverance. And now, *it was not you who sent me here, but God;* He has made me father to Pharaoh, master of his entire household, and ruler throughout the entire land of Egypt ... *God has made me master of all Egypt ...*'" (ibid., 45:3-9). *Sforno* paraphrases Joseph's statement as follows: "In view of Hashem's ultimate purpose, there is no doubt that the circumstances that preceded this outcome were also decreed by Hashem."

❦ ❦ ❦

Again, in the end of *Parashas Vayechi*, the verse says, "Joseph's brothers saw that their father was dead, and they said, 'Perhaps Joseph will nurse hatred against us and then he will surely repay us all the evil that we did him' ... But Joseph said to them, 'Fear not, for am I instead of God? Although *you* intended me harm, *God* intended it for good; in order to accomplish — it is as clear as this day — that a vast people be kept alive' " (ibid., 50:15-19). *Sforno* interprets this to mean, "Am I to pass judgment on His decrees? Who am I to punish the individuals who helped fulfill His decrees? True, you had malicious intentions against me because you considered me a threat to your welfare, but you were simply mistaken. What is important is that Hashem endorsed your actions."

Joseph's Test

The Talmud (*Yoma* 35b) says, "Poor people, rich people and wicked people will all be brought to judgment in Heaven in their time. The poor man will be asked, 'Why did you not engage in Torah study?' If he replies, 'I was poor, and was thus preoccupied with earning a living,' then he is told, 'Were you any poorer than Hillel?' For Hillel was extremely destitute, yet he made the necessary sacrifice to dedicate himself to Torah study and became the leading sage of his day. The rich man will be told, 'Were you any richer than Elazar ben Charsom,' who, despite his exceptional wealth, found the time to dedicate himself to Torah study? And the wicked man, if he argues, 'I was graced with beauty, and was preoccupied with indulging my evil inclination (*yetzer hara*),' is told, 'Were you more handsome than Joseph,' who, despite his attractive appearance, managed to conquer his evil inclination?"

We can learn from this *Gemara* to what extent Hashem deals fairly with His creations. If there had never been a Hillel to prove that it is humanly possible to withstand the trial of poverty, the poor man's excuse that he was faced with insurmountable hardship would have been accepted, and similarly for the rich and wicked men. It is only because history has provided evidence that these three "handicaps" can indeed be overcome that these people are judged for not having made the effort to do so themselves. Hillel realized that the Torah is the "source of life," that it is as precious as physical sustenance itself, and other poor people are expected to arrive at the same conclusion.

In *Sotah* 36b the Talmud tells us that "because Joseph sanctified the honor of Hashem in private, he merited to have one letter (ה) of the Divine Name added to his own name, as it says (*Psalms* 81:6), 'It was made a testimony through *Yehosef.*' " The Talmud continues, "Judah, who sanctified the honor of Hashem in public, merited to have his entire name made up of the letters of the Holy Name." This refers to Judah's admission of guilt when Tamar was about to be executed for harlotry. He was, after all, certainly interested in saving the life of his own daughter-in-law and unborn child. Nevertheless, his admission was considered to be a sanctification of Hashem's Name of such great proportions that his name was made up of the letters of Hashem's Name, for he could have probably found some other excuse to halt her execution, yet he chose to swallow his pride and publicly admit his guilt in the affair. *Maharsha* (ad loc.) asks the question: Wasn't Judah's name already given to him at birth — many years before this episode with Tamar? He answers that Leah should really have called him "Odeh," for the name was intended to be a reflection of the statement, "Now I will thank (*Odeh*) HASHEM" (*Genesis* 29:35). However, Hashem put the thought into her head to call him "Judah." Actually, *Rashi* interprets the Talmud's mention of Judah's "sanctification of Hashem's honor" to be a reference to the fact that Nahshon, the leader of the tribe of Judah, jumped into the Red Sea when he heard Hashem's command to Moses, "Speak to the Children of Israel and let them journey fourth [into the sea]" (*Exodus* 14:15). It was this brave act that entitled Judah to become the ruling tribe over Israel, the progenitor of David and the Messiah (see *Psalms* 114:2).

In the Manner that a Person Judges, So Is He Judged

The following interpretation is ascribed to R' Yitzchak Blazer, the disciple of R' Israel Salanter:

> The verse says, "And Joseph said to his brothers, 'I am Joseph! Is my father still alive?' But his brothers could not answer him because they were left disconcerted before him" (*Genesis* 45:3).

Now, at first glance, Joseph's question seems redundant, for that is the very question he asked the brothers upon their return from Canaan, as the verse says, "Is your aged father of whom you spoke at peace? Is he still alive?" At that time, the brothers assured Joseph, "Your servant our father is at peace, he still lives" (ibid., 43:27-28). Why, then, did Joseph repeat the question? Furthermore, why were the brothers left speechless? Why did they not answer once again, "Our father is at peace, he still lives"?

In order to comprehend, we must first elucidate the underlying thrust of Judah's plea to Joseph. Following Joseph's declaration that he would release all the brothers except Benjamin, Judah appealed to Joseph's sense of compassion, passionately describing to him the unbearable pain that Benjamin's disappearance would cause to Jacob, their elderly father. As Judah explained, "Your servant my father said to us, 'You know that my wife bore me two [sons]. One [Joseph] has left me, and I presumed that he has surely been torn to pieces, for I have not seen him since. So should you take this one [Benjamin], too, from my presence, and disaster befall him, then you will have brought down my hoariness in evil to the grave' " (ibid., 44:27-39). Thus, Judah, argued, even though Benjamin was indeed guilty of having stolen Joseph's cup, it would be unjust to imprison him, for this would surely bring about the death of a perfectly innocent man — namely, Benjamin's father Jacob.

Scripture describes Joseph's reaction: "Now Joseph could not restrain himself ... so he called out, 'Remove everyone from my presence!' ... And Joseph said to his brothers, '*I am Joseph! Is my father still alive?*' " (ibid., 45:1-3). In other words, Joseph countered, "When you judged *me*, you found me guilty and sold me to slavery *despite* the pain this would cause our father. You didn't care that your decision would cause him 22 years of utter misery! Why are you suddenly so concerned for our father's emotional well-being? You yourselves are guilty of the very thing that you accuse me!"

The brothers could not utter a single word in their defense. They were left totally speechless in the face of Joseph's incontestable retort.

With this insight, we may better understand the following *Midrash*: "R' Abba Cohen Bardla said: 'Woe to us on the Day of Judgment! Woe to us on the Day of Rebuke! If the rebuke of Joseph, who was the youngest of Jacob's sons, was too powerful for the brothers to withstand, how much more so when the Holy One, Blessed is He, *will rebuke each one of us in accordance with who we are*, as the verse says, 'I shall censure you and confront you with these charges' " (*Psalms* 50:21).

In other words, after describing in great detail the damaging effect that Benjamin's incarceration would have upon their father, the brothers clearly demonstrated that they possessed enough sensitivity to know what Joseph's disappearance would do to their father. All along, Joseph had been trying to make this quality of theirs come out into the open so that he could confront them with it. Finally, he held up a mirror to their souls, and the brothers recoiled from what they saw. The Sages referred to this kind of rebuke as "rebuke given in accordance with who they were." So too, in the future Hashem will "rebuke each one of us in accordance with who we are" — He will prove that we possessed all the qualities necessary for fulfilling every *mitzvah* in the Torah.

For example, if an individual were to be judged for not giving sufficient money to charity, he would most probably defend himself by saying, "But I'm always short of money, and to make matters worse, I'm a born miser!" Hashem will then show him all the lavish expenditures he happily incurred throughout his life in order to fulfill his own needs. Again, this is called "rebuke given in accordance with who we are" — our very actions invalidate our justifications.

In Scripture, we see this type of rebuke employed by the prophet Nathan when he confronted King David for the incident involving Bathsheba:

Nathan disarmingly asked the king how he would judge the following case: A poor man bought an animal with great difficulty, and then cared for it like one of his own children. As Nathan put it, "It ate from his food, drank from his cup, and slept in his bosom — it was like a daughter to him." In the same town lived a very wealthy man who owned many heads of livestock, but who was extremely miserly. When a guest came to the rich man, he stole the poor man's animal and served it to his guest.

King David's anger flared and he indignantly declared, "The wealthy man deserves to be put to death!"

"*You* are the man!" Nathan said to David. "Thus says HASHEM: 'I anointed you king over Israel, saved you from the hand of Saul, gave you your master's estate, your master's wives in your bosom, and the House of Israel and Judah . . . [Yet] you cut down Uriah with a sword and took his wife as your wife!" (*II Samuel* 12 ad loc.).

The next time we see a "terrible injustice" or notice another person's faults, let us remember that "rebuke is given in accordance with who we are." Let us remember that the faults we see in others are the very faults for which we ourselves will be held accountable on the Day of Judgment. For if we are sensitive enough to detect these shortcomings in others, it must be that we possess the necessary qualities to rectify these flaws in ourselves. What will we say when the mirror is held before our eyes? Woe to us on the Day of Judgment! Woe to us on the Day of Rebuke!

Be Impartial in Self-Judgment

Joseph's brothers were convinced that his dreams were nothing but wishful fantasies. That is why they taunted him, "Would you then reign over us? Would you then dominate us?" (*Genesis* 37:8), and then ultimately condemned him to death. They were certain that selling him into slavery would put an end to his dreams, and force him to finally come face to face with reality.

However, all their certainty vanished in an instant when Joseph declared, "I am Joseph your brother!" From one moment to the next, it became painfully clear to the brothers that they had been mistaken all along. Joseph's dreams had indeed been prophetic, reflecting the will of Hashem. They were so shocked by this realization that they were unable to utter a single word in response.

In reference to this the Sages said, "Woe to us on the Day of Judgment! Woe to us on the Day of Rebuke! If the rebuke of Joseph, who was the youngest of Jacob's sons, was too powerful for his brothers to withstand, how much more so when the Holy One, Blessed is He, *will rebuke each one of us in accordance with who we are*, as the verse says, 'I shall censure you and confront you with these charges' " (*Psalms* 50:21).

The Sages meant that just as the brothers were left speechless at the realization that they had erred all along, so will each one of us be left speechless on the Day of Judgment when we will be shown the errors we committed during the course of our lives. For undeniably we are all blinded by self-esteem, and invariably, we consider our actions impeccable and beyond reproach. As the Torah explicitly says, "You shall not accept a bribe, for the bribe *will blind the eyes of the wise* and make just words crooked" (*Deuteronomy* 16:19): If a monetary bribe blinds the eyes of a wise man, how much more so do the reassuring strokes of the ego incapacitate the average person's ability to introspect and evaluate the worthiness of his own deeds!

The Sages said: לְעוֹלָם יִרְאֶה דַיָּן עַצְמוֹ כְּאִלּוּ גֵיהִנֹּם פְּתוּחָה לוֹ מִתַּחְתָּיו, which is usually translated as, "A judge should always perceive himself as though [the gates of] *Gehinnom* are open below him."

However, according to the principles established above, the statement may also convey, "When judging *one's own actions*, a person should perceive himself as though [the gates of] *Gehinnom* are open below him." Unless a person scrutinizes his deeds with the utmost caution, he will invariably be blinded by the trappings of his self-esteem.

Jacob's Age

In *Genesis* 47:9 Jacob tells Pharaoh, "The days of the years of my sojourns have been one hundred and thirty years; the days of the years of my life have been few and miserable, and they have not reached the life spans of my forefathers ..." *Ramban* wonders why Jacob would take this seemingly inappropriate opportunity to complain about the hardship of his life before the august king of Egypt. Furthermore, he wonders, how did Jacob know that he would not reach the life span of his forefathers at this point in his life? *Ramban* suggests that Jacob, through all his sufferings, had acquired a very elderly appearance — in excess even of his 130 years — and this is what prompted Pharaoh, amazed at this ancient countenance (for most people at that time did not live to such an old age), to ask Jacob how old he was. Jacob's response was that he looked older than his 130 years because his days were "miserable," and that his age of 130 was not all that impressive when one takes into consideration that his forefathers lived much longer.

Daas Zekeinim mentions a *Midrash* which portrays Hashem as saying to Jacob, "I saved you from Esau and from Laban and brought back Dinah and Joseph to you, and you now complain about your life, that your days are 'few and miserable'! By your life, I will subtract from your life one year for every word of your complaint, from 'And he [Pharaoh] said' (ibid., v. 8) until 'in the days of their sojourns.' " For there are thirty-three words here, and you will find that Jacob's life was exactly thirty-three years shorter than that of his father.

This *Midrash* is difficult. The words of Jacob's complaint do not begin until v. 9, "And Jacob said to Pharaoh . . ." If so, why does the *Midrash* include the entire previous verse, which tells of *Pharaoh's* question to Jacob, into the number of words to be deducted from Jacob's life? The answer is apparently that Jacob was taken to task not only for the *words* of complaint that he uttered, but also for the *appearance* of discomfort that he exhibited, which led to Pharaoh's question in the first place. This is why the words of Pharaoh's question are also counted against him.

In a similar vein we find that Moses told the Children of Israel when they passed by the territory of Esau on the way to the Land of Israel that they should "purchase food from them with money . . . for HASHEM . . . has blessed you" (*Deuteronomy* 2:6, 7). *Rashi* explains, "Therefore (because 'HASHEM has blessed you'), do not show ungratefulness to Him by giving the impression that you are impoverished and cannot afford to buy your food. Rather, show the wealth and prosperity that are yours." Giving an impression of poverty would give the children of Esau the impression that Hashem had not properly cared for the Jews during their wanderings in the desert, which would be an ungrateful course of action for the Jews to take. It is the obligation of every person — especially someone on the lofty spiritual level of Jacob — to accentuate the good things that Hashem has done for him in his life, for this brings honor to Hashem's Name, showing that He looks after His servants. To do the opposite — to accentuate the negative in one's life — brings the opposite result — desecration of Hashem's Name.

Serving as the Object
of a Commandment

Just before his death, Jacob asked Joseph to promise that he would not be buried in Egypt (*Genesis* 47:29). *Rashi* (quoting the *Midrash*) explains the reason for this request: "So that they should not make his body an object of idolatrous worship. For when an idolater is punished for his sin, the object of his idolatry is also dealt with, as it says, 'I will perform judgments against all the gods of Egypt' " (*Exodus* 12:12). Jacob knew that the gods of Egypt would be destroyed along with those who worshiped them, and he therefore wanted to ensure that he would never be deified by the Egyptians. We see from this comment of the *Midrash* that despite the fact that Jacob had done nothing wrong — his being worshiped would have been done without his consent, or even knowledge — he would have suffered for having been the object or catalyst for other people's sins. As the Talmud in *Shabbos* (149b) puts it, "Anyone whose friend has been punished on his account is not allowed into Hashem's inner circle in the World to Come." We learn from this that even if a person passively becomes the object of his friend's sin, he is nevertheless subject to punishment.

However, we know that Hashem's mercifulness is much more forceful than His Attribute of Strict Justice (*Sanhedrin* 100a). Thus, we may infer that when a person passively becomes the object of his friend's observance of a commandment, he is deserving of a great reward for his role, although it was a completely unintentional one. This idea is mentioned in *Rashi's* comment on the verse "When you forget a bundle in the field, you shall not turn back to take it; it shall be for the ... orphan and the widow, so that HASHEM ... will bless you" (*Deuteronomy* 24:19). *Rashi*, quoting from *Sifrei*, notes: "Even though the food came into the hand of the poor without your performing an intentional, direct act of giving, [you are nevertheless entitled to Hashem's blessing]; how much more so if you give charity *directly* to a poor person. You may infer from this that if money falls out of someone's pocket and is found by a poor man, that person receives a blessing from Hashem."

We find this concept applying even to inanimate objects. We know that the site of Solomon's Temple was chosen by Hashem because it was the location where the Binding of Isaac (*Akeidah*) on the altar took place. The very dirt and stones of that mountain were endowed with sanctity merely by virtue of the fact that they served as the place where Abraham performed his supreme act of dedication to Hashem.

This theme appears again in *Sotah* 7b, where the Talmud tells us, "What is meant by 'May Reuben live and not die . . . and this is for Judah . . .' (*Deuteronomy* 36:6-7)? Judah's remains were in a state of unrest in his coffin because of the '*cherem*' he had imposed upon himself by saying to his father, 'If I do not bring [Benjamin] back to you . . . may I be considered a sinner before you for all days' (*Genesis* 43:9). This was the situation until Moses prayed on Judah's behalf: 'Master of the Universe! Who was the one who inspired Reuben to repent for his sin? Judah!' " Although Judah's behavior and admission of guilt in the episode of Tamar (ibid., 38:26) brought him great spiritual reward in its own right, as the Talmud discusses in *Sotah* 36b (see above "Joseph's test"), it was not enough to spare his body from unrest after death. For that, he needed the extra merit that was provided by the fact that his behavior served as an example for Reuben to emulate. This passive act, which was the catalyst for a righteous act on the part of another individual, was deemed to be more significant than his own righteousness!

Jacob's Blessings to His Sons

The verse says, "Then Jacob called for his sons and said, 'Assemble yourselves and I will tell you what will befall you in the End of Days'" (*Genesis* 49:1). Nowhere in the *parashah*, however, do we see any further reference to "what will befall you in the End of Days." Instead, Jacob proceeds to bless each of his sons.

Rashi explains that Jacob had originally intended to reveal to his sons the date when the Messiah would come, but the Divine Presence suddenly and inexplicably deserted him. Jacob, realizing that God must not want the time of the End to be revealed, proceeded to bless his sons.

When Jacob concluded blessing his sons, the verse says, "All these are the tribes of Israel — twelve — and this is what their father spoke to them and he blessed them; he blessed each according to his appropriate blessing" (ibid., v. 28). However, both *Rashi* and *Ibn Ezra* find it difficult to understand why Jacob's pronouncements are referred to as "blessings," since a number of his sons received nothing but scathing rebuke.

It would seem that the answer lies in redefining the term "blessing." Conventionally, "to bless someone" means to invoke God's favor upon a particular person. However, if this is all the term means, why did Jacob refuse to bless Joseph's sons in the manner Joseph desired? As the verse says, "Joseph saw that his father was placing his right hand on Ephraim's head, and it displeased him; so he supported his father's hand to remove it from upon Ephraim's head to Manasseh's head. And Joseph said to his father, 'Not so, Father, for *this* is the firstborn; place your right hand on *his* head.' But his father refused, saying, 'I know, my son, I know; he too will become a people, and he too will become great, but his younger brother shall become greater than he, and his offspring['s fame] will fill the nations' " (ibid., 48:18-19).

Jacob's explanation implies that blessing someone also connotes recognizing his natural disposition, including his strengths and weaknesses. For a blessing cannot reside upon an empty vessel — he who bestows a blessing cannot impart a quality to the recipient unless the recipient has already been endowed with a trace of that quality by Hashem. This principle is derived from the incident involving Elisha and the poor widow: Elisha wanted to bless her with prosperity, so he said, "What can I do for you? Tell me what you have in the house." Her answer was, "Your servant has nothing in the house but a jug of oil." At this, Elisha said, "Go and borrow vessels from the outside, from all your neighbors; empty vessels . . . Then go and close the door behind you and your children, and pour [the oil] into all the vessels and remove the full ones. She left him and closed the door ... They handed the vessels to her as she poured, and after the vessels were full, she said to her son, 'Give me another vessel,' *but he answered, 'There are no more vessels!' And the oil stopped"* (II Kings 4:1-6).

Similarly, we find that Moses prefaced his blessing to Israel by saying, "HASHEM came from Sinai — having shone forth to them from Seir, having appeared from Mount Paran, and then approached with some of the holy myriads — from His right hand He presented the fiery Torah to them" (*Deuteronomy* 33:2). As *Rashi* explains, Moses' intention was to demonstrate that Israel was *worthy* of receiving a blessing. Again, we see that a blessing cannot reside upon an empty vessel; rather, in order for a blessing to take effect, the recipient must already possess a trace of the attribute with which he is being blessed.

This, then, is the lesson Jacob imparted to his sons prior to his death. He taught them the importance of recognizing their own disposition, of coming to terms with the strengths and weaknesses with which they had been endowed by Hashem.

Hence, Jacob told Reuben, "You are my firstborn, my strength and my initial vigor, foremost in rank and foremost in power." As *Targum Onkelos* explains, Jacob in essence said, "You *should* have been entitled to three portions: the rights of the firstborn, priesthood ('foremost in rank') and kingship ('foremost in power')." Jacob then reveals to Reuben how he lost these three portions: "Water-like impetuosity — you cannot be foremost, because you mounted your father's bed; then you desecrated Him Who ascended my couch" (*Genesis* 49:4). *Rashi* interprets this to mean, "You lost your right to national leadership because of the impetuosity with which you rushed to vent your anger [in the incident with Bilhah, when you 'mounted your father's bed']." And even though the Sages said, "Whoever says that Reuben sinned is simply mistaken" (*Shabbos* 55), we *do* see that Jacob held him accountable for this almost imperceptible character flaw.

Similarly, Jacob declared, "Simeon and Levi are comrades, their weaponry is a stolen craft ... O my honor! For in their rage they murdered people and at their whim they maimed an ox. Accursed is their rage, for it is intense, and their wrath, for it is harsh ..." (*Genesis*

49:5-7). Jacob berated the two brothers for slaying the male inhabitants of Shechem following the incident involving their sister Dinah and Shechem the son of Hamor the Hivvite (see ibid., Ch. 34). The *Ramban* explains that even though the two brothers' "rage" on behalf of their sister's honor stemmed from the same exalted source as Phineas' zealousness for Hashem (see *Numbers* 25), Jacob berated them for indiscriminately killing *all* the Shechemite males, including those who were completely innocent. Furthermore, Jacob disapproved of the fact that "their weaponry is a stolen craft." As *Rashi* explains, Jacob considered Simeon and Levi's preoccupation with the weaponry of violence a trait that they "stole" from Esau. For it is Esau, not Jacob, who lives by the sword, as opposed to Jacob, whose weapon is prayer.

Thus, we see that the very act of identifying another person's strengths and weaknesses and sharing this information with him is the greatest blessing one can give. This idea can be illustrated through the following analogy: Imagine that your business has begun losing money. Your friends and acquaintances commiserate with you, wish you well, and bless you with success. One of them, however, does more — he takes a personal interest and asks you detailed questions about the running of your enterprise. Then, one day, he begins listing the reasons why your business is faltering. "You made this mistake, you made that mistake, this was an unwise decision, that was a bad investment . . ." His words are like arrows, your pride is in pieces. But what a blessing! Thanks to this person, you will get a realistic picture of your situation, and you will rectify your mistakes. In no time, you'll be making a profit again! The same is true of our spiritual "business" — the greatest blessing one can ever receive is to be informed of one's faults!

This, then, is the meaning of the verse, "All these are the tribes of Israel — twelve — and this is what their father spoke to them and he blessed them; *he blessed each according to his appropriate blessing*" — in other words, Jacob informed his sons of their underlying tendencies and defined their strengths and weaknesses. This was his blessing to them, for he knew that now they would be able to rectify their character and thereby perfect their service of Hashem.

In truth, we all have an obligation to realistically perceive our aptitudes and character makeup. How else can we ever expect to fulfill the commandment, "You shall love HASHEM, your God with all your heart, with all your soul and with all your resources"? Obviously, unless we know the extent of our spiritual "resources," we will never know how much we should expect of ourselves. Just as a person must know his financial situation in order to know how much charity to give, so must he know the dimensions of his spiritual potential in order to perceive when he has reached the limit. In the same way as a wealthy individual has not fulfilled the obligation to give charity unless he gives in accordance with his means, so a person endowed with great spiritual potential does not fulfill his purpose in life unless he serves Hashem in accordance with the faculties with which he was endowed.

The Sages said, "Do not judge your fellow until you stand in his place." The *Mabit* explains, "Even though at first glance it seems to you that you are greater than your fellow, do not judge him according to your standards. It is quite likely that you have fallen short of realizing your spiritual potential, whereas he, in accordance with the aptitudes with which he was endowed, *has* fulfilled his potential. In this case, he is actually greater than you."

Along the same lines, the *Chafetz Chaim* said, "People say 'Every fool is a wise man in his own eyes,' but the opposite is really the truth — 'Every wise man is a fool in his own eyes,' for a prisoner cannot release himself from his cell. We are so biased by our love for ourselves that it is almost impossible for us to discern the roots of our behavior. Every person does whatever he thinks is right without feeling the slightest pang of conscience!"

Judah's Supremacy

"The scepter shall not pass from Judah" (*Genesis* 49:10). Jacob, in these words of blessing, foretold of the supremacy of the tribe of Judah over all the others; the leaders of Israel would always come from Judah. *Ramban* asserts that according to this, all the kings of the Northern Kingdom of Israel (of the ten tribes), which split away from the reign of David's descendants, were acting against their patriarch's express wishes. They apparently relied on the prophecy of Achiyah the Shiloni, who had sanctioned the original split from Solomon's son (*I Kings* 11:31); but this was erroneous, for that was intended to be only a temporary measure. *Ramban* also suggests that it was for this reason that the Hasmonean dynasty was completely destroyed — they, being *Kohanim*, of the tribe of Levi, were punished for having assumed the mantle of kingship, which belonged by right exclusively to Judah.

Rambam (*Hilchos Melachim* 1:9) seems to agree with *Ramban's* interpretation, for he writes, "If a king should arise from one of the other tribes, it cannot be a permanent dynasty, as it is said in reference to Jeroboam (who led the original rebellion against David's house), 'I shall chasten the descendants of David . . ., but not forever' (*I Kings* 11:39)." However, *Raavad* (ad loc.) writes, "If Jeroboam and his descendants had been worthy kings, the kingship could have (theoretically) continued uninterrupted, although it would have been secondary to the House of David." *Ran*, in his *Drashos*, argues that Jacob's words were not meant as a commandment or even a request, but merely a prophecy of what would be in the future — that once the reign of Judah's descendants would begin, it would never be completely disbanded. The Hasmoneans, continues *Ran*, did nothing wrong by assuming the title of "king," because during that era the Jewish people were completely subservient to the powerful empires, with only a small measure of autonomy. Jacob did not mean to say that no member of another tribe would ever assume a post of importance; he meant only that such a person would never be an absolute monarch, which, as noted above, did not apply to the Hasmoneans.

Ramban in his commentary on our verse also deals with the problem of Saul's kingship. Saul, the first king to be anointed over Israel, was from the tribe of Benjamin, not Judah! This, explains *Ramban*, is because at the time of his appointment Hashem was displeased with the manner in which the people requested a king to lead them (*I Samuel* 8:7), and He did not wish at that time to grant them a king from the tribe of Judah, whose kingship would be firmly established for all times. He gave them Saul instead, who was killed along with his son a short time later. Actually, there is a verse (ibid., 13:13,14) which says, "HASHEM would have established your (Saul's) kingdom over Israel forever, but now your kingdom shall not endure," which implies that had Saul not sinned in the incident at Gilgal, his reign *would* have been permanent. *Ramban* explains that Saul would indeed have had some sort of permanent position of rulership over *part* of Israel, but not over the entire nation.

Supporters of Torah

"**Z**ebulun shall settle by seashores ... Issachar is a strong-boned donkey" (*Genesis* 49:13,14). The Sages explain that Zebulun would engage in commerce and donate a large portion of his earnings to the tribe of Issachar, who would apply their efforts to the toil of Torah study. Noting that Zebulun is mentioned before Issachar (although Issachar was older, and the other tribes are mentioned in order of age) both here and in Moses' blessings of *VeZos HaBerachah* (*Deuteronomy* 33:18), *Sforno* explains that since Issachar's study would have been impossible if not for the hard work and generosity of Zebulun — for "if there is no flour [for bread] there is no [study of] Torah" (*Avos* 3:17) — Zebulun is given priority over Issachar. We can learn from this to what extent those who enable Torah study with their financial assistance share in that commandment with those who do the actual studying! This, in fact, is the idea behind the Torah's commandments to the populace at large to supply the *Kohanim* and Levites with various gifts and awards (*terumah, bikkurim, maaser, reishis hagez*, etc.) — so that the general population could supply the necessary financial support to those who were in charge of studying and disseminating Torah knowledge throughout Israel, as it says (*Deuteronomy* 33:10), "They (of the tribe of Levi) will teach Your judgments to Jacob and Your Torah to Israel."

In the *Shulchan Aruch* (*Yoreh De'ah* 242) it is ruled that if someone has two lost objects to return — one to his father and one to his *rebbi* — the object of the *rebbi* should be attended to first. The *rebbe* is entitled to a higher degree of respect because "his father merely brought him into *this* world, while his *rebbi* brings him into the World to Come" (*Bava Metzia* 33a). *Rama* (*Yoreh De'ah* ibid., quoting *Sefer Chassidim*) rules that in a case where the father pays for the *rebbi* to teach his son, however, respect for the father takes precedence over respect for the *rebbi*. *Shach* (ad loc.) extends this idea even further: If there is a *third party* who pays for the boy's tuition, then that party is also entitled to a higher degree of respect than the *rebbi* who does the teaching. From this ruling we can see very clearly how Zebulun comes before Issachar!

Jacob Is Alive

The Talmud tells us (*Taanis* 5b) that Jacob never died. The verse says, "And [Jacob] expired and was gathered unto his people" (*Genesis* 49:33), but the expression "he died" is never used. *Rashi* (ad loc.) explains that it appeared to all those around him that he had died (and this is why they mourned him), but he was not really dead. *Ramban* points out that Jacob himself mentioned the word "death" in connection with his own situation — "Behold, I am about to die" (ibid., 48:21). This can be explained, suggests *Ramban*, as being due to his great humility; or perhaps Jacob himself thought (incorrectly) that he was about to die.

The deeper meaning of the Sages' assertion that "Jacob did not die" is explained by *Rabbeinu Bachya*. The soul of most righteous people, upon their demise, returns to its source. The souls of the greatest righteous people, however, remain near their bodies, hovering over them forever. Very few people achieve this exalted status, of course, but Jacob was one of them. We find that the Sages say (*Kesubos* 103a) concerning Rebbi as well that he used to appear regularly in his house after his death until his presence was detected by a neighbor, whereupon he decided not to come any more, so as not to "bring discredit upon the righteous men of previous days" (who did not merit this outstanding level of spirituality described by *Rabbeinu Bachya*).

In fact, the Talmud (ibid.) goes on to tell how Rebbi would recite *Kiddush* for his family on Shabbos (when he would appear to them after his death). There is a general rule that a person cannot fulfill his obligation by hearing someone else recite a prayer, unless the reciter himself has the obligation to perform that commandment. (Thus, for example, a woman cannot blow the *shofar* for a man, since women are exempt from the commandment of *shofar*, while men are obligated.) We must therefore conclude that the level of sanctity which Rebbi had achieved was so high that even after death he was considered, unlike dead people in general, to be bound by all the commandments of the Torah! Similarly, we find that one of the *Amoraim* was shocked to see the prophet Elijah in a cemetery, for he was a *Kohen* (who is forbidden to have any contact with a corpse). Apparently, even after death, Elijah's soul was on such a high level of holiness that he was bound to follow all the commandments of the Torah.

שמות
Shemos

Hashem's Design Shall Be Fulfilled

This *parashah* depicts the roots of the redemption from Egypt, Moses' birth, and his miraculous deliverance from death. The fundamental lesson it imparts to us is that no mortal being — even one as powerful as Pharaoh — is capable of resisting the will of the Almighty. Whatever Hashem decrees, that is what shall take place.

We learned the same lesson earlier, when Joseph revealed his true identity to his brothers. Joseph said to them, "Although you intended me harm, God intended it for good" (*Genesis* 50:20). Similarly, all the events that led up to the sale of Joseph were decreed by Heaven. As *Rashi* says in reference to the verse, "he sent him from the depth of Hebron" (ibid., 37:14) — "[Jacob sent Joseph] in fulfillment of the *profound, deep design that [HASHEM]* had confided to Abraham." When Joseph failed to find his brothers, Hashem sent an angel to direct him, saying, "They have journeyed from here, for I heard them saying, 'Let us go to Dothan' " (ibid., v. 17). Again, we see that nothing can stand in the way of a Divine decree. As *Ramban* says, "Scripture provides a lengthy description of how Joseph reached his brothers in order to emphasize that reality is dictated by Heavenly decrees, not by human endeavors."

Indeed, every single incident in Joseph's life was guided by the hand of Providence: First, he was sold as a slave to Potiphar, an influential courtier of Pharaoh. Then, Potiphar's wife fell in love with Joseph, causing him to end up in prison, but not just any prison — "Joseph's master took him and placed him in the prison . . . *where the king's prisoners* were confined" (ibid., 39:20). In prison, Joseph met the Chamberlain of the Cupbearers and accurately interpreted his dream, which in turn led the Chamberlain to mention Joseph's name to Pharaoh when the Egyptian ruler dreamt his disturbing dreams. Had any one of these events not occurred, Joseph would never have been appointed Pharaoh's second-in-command. And why, indeed, did it all have to happen? Because years earlier, Hashem had told Abraham, "Know with certainty that your offspring shall be aliens in a land not their own; they will serve them, and they will oppress them 400 years" (ibid., 15:13)!

With these introductory remarks, we may attempt to answer a question raised by several of the major commentators: Why does *Sefer Shemos* begin with the conjunctive clause וְאֵלֶּה שְׁמוֹת, "*And these are the names* . . ."?

The explanation would seem to be that Scripture informs us that *Sefer Shemos* and the *parashiyos* which precede it share a common underlying theme — namely, that Heavenly decrees are immutable and irrevocable, and that they will be fulfilled regardless of the circumstances. Just as the events in Joseph's life were guided by the immutable decree of "your offspring shall be aliens in a land not their own . . . and they will oppress them 400 years," so too, the events depicted in the beginning of *Sefer Shemos* were determined by the decree, "But also the nation that they shall serve, I shall judge, and afterwards they shall leave with great wealth" (ibid., v. 14).

Pharaoh's evil decrees were nothing more than means by which to expedite the fulfillment of Hashem's promise to Abraham. Thus, unwittingly, Pharaoh himself played an important role in bringing about Israel's redemption. Pharaoh said, הָבָה נִתְחַכְּמָה לוֹ פֶּן־יִרְבֶּה ("Come, let us outsmart [the Israelite nation] *lest* it become numerous") (*Exodus* 1:10), but Hashem amended his words to הָבָה נִתְחַכְּמָה לוֹ כֶּן־יִרְבֶּה ("Come, let us outsmart [the Israelite nation] for it *shall* become numerous"). At this point Jewish women began giving birth to sextuplets.

Similarly, Moses' life from beginning to end was one continuous miracle. The Sages teach that his mother Jochebed was no less than *130 years old* when she conceived him. He was born in the darkest era of the Egyptian exile, when Pharaoh, having failed to stem Jewish growth through slavery, ordered that every newborn Jewish male be cast into the Nile River. Just surviving this evil decree was miraculous enough, but the fact that he was saved by Batiah, *Pharaoh's own daughter*, and was raised under the doting care of *the very king who had ordered* the Jewish redeemer killed is simply astonishing.

Even more amazing is the fact that Moses was saved by being placed in the Nile, the very body of water through which Pharaoh had intended to kill him. And who nursed Moses? An Egyptian woman? No, Heaven forbid, for Moses refused to suckle the impure milk of an Egyptian. Instead, the verse tells us, "[Moses'] sister said to Pharaoh's daughter, 'Shall I go and summon for you a wet nurse *from the Hebrew women*, who will nurse the boy for you?' The daughter of Pharaoh said, 'Go' " (ibid., 2:7-8). Who was the "wet nurse from the Hebrew women"? None other than Jochebed, Moses' own mother! How incredibly ironical!

Ibn Ezra offers two reason why it was necessary that Moses grow up in Pharaoh's house: First, so that he become accustomed to the ways of nobility in preparation for his appointment as King of Israel; and second, so that he be revered by his fellow Jews.

However, in line with the concept that we have outlined above, there is a third reason: By growing up in Pharaoh's own home, Hashem conveyed to the Jews the power of Heavenly decrees. The Jews saw Pharaoh, the very person who had instigated Jewish infanticide as a means of preventing Israel's redemption, gently cuddling Israel's redeemer in his own hands! This sight etched an indelible impression in the minds of the Jewish people regarding the inexorable nature of Heavenly decrees.

We must internalize this lesson and realize that *all* events, including those we ourselves experience, are functions of the Divine will, and that nothing we do will alter it by one iota.

Repaying Kindness

There are several instances in the Talmud where particular individuals are accused of ungratefulness. The desert generation as a whole is accused of having been ungrateful for the manna

Hashem provided to them in the desert — they complained, "our soul is disgusted with this insubstantial food" (*Numbers* 21:5; see *Avodah Zarah* 5). *Rashi* explains that they considered the manna "insubstantial" because it did not activate the body's eliminatory system, since it contained no impurities and was completely absorbed into the limbs. Instead of being appreciative to Hashem for providing them with such pure food, they grieved. As a consequence, the Talmud calls that generation: "Ingrates, sons of ingrates!"

Pharaoh was also accused of this fault, as the verse says, "A new king arose over Egypt *who did not know of Joseph*" (*Exodus* 1:8) — according to one opinion, the verse does not mean that a new king was appointed, but rather that the existing monarch adopted a *new policy* of ignoring Joseph's monumental contributions to the country (*Sotah* 11a). The Sages said in reference to this, "Because Pharaoh did not show gratitude to Joseph, he ended up saying, 'I do not know HASHEM!' " (*Exodus* 5:2). Similarly, the Sages said, "He who denies the generosity of a fellow human being will ultimately deny the generosity of the Almighty."

This *parashah* deals extensively with the converse of ungratefulness — showing appreciation for acts of kindness. The *Midrash* says that when Hashem appeared to Moses amidst the burning bush and sought to appoint him as Israel's redeemer, Moses' immediate response was, "I cannot go without Jethro's permission. I am deeply indebted to him, for when I was fleeing in the wilderness from Pharaoh, he took me into his house as though I were his own son. Hence, I cannot go unless he gives his consent."

In truth, one should feel forever indebted to every person who has ever shown one a kindness, regardless of whether that person had ulterior motives in doing so. To illustrate this idea, let us take a closer look at Jethro's kindness to Moses, while keeping in mind Moses' sense of eternal gratitude towards him:

The verse tells us that "The minister of Midian had seven daughters; they came and drew water and filled the troughs to water their father's sheep. The shepherds came and drove them away. Moses got up and saved them and watered their sheep. They came to Reuel [Jethro] their father ... [They told him,] 'An Egyptian man saved us from the shepherds ...' He said to his daughters, 'Then where is he? Why did you leave the man? Summon him and let him eat bread' " (ibid., 2:16-20). *Rashi* explains that Jethro's real intention in inviting Moses to his house was to marry off one of his daughters to him. Indeed, the very next verse says, "and [Jethro] gave his daughter Zipporah to Moses." Despite Jethro's ulterior motives, Moses never forgot his kindness. The Sages say that Moses always thought, "All the trouble and inconvenience that Jethro put himself through was purely for my sake!" He gave Jethro the benefit of the doubt and assumed that his kind gesture stemmed from a sincere desire to help out a fellow human being; he did not focus on Jethro's self-seeking intentions. And what gratefulness! Moses felt so indebted to Jethro that he could not even commit himself to fulfill the Almighty's commandment to redeem his own brethren from the Egyptian house of bondage without first obtaining Jethro's consent. How great is our obligation to feel gratitude towards those who have been kind to us!

The failure to express gratitude for a kindness is judged very harshly by Hashem. We learn this from *Parashas Ki Seitzei*, where the verse says, "An Ammonite or Moabite shall not enter the congregation of HASHEM, . . . to eternity, *because of the fact that they did not greet you with bread and water* on the road when you were leaving Egypt, *and because he hired against you Balaam son of Beor* . . . to curse you" (*Deuteronomy* 23:4-5). *Ramban* explains that since these two nations were descendants of Lot, they owed their very existence to Abraham, for it was he who saved Lot from the four kings (see *Genesis* 14:12,16), and it was only on Abraham's merit that Lot had been led out of Gomorrah before that city's destruction. Thus, by rejecting the request of the Israelites — who are Abraham's direct descendants — the Ammonites and Moabites failed to express gratitude for the kindness that had been done to them. For this, Hashem eternally ostracized them from the Jewish people.

This incident delineates the extent to which we must feel gratitude towards those who have been kind to us — we should feel indebted even to the *descendants* of people who were kind to our *ancestors*. By failing to respond with kindness to the offspring of Abraham, Ammon and Moab proved that they were spiritually deficient, and it was thus decreed against them that they would never become a part of the Jewish people. This implies that feeling gratitude is an integral component of being a Jew.

It is for this reason that the Torah says, "You shall not reject an Egyptian, *for you were a sojourner in his land*" (*Deuteronomy* 23:8). As *Rashi* explains, even though the Egyptians brutally enslaved us and threw our male infants into the Nile, the Torah warns us that we must not spite them, for "you were a sojourner in his land" — we must be forever grateful to the Egyptians for giving asylum to Jacob and his children, our forefathers, during the severe famine that ravaged the world (see *Genesis* 47:5). Essentially, the Torah warns us to overcome the natural human reaction to forget past favors in the face of a more recent transgression.

The idea of showing gratitude is implicit in our *parashah*. We learn that "Moshe" was not Moses' real name, but the name given to him by Batiah, Pharaoh's daughter. Ostensibly, it is strange that the Torah refers to the greatest prophet the world would ever know by the name given to him by an Egyptian princess, especially since it was her own father's cruel decree that caused Moses to be cast into the Nile in the first place. The answer is that despite her father's wickedness, the Torah shows eternal gratitude to Batiah by using the name she chose for Israel's future redeemer.

Similarly, in explanation as to why Aaron and not Moses precipitated the plague of lice, *Rashi* says, "It would not have been appropriate for Moses to bring about the plague against the dust of the land, for it had protected him from discovery when he had used it to conceal the dead Egyptian (see *Exodus* 2:12)." It is for this same reason that Moses did not turn the waters of the Nile into blood or bring about the plague of frogs — Moses' life had been saved by being led adrift upon the waters of the Nile. If the Torah takes it for granted that one must show gratitude to inanimate objects, how much greater is one's obligation to show gratitude to a fellow Jew! And just as we must be grateful towards inanimate objects even though they do not explicitly demand this of us, so must we express gratitude to people who have been kind to us even if they do not explicitly ask us for anything in return.

At the end of his life, Moses once again demonstrated this trait. Hashem said to him, "Take vengeance for the Children of Israel against the Midianites; afterward, you will be gathered unto your people" (*Numbers* 31:2). The Sages point out that Moses did not postpone this military campaign even though its completion would mark the end of his life. Instead, Moses fulfilled the *mitzvah* with alacrity, as the very next verse says, "Moses spoke to the people, saying, 'Arm men from among yourselves ...' " Moses himself, however, did not participate in the war against the Midianites, but instead placed Phineas in charge of the army. Why? Because Moses could not take up arms against the nation which gave him asylum when he fled from Pharaoh.

The concept of showing gratitude has clear halachic ramifications. For example, the Sages say, "[If you find] your father's lost possession and also your Torah teacher's lost possession, your Torah teacher's lost possession takes precedence, for he brings you to the World to Come." Gratitude is also the basis of the *mitzvah* of honoring one's parents, as *Sefer HaChinuch* says: "The essence of the *mitzvah* is that a person recognize and reciprocate with kindness to those who have benefited him. He should not be rude, nor estrange himself, nor be ungrateful, for this is an evil and extremely loathsome trait to God and men."

Indeed, the Sages likened honoring one's parents to honoring Hashem Himself (*Kiddushin* 31). Citing the Talmud Yerushalmi, *Tosafos* adds, "The Holy One, Blessed is He, is more strict about honoring one's parents than about honoring Him. The verse says, 'Honor God with your possessions' — honor Him with what He has given to you; [only] if you have money must you [honor Him]. However, in regards to honoring one's parents, if you do not have enough money, you are obligated to ask for charity in order to sustain your mother and father."

Such importance is not attributed to any other *mitzvah* in the Torah. Why? Because if we would ponder for a moment how much pain and anguish a parent feels in the process of bringing up a child, we would realize how grateful we must be to our parents. Were it not that Hashem gives parents superhuman strength to endure the hardships of child-rearing, they would surely not be able to withstand it! Thus, we are bidden to recognize their generosity towards us and reciprocate their kindness.

In *Parashas Haazinu*, the Torah accuses the Jewish people of ungratefulness: "Is it to HASHEM that you do this, O vile and unwise people? Is He not your Father, your Master? Has He not created you and firmed you?" (*Deuteronomy* 32:6). Likewise, the Sages said that if a person does not recite a blessing prior to eating or drinking, it is considered as though he had stolen from God — failing to express one's gratitude to God for providing nourishment is an unforgivable act of ungratefulness.

The message is clear: We must make a greater effort to notice the favors that are done to us by others, and feel immense gratitude towards them.

Caring for One's Fellow Jew

The verse says, "Moses was shepherding the sheep of Jethro ... and he arrived at the Mountain of God, toward Horeb. An angel of HASHEM appeared to him in a blaze of fire ..." (*Exodus* 3:1-2).

In reference to this verse, the Sages said:

"The Holy One, Blessed is He, assessed two of the greatest individuals who ever lived — Moses and David — through their flock. He assessed David through his flock and found him to be a good shepherd, as the verse says, 'He chose David, His servant, and took him from the sheepfolds' (*Psalms* 78:70). David would keep back the larger [animals] and take out the smaller ones to pasture [first] so that they would eat the tenderest blades of grass. Then, he would take out the middle-sized [animals] so that they would eat the stiffer blades of grass, and finally, he would let out the largest [animals] so they would eat the hardest blades of grass. The Holy One, Blessed is He, said, 'Let he who knows how to guide his flock in accordance with the relative strengths of each member come and guide My flock!'

"So too, the Holy One, Blessed is He, assessed Moses through Jethro's flock. It once happened that a lamb ran away and Moses chased after it. The lamb reached a pool of water and stopped to drink. Moses said to it, 'I didn't know that you ran away because you were thirsty. You must be very tired!' Moses then picked up the lamb and carried it back to the flock on his shoulders. As Moses walked, the Holy One, Blessed is He, said, 'You showed mercy toward the flock of a human being — on your life, you shall guide My flock, Israel!' "

At first glance, it might seem strange that Hashem evaluated the leadership capabilities of David and Moses on the basis of such mundane criteria as the manner in which they cared for their sheep. However, as we all know from experience, it is often the little insignificant actions that reveal a person's true character. The fact that David and Moses showed so much concern for the welfare of their flock was a sign that they possessed the ability to sincerely care for their fellow Jews.

This aspect of Moses' character was revealed when he resolutely refused to act as Hashem's spokesman before Pharaoh. Moses was concerned that accepting this honor would be an affront to Aaron, his older brother, who was prophesying in Egypt and serving as the leader of the Jewish people. He could not fathom doing anything that would hurt someone else's feelings — especially his own brother — even though Hashem Himself was urging him to do so. Instead, Moses said, "Please, my Lord, send through whomever You will send" (*Exodus* 4:13) — that is, Moses beseeched Hashem to appoint Aaron as His messenger. Only when Hashem assured Moses, "Behold, [Aaron] is going out to meet you, and when he sees you, *he will rejoice in his heart*" (ibid., v. 14), did Moses acquiesce.

This trait of Moses also emerged when he fled from Egypt to Midian. A fugitive on the run from the Egyptian gallows, Moses had every reason not to get involved in the confrontation between the shepherds and Jethro's daughters (see ibid., 2:17-19). However, he simply could not stand idly by and watch Jethro's daughters be persecuted by the shepherds — his sincere concern for the welfare of his fellow human beings would not permit it. Moses possessed the trait of נוֹשֵׂא בְעוֹל, which literally means "sharing someone's burden." Significantly, by changing the order of the letters, these two words spell שׂוֹנֵא עָוֶל, or "one who loathes injustice."

When Moses was still in Egypt, the verse says, "It happened in those days that Moses grew up and went out to his brethren *and observed their burdens ...*" (ibid., v. 11). As *Rashi* explains, Moses' intention was to see the Jews' suffering and grieve along with them. The Sages add, "Moses would cry and say, 'How I pity you! If only

I would be taken instead of you!' He would then put his shoulder to the work and assist every single Jew in his backbreaking tasks." In addition to alleviating the Jews' physical labor, Moses worked alongside them in order to empathize with their pain. He knew that as long as he did not actually put his shoulder to the work, he would never feel the anguish of his brethren. In reference to Moses' gesture, Hashem declared, "You left your affairs and went to observe the burden of Israel. You acted like a brother towards them!"

The verse tells us that Moses "saw an Egyptian man striking a Hebrew man, of his brethren. He turned this way and that, and saw that there was no man, so he struck down the Egyptian and hid him in the sand" (ibid., vs. 11-12). This is the deeper intention of the verse, "HASHEM saw that [Moses] *turned aside to see*; and God called out to him from amid the bush and said, 'Moses, Moses' . . ." (ibid., 3:4) — Moses merited the vision of the burning bush because he "turned aside" to see his brethren's suffering.

Empathizing with the suffering of others is actually a Divine attribute. As the verse says: "HASHEM said, 'I have indeed seen the affliction of My people that is in Egypt and I have heard its outcry because of its taskmasters, *for I have known of its sufferings*' " (ibid., v. 7).

According to the *Midrash*, this is the reason why the Divine Presence appeared to Moses from the midst of the burning bush. Hashem in essence said to Moses, "Do you not perceive that I am overcome with anguish to the same degree as Israel? Then discern it from the place where I am speaking to you — from the midst of a thorny bush! See that I share their pain!"

Similarly, in explanation of the verse, "They saw the God of Israel, *and under His feet was the likeness of sapphire brickwork*, and it was like the essence of the heaven in purity" (ibid., 24:10), *Rashi* says: "Hashem kept a sapphire brick as a constant reminder of Israel's servitude to Egypt with brick and mortar. When the Jews were freed, Hashem's joy was as radiant as 'the very essence of Heaven.' "

The Sages also say in reference to the verse, "Yet when they were ill, I wore sackcloth" (*Psalms* 35:12) — "If a Torah scholar falls ill, one must become sick [with worry] for him. For King David said that when Doeg and Ahithophel fell ill, he was so concerned for their well-being that he himself became ill" (*Berachos* 12). Why did King

David become sick? Because he was so concerned for Doeg and Ahithophel that he felt as though he himself had contracted their disease. How great is our obligation to feel the pain of a fellow Jew!

A certain well-known *tzaddik* used to say that he learned the true meaning of feeling another person's pain from two drunkards. One of the men, intoxicated beyond control, began calling out to his companion, "I love you! I love you!" The recipient of this show of love replied, "If you really love me, tell me what I lack. And if you don't know, then you don't really love me!"

At any rate, we see that Hashem chose Moses to lead Israel out of Egypt only on the merit of his ability to feel the pain of his fellow Jews. Although, as *Ramban* points out, Moses already possessed great wisdom when he was in Midian, he was chosen to be Israel's redeemer only because "he turned aside to see" the anguish of his fellow Jews.

The trait of caring for the welfare of one's fellow Jews was exemplified by the prophet Jonah. As *Radak* explains, Jonah fled to Tarshish because he feared that Hashem would appear to him once again, this time explicitly commanding him to go to Nineveh and rebuke the city's inhabitants. Jonah did not want to fulfill this commandment, for he suspected that the Ninevites would indeed heed his warnings and repent. This would reflect negatively upon the Jewish people: Here a gentile city repents after hearing the rebuke of a single prophet, yet the Jewish people persist in their evil ways despite having heard the scathing reproof of countless prophets and sages! Thus, for the sake of his fellow Jews, Jonah relinquished the spiritual ecstasy of prophecy and risked incurring God's wrath. He fled to Tarshish because he thought that prophecy could only occur within the territorial boundaries of the Holy Land. How great was Jonah's concern for the welfare of his fellow Jews!

The manifestation of this trait has actual halachic ramifications. For example, the Sages said that if someone's tree should shed its leaves out of season, he should paint the tree with *sikra*, a red dye. This will attract the attention of passersby, who, noticing the tree, will surely stop to beseech Hashem to have mercy upon it. The *Saba miKelm* would often cite this ruling to illustrate the immense obligation incumbent upon us to show concern for our fellow Jews — the Sages assumed that any Jew who would see the afflicted tree would naturally stop and pray to Hashem to have mercy upon the tree's owner.

If we are bound to show this much concern for our fellows' *physical possessions*, how much more are we obligated to take an interest in their spiritual well-being. This obligation prompted Abraham to risk his life by disseminating faith in the One God in a rabidly pagan society, and by making attempts to convert sworn idol worshipers to monotheism. Abraham was driven by the obligation of נוֹשֵׂא בְעוֹל עִם חֲבֵרוֹ, or feeling responsible for others. Just as we have an obligation to return someone's possession *even if he is totally unaware that he has lost it*, so must we try to rectify a person's spiritual makeup even if he is unaware that he has gone astray. In fact, the responsibility to show concern for another Jew's spiritual condition exceeds that of caring for his physical condition, for his spiritual shortcomings will cause him irreparable damage in this world as well as in the World to Come. And as the Sages said, "He who does not show compassion for people, it is certain that he is not from the seed of our father Abraham" (*Beitzah* 32).

The verse says, "[Moses] went out the next day, and behold, two Hebrew men were fighting. He said to the wicked one, 'Why would you strike your fellow?' He replied, 'Who appointed you as a dignitary, a ruler, and a judge over us? Do you propose to murder me, as you murdered the Egyptian?' Moses was frightened and he thought, *'Indeed, the matter is known!'* " (*Exodus* 2:13-14). In explanation, *Rashi* quotes the *Midrash*: "It now became known to Moses why the Jews deserved to suffer so — because they quarreled and slandered each other."

In light of the fact that the Jews in Egypt had descended to the 49th level of spiritual impurity, it is difficult to understand why Moses concluded that the root of their troubles was their internal strife. As *Ramban* writes, "It is well known that while in Egypt, the Jews were extremely wicked and sinful." Surely transgressions such as idol worship by far outweighed the negative aspects of social discord. Why, then, did Moses attribute Israel's troubles to internal strife?

The answer is that the obligation to show concern for the welfare of others is even greater in times of widespread adversity.

At such times, the common anguish experienced by all should evince a stronger sense of solidarity than usual. A feeling of brotherhood should naturally emerge, bonding every Jew closer to his fellow. Thus, when Moses saw the two Jews fighting with each other despite the Jewish people's wretched condition, he suddenly realized that they were not worthy to be redeemed, for if they could not show concern for each other under these horrific conditions, they certainly would not be able to do so when freed from their bondage.

If you take this lesson to heart you will reap great reward, for the Sages said, "Whoever prays on behalf of his fellow, he shall be answered first." If you seek to realize your aspirations, first become more sensitive to the needs of others — Hashem will reward you by answering your prayers first.

Appreciating Miracles

The verse says, "God called out to [Moses] from amid the bush and said, 'Moses, Moses,' and he replied, 'Here I am!' He said, 'Do not come closer to here, remove your shoes from your feet, for the place upon which you stand is holy ground.' And He said, 'I am the God of your father, the God of Abraham, the God of Isaac, and the God of Jacob.' *Moses hid his face, for he was afraid to gaze toward God*" (*Exodus* 3:4-6).

In *Berachos* (7) the Sages say that in reward for hiding his face, Moses merited a radiant countenance. In return for being "afraid," he merited the spiritual brilliance that made the people "afraid to approach him" (see ibid., 34:30). In return for not gazing toward God, he merited the verse "at the image of HASHEM does he gaze" (see *Numbers* 12:8).

The Sage Ben Karchah, however, disagrees with this opinion. According to him, Moses was *punished* for averting his gaze from the Divine Presence in the burning bush — for when Moses pleaded with Hashem, "Show me now Your glory" (*Exodus* 33:18), Hashem responded, "When *I* wanted to [show you My glory,] *you* did not want [to look]. Now that *you* want, *I* do not want!"

Ostensibly, Ben Karchah's opinion defies understanding. As the verse clearly states, Moses did not purposely avert his face from the Divine Presence. The only reason he did so is because "*he was afraid to gaze toward God.*" Moses' involuntary reaction to the resplendent scene unfolding before him seems quite an understandable human response. What crime did he commit? What did he do to deserve this punishment?

The answer lies in the premise of this very difficulty: We tend to think that we are not responsible for having "normal" human reactions — as a matter of fact, we refer to them as "involuntary." In truth, however, we *do* have the potential to gain total control over every single aspect of ourselves. Moses was presented with an opportunity to do so when the Divine Presence revealed itself to him at the vision of the burning bush. Had he overcome the natural human fear of the unknown at that time and gazed at the Divine Presence, he would have immediately been transported to a new realm of consciousness. Unfortunately, however, he failed. Thus, later on, when he sought to reach this supernal awareness of the Divine, Hashem turned him down. As Ben Karchah said, "When I wanted to, you did not want. Now that you want, I do not want!"

This serves as a valuable lesson to us all. How often do miracles occur on our behalf? Anyone who looks closely will agree that they happen constantly, almost at every moment. But how many of us notice them? Of course, it can be argued that it is "humanly impossible" to notice miracles all the time, especially when taking into account the myriad distractions that constantly bombard us from every direction. "Since we do not *purposely* disregard miracles, we cannot be held accountable," we say in our defense.

Ben Karchah teaches us otherwise — we *are* held accountable for disregarding the miracles Hashem performs on our behalf, and unless we do something about it, our "spiritual eyesight" will steadily diminish and we will be rendered totally incapable of witnessing the workings of Providence in our daily lives.

Deepest Darkness Precedes Light

After Moses finally agreed to act as Hashem's messenger to redeem Israel, he and Aaron came before Pharaoh and demanded, "So said HASHEM, the God of Israel: 'Send out My people that they may celebrate for Me in the wilderness' " (*Exodus* 5:1). Not only did Pharaoh refuse, saying, "I do not know HASHEM, nor will I send out Israel!" but he also ordered his taskmasters, "You shall no longer give straw to the [Jewish] people to manufacture the bricks ... let them go and gather straw for themselves" (ibid., v. 7). As a result, "the foremen of the Children of Israel, whom Pharaoh's taskmasters had appointed over them, were beaten ..." (ibid., v. 14).

Scripture then tells us that "the foremen of the Children of Israel came and cried out to Pharaoh, saying, 'Why do you do this to your servants?' " (ibid., v. 15). But their protestations fell on deaf ears.

As they were leaving Pharaoh's royal chamber, they met Moses and Aaron. The foremen held the two leaders directly responsible for the new state of affairs. They angrily said to them, "May HASHEM look upon you and judge, for you have made our very scent abhorrent in the eyes of Pharaoh and the eyes of his servants, to place a sword in their hands to murder us!" (ibid., v. 21).

Moses could not endure any more. The verse says that he "returned to HASHEM and said, 'My Lord, why have You done evil to this people, why have You sent Me? From the time I came to Pharaoh to speak in Your Name, he did evil to this people, but You did not rescue Your people!" (ibid., vs. 22-23).

The commentaries go to great lengths in explaining Moses' complaint:

Ibn Ezra points out that since Hashem explicitly warned Moses, "I know that the king of Egypt will not allow you to go, except through a strong hand" (ibid., 3:19), Moses' statement is somewhat difficult to understand. *Ibn Ezra* suggests the following explanation: Moses realized that Pharaoh would not *free* the Jews outright, but he *did* expect that Pharaoh would at least lighten their work load somewhat in order to appease them. Hence, when Pharaoh proceeded to increase the Jews' work load, Moses called into question Hashem's earlier statement, "I have indeed seen the affliction of My people that is in Egypt, and I have heard its outcry ... for I have known of its sufferings" (ibid., v. 7).

Sforno takes a different approach. Moses did not question whether the Jewish people deserved the evil decree, but only why it had come as a direct consequence of his intervention. Moses could not understand why he had been chosen to be the vehicle for this evil mandate.

Alternatively, *Ramban* explains that Moses could not understand why Hashem sent him to Pharaoh prematurely, before the appointed time of the Redemption had arrived. There seemed no point in aggravating Pharaoh unnecessarily, especially in view of the fact that as a result, the Jewish people were subjected to even more torture.

Nevertheless, none of the above interpretations seems to fit in with Hashem's answer to Moses: "Now you will see what I shall do to Pharaoh, for through a strong hand will he send them out, and with a strong hand will he drive them from his land" (ibid., 6:1). How does this response address Moses' question?

The explanation is as follows:

The answer that Hashem conveyed to Moses was that He purposely intensified the Jewish people's suffering so that they would gain a greater appreciation of the imminent redemption. Just as light cannot truly be relished except by one who has been enshrouded in deep darkness, so too, freedom cannot truly be appreciated except by someone who has been subjected to brutal enslavement. When the redemption finally occurred, the sharp contrast between the Jewish people's new state and their dismal condition of the past prompted them to burst out in joyous song and praise to Hashem. By being subjected to one final plunge into the deepest recesses of the Egyptian exile, they gained heightened awareness of the miraculous nature of the redemption, and realized beyond doubt that their freedom had been granted to them by Hashem.

The Clutches of Sin

The *parashah* begins, "HASHEM said to Moses, 'Come to Pharaoh, for I have made his heart and the heart of his servants stubborn so that I can put these signs of Mine in his midst. And so that you may relate in the ears of your son and your son's son that I made a mockery of Egypt and My signs that I placed among them — that you may know that I am HASHEM'" (*Exodus* 10:1-2).

As we all know, this verse conveys the *mitzvah* of describing the Exodus from Egypt (*sippur yitzias Mitzrayim*), which we fulfill during the Pesach *Seder*. The recognition that Hashem took us out of Egypt is the foundation stone of the First Commandment, "I am HASHEM your God, Who has taken you out of the land of Egypt, from the house of slavery" (ibid., 20:2). However, there is another lesson of great value to be gleaned from this verse.

To begin with, note the interesting choice of words, "I made *a mockery* of Egypt ..." The verse refers to Pharaoh, who fluctuated between unparalleled defiance and quivering submissiveness before Hashem. Pharaoh initially said, "Who is HASHEM that I should heed His voice?" (ibid., 5:2). After the plague of hail, however, Pharaoh "sent and summoned Moses and Aaron and said to them, 'This time I have sinned; HASHEM is the Righteous One, and I and my people are the wicked ones'" (ibid., 9:28). At this point, Pharaoh finally came to terms with reality and realized "Who is HASHEM." But this lucid state did not last for long. A few verses later the Torah tells us that "Pharaoh saw that the rain, the hail, and the thunder ceased, and he continued to sin; *and he made his heart stubborn*, he and his servants. *Pharaoh's heart became strong* and he did not send out the Children of Israel, as HASHEM had spoken through Moses" (ibid., vs. 34-35).

In reference to God deliberately making Pharaoh's heart "stubborn," the *Midrash* says:

"R' Yochanan said: This provides an excuse to apostates — no transgressor can ever repent, as the verse says, 'I made [Pharaoh's] heart stubborn.'

"Reish Lakish answered: Let the apostates' mouths be shut! The verse says, 'At scoffers he scoffs' (*Proverbs* 3:34) — the Holy One, Blessed is He, warns a person once, twice, three times; if he still does not repent, He seals his heart from repenting, thereby exacting punishment for his sin.

"So too with Pharaoh. After sending him [a clear message] five times to no avail, the Holy One, Blessed is He, in effect said to him, '[Because] you stiffened your neck and made your heart stubborn, I shall add even more impurity upon you!' This is the intention of the verse, 'I made [Pharaoh's] heart stubborn.' "

Of course, this is not to say that Hashem took away *all* free choice from Pharaoh. He must have had the capability — however slight it may have been — of repenting for his sin, for the Torah says, "See, I have placed before you today the life and the good, and the death and the evil" (*Deuteronomy* 30:15). In fact, we see that even after Hashem "made his heart stubborn," Pharaoh had several moments of spiritual clarity. At such times, when the clouds of darkness enveloping his heart would momentarily part, Pharaoh would make such statements as, "This time I have sinned; HASHEM is the Righteous One, and I and my people are the wicked ones" (*Exodus* 9:27).

Thus, even though Hashem withheld a significant measure of spiritual sensitivity from him, Pharaoh was still in control. He could have changed his ways had he wanted to, but he deliberately chose to follow the impulses of his evil inclination (*yetzer hara*). As a consequence, his sudden realization of Hashem's omnipotence became obscured, as the verse says, "Pharaoh saw that the rain, the hail, and the thunder ceased, and he continued to sin; and he made his heart stubborn, he and his servants ... Pharaoh ... did not send out the Children of Israel, as HASHEM had spoken through Moses" (ibid., vs. 34,35).

A lesson of great importance is to be gleaned from the Torah's account of Pharaoh's demise: We must never underestimate the power of the evil inclination. It is capable of making a person fixate on his physical desires to the point that his decision-making process becomes impaired. When a person falls into the clutches of the evil inclination, he will begin to think and act in a completely irrational manner, as though deranged. Why else would Pharaoh have chased the Israelites into the Red Sea? As *Ramban* explains, Pharaoh was afflicted by a type of insanity.

This demented state does not develop from one day to the next, but grows incrementally with each passing sin. For when a person commits a transgression, he distances himself from his Creator. As the sins accumulate, the person becomes so distant that he approaches the point of no return, when the realistic chances for him to repent are almost nil. To repent for his sins and return to the ways of the Torah from such a spiritual wasteland would take a miracle.

And yet, the path to this "miraculous return" is constantly within a sinner's reach. The verse says, "HASHEM, HASHEM, God, Compassionate and Gracious . . ." (ibid., 34:6). The Sages explain that the repetition of the Divine Name "Hashem" teaches that He is Hashem before the sin, and He is Hashem after the sin" (see *Rosh Hashanah* 16). Hashem may close the gates of repentance before a sinner, but He always leaves them ajar. In His great mercy, Hashem gives every sinner the opportunity to repent, no matter how far he may have strayed. All he needs to do is make the effort, and Hashem will assist him. As the Sages said, "He who comes to purify himself will receive Heavenly assistance."

It is because of the cumulative damage of sin that the Sages warned, "Flee from sin, for a sin brings another sin in its wake." With each additional sin a person's spiritual arteries increasingly constrict and obstruct the light of Divine supervision in his life. Before he knows it, he is overcome by a feeling of spiritual emptiness and emotional darkness. His perception becomes so impaired that he even fails to realize that his spiritual barrenness is a natural consequence of having distanced himself from His Creator.

With this understanding, the verses, "Come to Pharaoh, for I have made his heart and the heart of his servants stubborn so that I can put these signs of Mine in his midst. And so that you may relate in the ears of your son and your son's son that I made a mockery of Egypt and My signs that I placed among them — that you may know that

I am HASHEM" (*Exodus* 10:1-2), take on new meaning. In addition to describing the awesome wonders that Hashem brought about during the redemption from Egypt, the verses also illustrates the dire repercussions of committing sin — Hashem makes the sinner's heart "stubborn," and ultimately makes a mockery of him by causing him to think and act irrationally. This lesson, too, must we "relate in the ears of our sons and our son's son" during the Pesach *Seder*!

Rambam (*Hilchos Teshuvah* Ch. 6, Law 4) writes: "Along the same lines, righteous individuals and prophets beseeched Hashem to help them towards the truth. As King David said, 'HASHEM, teach me Your ways' — in other words, 'Let not my sins impede me from the way of truth, through which I will come to know Your ways and the unity of Your Name.' This was also his intention when he said, 'Let a noble spirit reside upon me' — that is, 'Let my spirit do Your will, and do not allow my sins to impede me from repentance.' Rather, present me with the opportunity to repent, that I may know and understand the way of truth."

If the most righteous individuals and the greatest prophets who ever lived saw it necessary to plead to Hashem that their sins not obstruct them from doing *teshuvah*, how much more must we feel concern over this eventuality!

The idea of minimizing one's own chances to repent with each passing transgression is frequently mentioned in the Talmud. For example, the Sages said, "If you leave [Torah] for one day, *it* will leave you for two days. If you neglect it, numerous obstacles will arise against you."

Rashi alludes to this phenomenon in *Parashas Bechukosai*. The first verse says, "If you will follow My decrees and observe My commandments . . ." (*Leviticus* 26:3). As *Rashi* explains, "My decrees" refers to Torah study. In a later verse we are warned, "But if you will *not* listen to Me and *will not* perform all of these commandments; if you consider My decrees loathsome, and if your being rejects My ordinances, so as not to perform all My commandments, so that you annul My covenant" (ibid., vs. 14-15). *Rashi* explains the logical progression of the verse as follows: "If you will not listen to Me" — that is, if you do not toil in Torah study — then you "will not perform all of these commandments" — i.e., you will stop observing mitzvos. Next, "you will consider My decrees loathsome" — i.e., you will loathe individuals who do observe mitzvos — until eventually "your being shall reject My ordinances" — meaning, you will come to detest Torah scholars — and you will "not perform all My commandments" — i.e., you will try to prevent others from following My commandments. You will reach your lowest point when "you annul My covenant" — when you will deny that I commanded the mitzvos.

Now, at first glance, one may rightly wonder why the verse takes such an extreme view of Divine service — just because a person neglects Torah study ("If you will not listen to Me") means that he will come to deny the Divine origin of mitzvos? This seems to be a rather harsh approach! However, in light of the "spiritual obstruction/constriction" principle outlined above, the verse's intention is crystal clear — one transgression generates the next.

How careful we must be!

The Korban Pesach

The Torah tells us that "Moses called to all the elders of Israel and said to them, 'Draw forth and take for yourselves sheep . . . and slaughter the pesach-offering' " (Exodus 12:21). The Mechilta explains the expression "draw forth" as being a warning that the people must "draw themselves away" from their idolatrous practices which they had adopted in Egypt before performing the pesach-offering. It is interesting to note that when Hashem had originally given Moses this commandment, the wording was somewhat different: "They shall take for themselves, each man, a lamb or kid . . ." (ibid., v. 3). Why did Moses see fit to add the message of "drawing forth" (or "drawing apart") when he repeated Hashem's commandment to the people? (See Ohr HaChaim, who also raises this question.)

Perhaps the answer lies in a statement that Moses had made once before, when speaking to Pharaoh, when the latter had offered him to allow the Children of Israel to perform their sacrifice within the land of Egypt: "We will be sacrificing the deity of Egypt to HASHEM; if we sacrifice the deity of the Egyptians in their presence, will they not stone us?" (ibid., 8:22). One of the main points of the *pesach*-offering was thus to serve as a repudiation of the Egyptian deity. The Jews were to take the very symbol of Egyptian idolatry and slaughter it unto Hashem. As Hashem Himself had said, the *pesach*-offering was to commemorate the fact that "I shall pass through Egypt on that night, and I shall strike down every firstborn in Egypt ... and I shall administer justice to all the gods of Egypt; I am HASHEM ... And when I see the blood (of the *pesach*) I will pass over your [houses]" (ibid., 12:12,13). The *Haggadah* points out the repeated use of the pronoun "I" in this verse; Hashem was emphasizing that the miracles involved in the redemption from Egypt were carried out by Him, without the agency of angels. The *pesach*-offering was thus intended to be a lesson in the clear recognition of Hashem's power in the world, and the total worthlessness of Egypt's deities. It was thus entirely appropriate that Moses incorporated into his repetition of Hashem's command the need for the people to "draw themselves away" from Egyptian idolatry. This was, after all, the major theme of the *pesach*-offering.

The Splitting of the Red Sea

We learn in our *parashah* that soon after the Israelites left Egypt, Hashem commanded them to retrace their steps and move back towards Egypt. At the same time, Hashem hardened Pharaoh's heart and induced him to assemble a formidable array of cavalry and troops and chase after the Israelite nation. Pharaoh's detachment closed in on the Israelites, who were encamped on the shores of the Red Sea. Trapped between the advancing army and the sea, the Israelites could do nothing but pray. As the verse says, "Egypt pursued them and overtook them, encamped by the sea — all the horses and chariots of Pharaoh, and his horsemen and army . . . [As] Pharaoh approached, the Children of Israel cried out to HASHEM" (*Exodus* 14:9-10). Moses began praying as well.

Hashem's response to Moses' plea was, "Why do you cry out to Me? Speak to the Children of Israel and let them journey forth!" (ibid., v. 15). Citing a *Midrash*, *Rashi* interprets Hashem's words to mean, "All they have to do is journey forth, for the sea shall not stand in their way. Their forefathers' merit, together with the fact that they had faith in Me and went out [of Egypt], is sufficient to split the sea for them!"

Nevertheless, the Sages (*Sotah* 37) say that the sea did not split until Nahshon ben Aminadav (the tribal prince of Judah) jumped in the water and prayed, "Save me, God, for the waters are about to take my soul!" (Incidentally, Nahshon's courageous deed earned the tribe of Judah the eternal leadership over Israel, as the verse says, "Judah sanctified Him [and] Israel came under his dominion.")

At first glance, the Sages' statement contradicts the *Midrash* cited by *Rashi*: If the merit of the Israelites and of their forefathers was sufficient to split the sea for them, why did it not split until Nahshon jumped in?

The answer may be as follows: According to the Sages, the Red Sea initially refused to split before the Israelites — it "argued" that such an act would constitute a gross violation of the laws of nature, and was therefore unwarranted. How could the Israelites counter such a logical argument? They had reached an impasse; there seemed no way out.

At this point Nahshon jumped in the water. Through this selfless act, *which violated the inherent human sense of self-preservation*, Nahshon demonstrated that the laws of nature were not etched in stone. If the circumstances at hand called for "supernatural" events, the laws of nature could be temporarily suspended. Nahshon's personal example hit home, and the Red Sea consented to become the stage for some of the most astounding miracles that ever occurred.

A very important lesson emerges from Nahshon's courageous deed: We cannot expect miracles to happen unless we ourselves are disposed to act with self-sacrifice (*mesiras nefesh*). If we would exhibit "superhuman" qualities, Hashem would reciprocate by performing "supernatural" occurrences for our sake. As the Sages said, "A man is judged in accordance with his own yardstick."

This principle is discussed in the Talmud (*Berachos* 20). Abaye asked R' Pappa, "Why is it that miracles occurred on behalf of earlier generations, while we cry out to Hashem and [seemingly] no one listens to us? If it is because of Torah study, we learn even more than they did!"

R' Pappa answered, "Earlier generations sacrificed themselves to sanctify God's Name, but we do not."

Again, we see that unless we ourselves show a willingness to go beyond human nature for the sake of serving Hashem, we should not expect Him to perform events that defy the laws of nature on our behalf.

The Contiguity of Redemption and Prayer

The Sages said, "Who will have a portion in the World to Come? He who [recites the blessing] of redemption adjacent to prayer" (*Berachos* 4). This statement is the basis for the well-known law prohibiting speech between the recitation of the blessing "Blessed are You, Hashem, Who redeemed Israel" and the *Amidah* during the Morning Prayer Service.

Rabbeinu Yonah explains the reasoning behind the Sages' statement in the following manner:

The main reason why Hashem took us out of Egypt was in order that we should become his slaves. As the verse says, "For they are My servants, whom I have taken out of the land of Egypt . . ." (*Leviticus* 25:42). Similarly, the verse says, "I am HASHEM, your God, Who has taken you out of the land of Egypt, from the house of slavery" (*Exodus* 20:2) — according to *Rashi*, the verse conveys: "therefore, in light of the fact that I took you out, it would be appropriate that you subjugate yourselves to Me."

When we recite the blessing "Blessed are You, Hashem, Who redeemed us," we recognize and express gratitude for the great kindness the Creator performed on our behalf in Egypt. Next we recite the *Amidah*, the silent prayer that stands in place of the Temple service, the epitome of Heavenly worship. By reciting these two prayer sections contiguously, we behave in the same manner as a slave before his master: Just as the slave feels bound to carry out his master's will, so too, when we recite the blessing "Blessed are You, Hashem, Who redeemed us," we recognize that Hashem is our Master and we feel bound to serve Him. And how do we serve Him? by performing His *Avodah* — or Divine service — which is contained in the word of the *Amidah*. For this level of devoted service, one earns a portion in the World to Come.

We may also explain the Sages' statement as follows: In reference to the verse, "Israel saw the great hand that HASHEM inflicted upon Egypt; and the people revered HASHEM, and they had faith in HASHEM and in Moses, His servant" (ibid., 14:31), the *Midrash* says, "When the Israelites saw the great miracles that the Holy One, Blessed is He, performed for their sake, they 'had faith in HASHEM.' " Hence, by reciting the blessing of redemption, we invoke our forefather's faith in Hashem. Then, by immediately praying to Hashem for our own needs, we demonstrate that we share the faith of our forefathers in Him, for we would not make requests of Hashem unless we had complete faith in Him. In return for this display of faith, we merit a portion in the World to Come.

Alternatively, the explanation may simply be that the redemption blessing reminds us that everything is under God's control, as the verse says, "And on that day I shall set apart . . . so that you will know that I am HASHEM in the midst of the land" (ibid., 8:18). This instills within us the knowledge that we have nothing to rely upon but God, a concept that comprises the basic foundation of belief. By immediately turning to God and requesting that He grant our daily needs, we demonstrate that we have internalized this concept. This explains why in every prayer we first praise Hashem and only afterwards request our needs — in order to be sincere in our requests, we must first come to the realization that there is no one to trust in but Him, "that there is none other than Him."

The Elements of Piety

"R' Yehudah said: If a person wants to become a pious person, he should carefully observe the laws of monetary matters. Rava said he should observe the rules [of proper conduct] set down in *Pirkei Avos*. Others say he should observe the matters of *Berachos*."

When R' Yehudah said that the key to piety lies in the strict observance of monetary matters, he meant such issues as being careful not to cause any harm to others directly or indirectly, even in such cases where he would be exempt from reimbursing the person for damages because of technical reasons. Also included would be observing the rules of good neighborliness, showing respect for the rights of others, refraining from speaking ill of other people, etc.

Included in Rava's advice — to observe the rules of *Avos* — would be acting in a spirit of generosity and humility, avoiding such negative traits as jealousy, overindulgence in material pleasures, self-centeredness, etc.

"The matters of *Berachos*" refers to the constant awareness of Hashem's hand in bringing about all our daily needs — the idea encapsulated in the *Gemara*'s dictum: "Whoever derives benefit from anything in this world without praising Hashem for it is tantamount to being a thief [because he is taking it from Hashem 'without permission']." Another major theme of *Berachos* is the idea that we must give thanks to Hashem before performing one of His commandments, expressing our appreciation for the extra measure of sanctity with which He has graced the Jewish people.

In truth, these three facets of "the pious life" are not three divergent opinions of three separate Talmudic Sages; they are actually three parts which together form one unit. It is impossible to arrive at a meaningful level of righteousness in life without adhering to all three of these principles.

The interrelationship among these three themes may be seen in another *Gemara*, in *Shabbos* 133b: " 'This is my God and I will glorify (or beautify — וְאַנְוֵהוּ) Him' (*Exodus* 15:2) — adorn yourself before Him with the commandments. Make your *sukkah* beautiful, make an attractive *sefer Torah*, wear nice *tzitzis*, etc. Abba Shaul interprets וְאַנְוֵהוּ in a different sense: Strive to resemble God in His ways — just as He is gracious and merciful, so should you be gracious and merciful towards others, etc." It would seem that here, too, the two interpretations of וְאַנְוֵהוּ are to be understood as being complementary to each other, not as opposing opinions. The explanation is as follows. We are told that the revelation of Hashem's might and glory at the splitting of the Red Sea was so manifest that even the lowest of the people experienced a vision on a higher level than that of Ezekiel, who was the prophet who witnessed and described the "work of the Divine Chariot." This assertion is derived from the fact that the people exclaimed, "This is my God . . .," as if they actually saw Him and pointed to Him. As a result of this supreme spiritual experience the people's reaction was, ". . . and I will glorify Him"; they realized that experiencing such a revelation demanded of them that they dedicate themselves to the honor of God, Who had shown His glory to them so openly. They could not suffice themselves with a mere observance of His commandments according to the letter of the law, but they felt compelled to go beyond that and find ways to beautify and embellish the performance of the commandments. This is the message that the *baraisa* derives from the verse "This is my God and I will glorify Him." Abba Shaul agrees with the basic premise of this interpretation, but he adds that it is not enough to enhance one's performance of the commandments "between man and God"; one must also enrich his fulfillment of the laws "between man and man." The lesson that this *Gemara* teaches us, then, is that the greater one's appreciation of Hashem's involvement in the affairs of the world (the idea embodied in "the matters of *Berachos*" recited over deriving pleasure from the world), the greater his expression of devotion to Hashem must express itself in terms of his eagerness in serving Him with the performance of the commandments (the idea embodied in "the matters of *Berachos*" recited before the performance of commandments), and in terms of his meticulousness in his dealings with his fellow man (the idea embodied in "the laws of monetary matters" and the "rules set down in *Pirkei Avos*").

Amalek

In our *parashah* the verse says, "Amalek came and battled Israel in Rephidim . . . Joshua weakened Amalek and its people with the sword's blade. Hashem said to Moses, 'Write this as a remembrance in the Book and recite it in the ears of Joshua, that I shall surely erase the memory of Amalek from under the heavens.' Moses built an altar and called its name 'HASHEM is My Miracle'; and he said, 'For the hand is on the throne of God; HASHEM maintains a war against Amalek, from generation to generation" (*Exodus* 17:8-16).

Similarly, in *Parashas Ki Seitzei* we learn, "It shall be that when HASHEM, your God, gives you rest from all your enemies all around, in the Land that HASHEM, Your God, gives you as an inheritance to possess it, you shall wipe out the memory of Amalek from under the heaven — you shall not forget" (*Deuteronomy* 25:19).

It is well known that the *mitzvah* of exterminating Amalek may only be carried out under the auspices of a Jewish king, and is therefore not applicable today. However, the *mitzvah* to *remember* what Amalek did to us in the desert may be performed at any moment. The *Rambam* (*Hilchos Melachim* Ch. 5) states: "It is a positive commandment to constantly remember [Amalek's] evil deeds in order to awaken hatred against him. Amalek's sin is explicitly mentioned in the Torah — 'Amalek came and battled Israel in Rephidim.' "

Rashi explains the juxtaposition of the section describing Amalek's unprovoked attack against Israel with the previous section — which portrays the Israelites' insubordination against Hashem at *Massah U'Meribah*: Because the Israelites wondered aloud "Is HASHEM among us or not?" (*Exodus* 17:7), the very next verse begins, "Amalek came and battled Israel . . ." To illustrate the point, *Rashi* quotes a *Midrash* that likens the Israelites to a child whose father carried him on his shoulders and fulfilled his every request. Then the child asked a passerby, "Have you seen my father?" Angered, the father said, "Don't you know where I am?" and cast his son to the ground, where he was bitten by a dog. Similarly, because after all the miracles and salvations Israel still had the gall to wonder whether God was really with them, He "cast them off" and left them vulnerable to attack. Hashem in effect said to the Jews, "On your life, let the dog [Amalek] come and bite you, and make you scream out to Me! Then you will know where I am!"

It is very difficult to understand how the Israelites could have wondered whether Hashem was in their midst. Such a short time had elapsed since the cataclysmic miracles that Hashem performed for their sake in Egypt, and the mind-boggling events at the Red Sea were still fresh in their minds. What went wrong? What made them lose perspective?

The answer is that one of the most powerful weapons of the evil inclination is the human tendency to take for granted things that come easily. If we would try to list all the astounding miracles that occur every time we take a breath of air, we would use up all the ink and paper. Yet, how often do we feel gratitude towards God for such things?

At *Massah U'Meribah*, Hashem wanted to train the Israelites to turn to Him in prayer whenever they were faced with deprivation. Instead of turning on Moses as if he controlled the water supply, they should have realized that God was their Healer and Provider, and thus pray to Him. They failed the test, and Moses had to ask God to intercede before they stoned him, for it was clear to him that they would not pray. Their parched throats caused them to swiftly forget the miracles in Egypt and the Red Sea, to the point that they wondered, "Is HASHEM among us or not?"

Generations later, the Jewish people were punished for this sin when Ahasuerus slipped off his signet ring and gave it to Haman. The test of *Massah U'Meribah* was reenacted. With their lives at stake, would the Jews turn to God in prayer, or would they once again wonder, "Is HASHEM among us or not?" This time, they passed the test.

In its account of the Israelites' struggle against Amalek, the Torah describes that evil nation's sin: "Remember what Amalek did to you, on the way when you were leaving Egypt, that he happened upon you on the way [אֲשֶׁר קָרְךָ בַּדֶּרֶךְ] and he struck those of you who were hindmost, all the weaklings at your rear, when you were faint and exhausted, and he did not fear God" (*Deuteronomy* 25:17-18). *Rashi* associates the words אֲשֶׁר קָרְךָ בַּדֶּרֶךְ (lit., "that he happened upon you on the way") with קָר, or "cold." This conveys that by attacking Israel, Amalek dispelled the aura of invincibility that surrounded the Jewish people. Prior to Amalek's attack, no nation on earth would have dared raise a hand against Hashem's Chosen people. Amalek's attack proved that they were not invulnerable. *Rashi* likens this to a person who jumps into a tub of boiling water — even though he scalds himself, he cools the water sufficiently to enable others to go in after him.

The repercussions of Amalek's transgression are very great. The verse says, "Write this as a remembrance in the Book and recite it in the ears of Joshua, that I shall surely erase the memory of Amalek from under the heavens ... For the hand is on the throne of God; HASHEM maintains a war against Amalek, from generation to generation" (*Exodus* 17:14-16). *Rashi* explains: "Moses declared that God had sworn by placing His hand on His throne, as it were, that He would continue the war against Amalek forever, until the memory of that evil nation is obliterated. In expressing the oath, Moses used an abbreviated form for 'throne' — כֵּס instead of כִּסֵּא — and he used the two-letter Divine Name [יָהּ] instead of the full Name [י-ה-ו-ה]. This indicates that God's Name and throne are diminished as long as Amalek exists."

The scope of Amalek's actions explains why we have a constant *mitzvah* to remember the evil deeds that nation perpetrated against us in the desert. Following the awesome miracles that Hashem performed on behalf of the Israelites, the entire world trembled before God and His Chosen People. There was no room to question whether

God existed — it was a palpable and undeniable fact. Amalek, however, changed the world's frame of mind by brazenly attacking Israel at the height of their distinction. Although the Israelites repelled the Amalekites' attack, the very fact that they survived the armed conflict with God's nation made the world's inhabitants reconsider their belief in God. "Perhaps He does not exist after all," some people began to wonder.

This explains why, according to *Rashi*, "God's Name and throne are diminished as long as Amalek exists" — the nation's very presence leaves room for doubting God's existence. That is why we have a *mitzvah* to exterminate the entire nation. And even when we are incapable of actually fulfilling this *mitzvah*, we are still bidden *to remember* Amalek's deeds and thereby uproot the seeds of heresy that he sowed in the depths of the human psyche.

Amalek's spiritual poison affected not only the nations, but also the spiritually weak members of Israel. The verse says, "and he struck those of you who were hindmost, all the weaklings at your rear, when you were faint and exhausted, and he did not fear God" (*Deuteronomy* 25:18). *Rashi* explains that "the weaklings at your rear" refers to those Jews who were spiritually weak as a consequence of their sins. Amalek's attack inflicted the greatest theological damage among members of this group, who had already been wavering in their commitment to fulfill God's commands. The fact that Amalek managed to engage Israel in battle and come out alive strengthened the doubts of these spiritual "weaklings," and thus the seeds of discontent and heresy were sown in the Israelite camp.

The vulnerability of these Israelite stragglers teaches us a very important lesson: Uncertainty regarding matters of faith is a fertile environment for sin to strike roots. This principle may be inferred from the *mishnah* in *Pirkei Avos*, which teaches that if one would ponder the following three things, one would never come to sin: that an eye observes, an ear hears, and every single deed is recorded in a book. If a person loses sight of these three things, however, he will surely sin.

Indeed, the battle against Amalek was fought in both corporeal and spiritual realms. The verse says, "It happened that when Moses raised his hand, Israel was stronger, and when he lowered his hand, Amalek was stronger. Moses' hands grew heavy, so they took a stone and put it under him and he sat on it, and Aaron and Hur supported his hands, one on this side and one on that side, and he remained with his hands in faithful prayer until sunset" (*Exodus* 17:12). Concerning this verse, the Sages ask, "Was it Moses' hands that won or lost the battle? Rather, [the Torah] teaches that as long as Israel looked heavenward and subjected their heart to their Father in Heaven, they would prevail. But if they would not — they would fall" (*Mishnah, Rosh Hashanah* 3:8).

From the Sages' words we see that the battle was primarily a spiritual one. Moses' raised hands strengthened Israel's belief in the Almighty, but when he lowered them, Amalek's heretical beliefs would grow stronger. The forces of faith and belief were pitted against the forces of heresy and evil. It is for this reason that the verse says, "HASHEM maintains a war against Amalek" (*Exodus* 17:16), and not "Israel maintains . . ." — the war was primarily between God and the forces of evil.

Another fact that illustrates the unconventional character of this war is the criteria by which the soldiers were selected: "Moses said to Joshua, 'Choose people for us and go do battle with Amalek . . .' " — according to the Sages, "choose *people*" meant God-fearing people who knew, felt, and recognized their obligation, as well as the severity of Amalek's transgression. The Jewish soldiers were not selected for their fighting prowess, but for their belief in and adherence to Hashem. Had the soldiers not been selected according to these criteria, they might have won the battle, but surely lost the war. That is, they theoretically *could* have defeated Amalek on the battlefield, but had they attributed their victory to their own strength and not to God, they would have lost the vastly more important spiritual struggle against that evil nation. The Jewish fighters were therefore picked for their belief in the Almighty, and not for their belief in their battle skills. This also explains why the Israelite troops *fasted* on the day of battle — they realized that the war was essentially being fought on the spiritual plane. Hence, they prepared themselves spiritually, totally disregarding the physical aspects of the war.

Similarly, the battle between the Jews of Mordechai's generation and the Amalekite anti-Semites of Ahasuerus' kingdom contained the same aspects as the battle in the desert between the Israelites and the Amalekites. Like their ancestors before them, the Jews of

Mordechai and Esther's day prepared themselves spiritually for their upcoming battle against the descendants of the Amalekites. They, too, fasted prior to the battle, this time for *three days*.

The Sages teach that the main reason why Esther invited Haman to her feast was in order to induce the Jews to rely solely on Hashem for their salvation, and not on her. Until this point the Jews had felt secure in the knowledge that Esther — a secret Jewess — would watch over them and protect them from harm. However, when she invited Haman to her feast, the Jews were horror stricken, for they were convinced that Esther had betrayed them and formed an alliance with the enemy. With nowhere left to turn, the Jews desperately beseeched Hashem to have mercy on them. Again, we see that the war against Amalek could only be fought on the spiritual plane. Had it been otherwise, the Jews would have attributed their victorious battle to their superior fighting skills, and the theological war would have been utterly lost.

Hence, we see that the essential obligation on Purim is to uproot the heretical thoughts sown into our minds by Amalek. We must internalize the concept that Hashem is always in our midst, regardless of whether we perceive His presence. We must rectify the sin of wondering, "Is HASHEM among us or not?" by acknowledging beyond any doubt that He always resides among us.

The Sages ask, "Where in the Torah do we find an allusion to Esther [אֶסְתֵּר]? In the verse, 'But I will surely have concealed My face on that day' [וְאָנֹכִי הַסְתֵּר אַסְתִּיר פָּנַי בַּיּוֹם הַהוּא]" (*Deuteronomy* 31:18). In other words, Esther symbolized the era of Divine concealment, when the Jewish people were unaware of His presence among them. However, by reading the account of the miracles recorded in *Megillas Esther*, the Jewish people merit to realize that there is none other than Him. It is for this end that we are bidden to publicize the miracles of Purim.

The Greatness of Peace

The *Shelah* writes, "In three places we find that Hashem overlooked the sin of idol worship (*avodah zarah*). He did not overlook the disruption of the harmony between men — He forgave the people for the sin of the Golden Calf, yet He did not forgive them for the sin of the rebellion of Korah."

In addition to the above, we find that peace and harmony were prerequisites to the giving of the Torah, for the Torah tells us that when the Children of Israel arrived at Mount Sinai, "it" encamped there (*Exodus* 19:2). The use of the singular verb (וַיִּחַן) is intended to emphasize that part of the people's preparation for the acceptance of the Torah was their feeling of unity and mutual cooperation.

Another reference to the importance of peace and harmony among the various camps in Israel is found in *Yevamos* 14b. There is a disagreement between *Beis Shammai* and *Beis Hillel* as to the permissibility of a man performing the commandment of levirate marriage (*yibbum*) in a certain case called *tzaras ervah*. According to *Beis Hillel*, a *tzaras ervah* is considered a regular sister-in-law, and marrying her would be considered an act of incest. According to *Beis Shammai*, however, she may — and should — be married to this man. The individual members of each school followed their own opinion, and this would undoubtedly lead to some members of *Beis Shammai*'s group becoming, over the generations, descendants of incestuous relationships (*mamzerim*) according to the view of *Beis Hillel*. Nevertheless, the Talmud tells us, the members of one school never hesitated to marry into the families of the other school, because they would be careful to keep track of the "problematic" families and notify the members of the other faction that a particular mate was not permissible according to their opinion. Thus, although *Beis Shammai* were quite certain about the correctness of their own view, and they followed it for themselves unhesitatingly, they assigned an even higher value to the principle of the importance of harmony and peaceful coexistence between the diverse groups making up the people of Israel.

The Torah says, "There was a King in Jeshurun, when the heads of the people gathered, when the tribes of Israel were together" (*Deuteronomy* 33:5). *Daas Zekeinim* explains that only when the tribes of Israel are harmoniously united is Hashem king over them, but when they are divided, as it were, Hashem does not rule over them.

When the Tabernacle (*Mishkan*) was dedicated, each of the twelve tribal leaders brought a large offering, as part of the twelve-day inauguration ceremony. Each leader brought a specified number of articles, including gold and silver utensils, and sacrificial animals. One of the items brought was wagons for use in transporting the parts of the Tabernacle from one encampment to another. Interestingly, however, the twelve leaders brought a total of only *six* wagons. *Sforno* explains that this was done as a demonstration of unity among the tribes. They could easily have donated one wagon per tribe, but they specifically chose to share the wagons as a symbolic gesture that at this time, when the Divine Presence (*Shechinah*) was just beginning to dwell within the Israelite camp — when the King was about to begin his reign over Jeshurun — all the various factions that comprised the Jewish people would be united and joined together in harmony.

It was said that R' Yochanan ben Zakkai was never preempted in greeting people, even when it came to non-Jews whom he met in the street; *he* was always the first to offer his words of salutation, so great was his dedication to the principle of peace between men. In fact, peace between disparate elements is basic to the very creation of the universe, as it says, "He makes peace in His lofty abode" (*Job* 25:2). As *Rashi* explains (*Genesis* 1:8), the heavens were created by combining the elements of fire and water, which normally do not coexist harmoniously in nature; Hashem "forced" this unnatural combination of elements in order to emphasize the importance of peace between disparate forces, by incorporating this phenomenon into the very fabric of creation.

It should also be remembered that the Torah itself is based on the ideal of peace — "Its ways are the ways of pleasantness and all of its paths are peace" (*Proverbs* 3:17).

Fulfilling One's Wisdom

In *Song of Songs* (4:3) we read, "Your forehead (or temple — *rakkah*) is like a section of a pomegranate." The Sages interpret homiletically, "Even the empty (*rekan*) people among you are as full of commandments as a pomegranate is full with seeds." This statement requires some explanation. If we are referring to people who are full of commandments, in what sense are they "empty" people?

Perhaps this comment can be better understood by referring to another statement of the Sages (quoted above): "The commandments were only given in order for man to become purified through them." This teaches that the purpose of commandments is to provide one with a vehicle to spiritual uplifting, to the sanctification of the soul. Thus, it is possible for a person to fulfill many commandments according to the letter of the law, yet still remain on a low spiritual plane. He may be "full of commandments," but he is nevertheless "empty" of true spiritual content. Sometimes, a person acts in a way which he believes to be a commandment, but his conduct in reality runs contrary to the ways of Torah.

Let us consider an example. The Torah speaks of two commandments in *Exodus* 23:5 and *Deuteronomy* 22:4 — one is to assist a fellow Jew whose load has fallen off his donkey and requires help in lifting it back into place, and the other is to assist someone whose animal is overburdened, to unload the animal. The Torah gives precedence to the commandment of "unloading" over that of "reloading," because the former involves not only a kindness to one's fellow man, but the alleviation of an animal's suffering as well. Nevertheless, if someone is confronted with both commandments, and the "reloading" case involves someone he hates, while the "unloading" involves a friend, the Torah gives preference to the "reloading" in this instance. This is in order to teach a person to overcome his hatred for his fellow Jew by helping him in his distress. This is considered a more important concept than the "unloading" of the animal's burden. As *Tosafos* in *Pesachim* 113b points out, the "hated man" described in this verse is actually someone who is known to his hater to have acted immorally (but without witnesses, so he could not be prosecuted) — someone whom we are permitted, and even encouraged, to hate. Nevertheless, *Tosafos* explains, hatred which begins as hatred sanctioned and mandated by the Torah inevitably deteriorates into personal, subjective spite. It is this added dimension of hatred between Jews that the Torah wants us to overcome by offering assistance to such an individual. Now, if a person would face such a situation, and be confronted simultaneously by both of these commandments — assistance to his hated enemy, and unburdening the animal of his friend — if he would choose to help his friend and his friend's animal, instead of his enemy, he would be guilty of acting contrary to the intentions of the Torah. For the Torah wanted him to learn the lesson of tolerance by helping his enemy. Externally, it would seem that he performed a commandment, but because his intentions went against the Torah's intentions, he gave precedence to the wrong commandment, and thus did not perform a commandment at all! Thus, we learn that if a commandment is carried out with the wrong intentions, it may lead to the annulment of the merit of that commandment altogether.

Perhaps this is the message of the arrangement of the first two sections of *Krias Shema*: "Why is *Shema* recited before *Vehaya Im Shamo'a*? So that a person should first accept upon himself the yoke of Heaven, and only afterwards the yoke of commandments" (*Berachos* 13a). The goal of keeping the commandments is the attainment of the fear of Hashem. Without this, the act of a commandment is no more than an empty, hollow deed. As *Rashi* comments at the end of *Parashas Kedoshim*, "A person should not have the attitude that 'I despise pig's meat; I have no desire to wear garments made of wool and flax.' Rather, he should think, 'I *do* have a desire for these things, but my Father in Heaven has forbidden them to me.' " Refraining from forbidden actions must be done for the sake of accepting upon oneself the yoke of Hashem, for if someone fulfills the laws of the Torah without this intention, he may be "full of commandments," but he is nevertheless considered an "empty person."

The Ten Commandments

The introductory verse to the Ten Commandments says, "*God spoke all these statements . . .*" (*Exodus* 20:1). In *Parashas Va'eschanan* we learn that "HASHEM spoke to you from the midst of the fire; you were hearing the sound of words, but you were not seeing a form, only a sound. He told you of His covenant that He commanded you to observe, the Ten Declarations, and He inscribed them on two stone Tablets" (*Deuteronomy* 4:12-13).

Ibn Ezra notes that these two verses imply that the entire congregation of Israel heard *all Ten Commandments* directly from Hashem.

However, the syntax used in the first two commandments ("*I am* HASHEM, your God, Who has taken you . . . You shall not recognize the gods of others in *My* presence . . .") differs drastically from that of the other eight ("You shall not take the Name of *HASHEM*, your God, in vain, for *HASHEM* will not absolve anyone who takes *His* Name in vain"). While the first two commandments are phrased as a direct dialogue between Hashem and the Jewish people, the other eight are more like a narration by a third party. This suggests that the entire congregation of Israel heard only *the first two commandments* directly from Hashem, while the last eight were conveyed to the Israelites through an intermediary — namely, Moses. Indeed, this is implicit from the Sages' statement, "[The Israelites] heard 'I am HASHEM, your God' and 'You shall not recognize the gods of others in My presence' directly from Hashem" (*Makkos* 24) — the inference is that they *did not* hear the other eight commandments from Him.

Ramban resolves this apparent contradiction as follows: Undoubtedly the Israelites *heard* all Ten Commandments directly from God, as the plain meaning of the verses suggests, but they were only capable of *comprehending* the first two. As far as the other eight, Moses had to translate and explain them to the people. Thus, the people would first hear God's voice, and then Moses would elucidate what had been said — this is the intention of the verse, "Moses would speak, and God would respond to him with a voice" (*Exodus* 19:19).

One may rightly wonder why all the commandments were not

transmitted in the same manner. Why weren't all ten transmitted directly by Hashem, or alternatively, by Moses? Why did Hashem instead allow every single member of the Jewish people to hear and understand the first two commandments, but not the rest? The answer is that the Israelites were not on the spiritual level to hear the Divine voice directly. Even so, Hashem enabled them to hear the first two commandments in order to impart to all Jews a prophetic, personal experience of what it means to have faith in God and shun idol worship. Since these two commandments are the foundation stones of the entire Torah, each Jew had to have them indelibly etched into his consciousness by Hashem's own voice.

The Jewish people's prophetic experience was further amplified by the miracles and wonders that took place at Mount Sinai. As the verse says, "The entire people saw the thunder and the flames, the sound of the shofar and the smoking mountain; the people saw and trembled and stood from afar" (ibid., 20:15). *Rashi* interprets the words "the people . . . stood from afar" to mean that the Jews were flung backwards 12 *mil*, and that ministering angels helped them find their way back to Mount Sinai. Similarly, in *Parashas Va'eschanan* the verse says, "You have been shown in order to know that HASHEM, He is the God! There is none beside Him!" (*Deuteronomy* 4:35). *Rashi* explains, "When God gave the Ten Commandments, He opened the heavens above and the nether regions below, so that it would be clear to every Jew that there is only one God." The *Midrash* adds, "When the Holy One, Blessed is He, gave the Ten Commandments, birds did not chirp, fowl did not fly, angelic beings did not sing songs of praise to God — the world was in complete silence. And then a voice was heard saying, 'I am HASHEM your God . . .' "

According to *Ibn Ezra*, another reason these miracles were necessary was in order to dispel some people's doubts concerning the authenticity of Moses' prophecies. The fact that these doubts existed is implicit from the verse, "Behold, I come to you in the thickness of the cloud, *so that people will hear as I speak to you, and they will also believe in you forever*" (*Exodus* 19:9). Evidently, some people doubted Moses.

Ramban, however, disagrees with *Ibn Ezra*'s premise. In his opinion, it is unthinkable that any member of the Jewish people ever doubted Moses' prophecies. Instead, *Ramban* explains, the Jews were shown all these miracles in order to raise each and every one of them to an exalted prophetic state. In this manner Hashem ensured that if a false prophet would ever emerge among the Israelites and attempt to lead them astray, they would immediately rise up against him — since they perceived the prophecies given to Moses with their own senses, they would never consent to amend them by even one iota.

Rambam's opinion (*Hilchos Yisodei HaTorah* Ch. 8) is as follows: The people were not fully convinced by the signs and wonders Moses performed in Egypt (see *Exodus* 4:1-9), for such marvels can never be considered absolutely conclusive evidence that Moses' prophecies were authentic. When did they fully believe in Moses? When HASHEM appeared upon Mount Sinai. At that time, our eyes saw and our ears heard the fire and thunder — we saw Moses approach the mist, and God's voice speaking to him, saying, "Moses, Moses, tell them the following . . ."

However, *Ohr HaChaim* objects to *Rambam's* interpretation on the grounds that an explicit verse in the Torah clearly states that the people *did* believe in Moses — regarding the splitting of the Red Sea the verse says, "Israel saw the great hand that HASHEM inflicted upon Egypt; and the people revered HASHEM, *and they had faith in HASHEM and in Moses*, His servant" (ibid., 14:31). Why, then, did Hashem perform all the miracles at Mount Sinai? Because although the people believed that Moses was Hashem's *servant*, they were not aware of Moses' exalted level of prophecy, about which Hashem Himself testified, "Mouth to mouth do I speak to him, in a clear vision and not in riddles, at the image of HASHEM does he gaze" (*Numbers* 12:8). At Mount Sinai, however, the people became aware of this heretofore unknown facet of Moses.

A practical lesson emerges from this discussion: We must firmly believe in every word of the Torah that Moses handed down to us as though we had heard it with our own ears. We must not allow any "false prophet" — in whatever form he may appear in modern times — to lead us astray from the ways of the Torah. We must affirm our belief that the Torah is perfect and complete, and disclaim the doubts concerning its authenticity that the heretics and apostates of this day try to disseminate among the Jewish people.

The Reception of the Torah at Mount Sinai

The last of the Ten Commandments is: "You shall not covet your fellow's house. You shall not covet your fellow's wife, his manservant, his maidservant, his ox, his donkey, nor anything that belongs to your fellow" (*Exodus* 20:14). *Ibn Ezra* raises the question, "How is it possible to observe this commandment? Can a person really control his emotions to such an extent?"

He answers that it is indeed possible to prevent oneself from coveting another person's possessions. We see, for example, that people do not covet things that they know are beyond their reach — a pauper does not harbor a desire to marry a king's daughter for the simple reason that he knows that such an eventuality could never come about. Similarly, people who smoke do not have a strong urge to do so on Shabbos because they know that it is absolutely forbidden by the Torah. After the sun sets, however, their thoughts suddenly turn to inhaling tobacco.

Thus, *Ibn Ezra* says, if we would reflect upon the idea that everything has been decreed in Heaven, we would never come to covet another person's possessions. If we would only realize that each person's fate was cast in accordance with his own individual and highly complex spiritual makeup, and that other people's possessions are as beyond our domain as the proverbial king's daughter is to the pauper, we would never violate this Tenth Commandment.

This idea is actually implicit in Moses' reassurances to the Jewish people: In its description of the Divine revelation at Mount Sinai, the verse says, "The entire people saw the thunder and the flames, the sound of the shofar and the smoking mountain; the people saw and trembled and stood from afar. They said to Moses, 'You speak to us and we shall hear; let God not speak to us lest we die.' Moses said to the people, 'Do not fear, for in order to elevate you has God come; so that awe of Him shall be upon your faces, so that you shall not sin" (ibid., vs. 15-17). Clearly, then, if a person would truly fear God, he could not even entertain the possibility of sinning.

We see a similar concept in Moses' dialogue with Hashem:

> HASHEM said to Moses, "Descend, warn the people, lest they break through to HASHEM to see, and a multitude of them will fall. Even the Kohanim who approach HASHEM should be prepared, lest HASHEM burst forth against them."
>
> Moses said to HASHEM, "The people *cannot ascend Mount Sinai, for You have warned us*, saying, 'Bound the mountain and sanctify it' " (ibid. 19:21-23). What did Moses mean by saying "The people *cannot* ascend . . ."? True, Hashem had *prohibited* them from climbing the mountain, but in theory, they still *could* have violated this commandment. The answer is that Hashem's word was so revered by the Israelites that they could not even entertain the *possibility* of violating it. Therefore Moses did not see the point in warning them a second time against climbing up Mount Sinai.

This is what the Sages meant when they said, "Whoever is not naturally humble, it is certain that his ancestors did not stand at Mount Sinai." The fear of God that was instilled into the Isralites at Mount Sinai became an integral component of their spiritual being. Our conscious mind may have forgotten this experience, but it was so powerful that it remains permanently ingrained in the fabric of our souls forever more. This explains why the Sages include humility among the characteristic traits of the Jewish people.

We learn from this a lesson of great importance: We must relate to the Torah's commandments as exactly what they are — *commandments*. They are not suggestions, good advice, codes of proper conduct, but outright *commandments*, which must be observed regardless of the consequences. The way to tell whether one has reached this level of Divine service is to pay attention to the internal dialogue that goes on in one's mind when faced with a difficult *mitzvah* — if you consider even for a fleeting moment the possibility of not fulfilling it, you still have some work ahead of you.

Honoring One's Fellow

Parashas Yisro concludes thus: "An Altar of earth shall you make for Me ... And when you make for Me an Altar of stones, do not build them hewn, for you will have raised your sword over it and desecrated it. You shall not ascend My Altar on steps, so that your nakedness will not be uncovered upon it" (*Exodus* 20:21-23).

Rashi explains that if the *Kohanim* would mount the Altar on steps, the movement of their legs would *seem* to expose their private parts to those steps, and the Torah frowns upon even the slightest suggestion of immodesty. In order to avoid this problem, the *Kohanim* walked up the Altar on a ramp. These verses teach us a profound lesson: Even though the Altar and steps are inanimate objects which would not be aware of the pounding of iron or the "immodest" gesture of the *Kohanim*, the Torah nevertheless commands us to refrain from "shaming" them. How much more, then, must we be careful not to cause shame or embarrassment to living, breathing human beings who are created in the image of God.

Midrash Rabbah (*Bereishis* 24) expresses this concept as follows: "R' Akiva said, 'You shall love your fellow as yourself (*Leviticus* 19:18) — this is a fundamental Torah principle of great importance.'" Indeed, all the interpersonal obligations delineated in the Torah stem from this tenet. To illustrate, the Talmud recounts that a prospective convert once asked Hillel to convert him and "teach him the entire Torah on one leg." Hillel consented. After converting the man, Hillel taught him, "Do not do to your fellow that which you yourself dislike — that is the entire Torah, while the rest is just elucidation of this principle" (see *Shabbos* 31).

In truth, however, it is difficult to understand why such great importance is ascribed to the manner in which we behave towards others. True, we have a great responsibility towards our fellow Jews, but how does proper behavior towards other human beings fulfill our obligations to HASHEM? Both R' Akiva and Hillel said that loving one's fellow is the basis of the entire Torah, but isn't the fear of God a more basic principle of belief?

The answer lies in the Talmud, which quotes Ben Azzai as saying,

"The most important Torah principle is 'This is the account of the descendants of Adam — on the day that God created man, *He made him in the likeness of God'* (*Genesis* 5:1). This warns you against thinking, 'Since I have suffered embarrassment, let my friend feel embarrassment as well!' [The verse essentially says to us,] 'Know Whom you are embarrassing — He made him in the likeness of *God!* ' " Ben Azzai warns us that by disgracing a fellow human being, we shame God as well, for every human was made in His image. This idea is further illustrated by the Talmudic account of a certain *Tanna* who, upon seeing a particularly ugly individual, exclaimed, "What a repulsive man!" The target of this insult retorted, "Go to the One Who created me and tell Him, 'What an ugly object You created!' " When the *Tanna* asked forgiveness for insulting him, the man agreed, but only on one condition — that the *Tanna* promise him that from that day on, he would never again disgrace the handiwork of the Creator (see *Taanis* 20).

Hence, we see that proper conduct towards our fellow human beings encompasses both the interpersonal and the human-Divine realm of responsibilities. When we honor our fellow men, we also honor the Entity that they mirror — Hashem, the Master of the Universe. On the other hand, when we belittle our fellow men, God forbid, we unknowingly disgrace the Creator. How careful we must be in our conduct toward others!

The harshness of the punishment incurred for humiliating others may also be discerned from the following incident involving David and Saul. The verse tells us that during his last years of life, "King David was old, advanced in years; they covered him with garments, but he did not become warm" (*I Kings* 1:1). The Sages say that this condition came upon him as punishment for having embarrassed King Saul, as the verse says, "Saul took three thousand men from all Israel and pursued David and his men ... There was a cave there, and Saul entered it to relieve himself ... David got up, and proceeded to stealthily cut the corner of Saul's cloak" (*I Samuel* 24:2-4). The Sages' statement is truly astounding! Even though David spared Saul's life and did not cause him physical harm, he received harsh punishment for merely embarrassing him!

In the next *parashah* — *Mishpatim* — the Torah conveys the importance of honoring one's fellow Jews by delineating the laws pertaining to Jewish slaves. We learn that one of the ways of becoming a Jewish slave is by being found guilty of theft, as the verse says, "If the thief is discovered . . . He shall make restitution; if he has nothing, he shall be sold for his theft" (*Exodus* 22:1-2). Nevertheless, the Torah dictates that [the slave's] master treat him with utmost dignity and respect. For example, if the master drinks fine wine, he must not serve his slave wine of inferior quality; if he eats fine food, he must serve his slave the same. In fact, a slave-owner's obligation is so great that the Sages said, "He who purchases a Jewish slave, it is as though he had acquired a master over himself." *Tosafos* point out that if a master owns only one pillow, he must give it to his slave, while he himself should do without. And why must one pay so much honor to a person who was nothing but a common thief? In order to spare him embarrassment. How respectful is the Torah towards every Jew! We, too, are bound to emulate this attitude in our dealings with people.

To illustrate, the Talmud recounts the following incident: "Rebbi sat and began teaching. He [suddenly] smelled garlic. 'Whoever is eating garlic, please go outside!' he said. R' Chiya stood up and went outside. Presently, everyone else stood up and followed him outside. The next morning, R' Shimon the son of Rebbi met R' Chiya. He said to him, 'Are you the one who upset my father?' R' Chiya answered, 'Such things shall not occur in Israel!' " (*Sanhedrin* 11). *Maharsha* explains that R' Shimon — Rebbi's son — accused R' Chiya of deliberately having stepped outside even though he had not been chewing garlic. The interruption of the lesson, and the consequent neglect of Torah study, tormented Rebbi to no end. R' Chiya countered that although it was certainly a pity that the Torah session had to be interrupted, there could not be a worse transgression than causing embarrassment to a fellow Jew. Such an offense, even coming from a saintly individual such as Rebbi, was simply inexcusable!

Perhaps the most well-known narrative that illustrates the severity of embarrassing a fellow Jew is the story of Kamtza and Bar Kamtza. Sadly, however, we frequently forget its straightforward lesson. The Sages' summary of the lesson to be learned from Kamtza and Bar Kamtza seems an appropriate way to conclude this exposition: "R' Eliezer said: 'Come and look at the [destructive] power of causing someone embarrassment. The Holy One, Blessed is He, assisted Bar Kamtza [in his plot to avenge his embarrassment], and destroyed His Temple and burned His Sanctuary!' "

"We Will Do and We Will Obey"

This *parashah* describes the covenant that was sealed between
Hashem and the Jewish people:
"Moses came and told the people all the words of HASHEM and all
the ordinances, and the entire people responded with one voice and
they said, 'All the words that HASHEM has spoken, we will do!'
"Moses wrote all the words of HASHEM. He arose early in the morning and built an Altar at the foot of the mountain, and twelve pillars
for the twelve tribes of Israel. He sent the youths of the Children of
Israel and they brought up elevation-offerings to HASHEM. Moses took
half the blood and placed it in basins, and half the blood he threw upon
the Altar. He took the Book of the Covenant and read it in earshot of
the people, and they said, 'Everything that HASHEM has said, we will
do and we will hear!' Moses took the blood and threw it upon the
people, and he said, 'Behold, the blood of the covenant that HASHEM
sealed with you concerning all these matters' " (*Exodus* 24:3-8).
There is disagreement among the commentators regarding the
chronology of these events:
According to *Rashi*, this ceremonial pact took place *before* the
Jewish people received the Ten Commandments. This would mean
that the revelation at Sinai recorded in Chapter 20 happened after the
narrative given here, four chapters later. However, this does not
present a difficulty, for the Sages said, "The Torah is not necessarily
written in chronological order." What, then, does the verse mean by,
"Moses came and told the people all *the words of HASHEM and all the
ordinances...*"? At first glance, this would seem to be referring to the
Ten Commandments! *Rashi* interprets these words as follows: "[The
verse refers to] the Seven Noahide Laws, to [the laws of] *Shabbos*, to
[the *mitzvah* of] honoring one's father and mother, to [the laws
regarding] the red cow (*parah adumah*), and the ordinances that were

given to them at *Marah*." What, then, does the verse mean by: "He took the *Book of the Covenant* and read it in earshot of the people"? Is this not a reference to the Torah? *Rashi* explains, "[It refers] to the early portions of the Torah — from *Parashas Bereishis* until the reception of the Torah at Sinai."

Ramban, however, maintains that this pact took place *after* Israel received the Ten Commandment. On the very same day when HASHEM revealed Himself on Mount Sinai, He said to Moses, "So shall you say to the Children of Israel, 'You have seen that I have spoken to you from heaven. You shall not make [images of] what is with Me; gods of silver and gold shall you not make for yourselves" (ibid., 20:19-20). Hashem then proceeded to command the Israelites, "And these are the ordinances that you shall place before them . . ." (ibid., 21:1). The Jewish people's joyous response was, "Everything that HASHEM has said, we will do!"

Moses recorded all the laws and ordinances that Hashem had given to the Jewish people and compiled them in one book — "the Book of the Covenant." The next morning, Moses rose early and sealed the pact between the Jewish people and Hashem. He read the book that he wrote on the previous night to the people, and they responded by saying, "Everything that HASHEM has said, we will do and we will hear [נַעֲשֶׂה וְנִשְׁמַע]!"

Ramban interprets Israel's response as follows: "We will do" meant that the Israelites agreed to keep the laws they received at Mount Sinai (as outlined in *Parashas Mishpatim*); "we will hear" meant that they agreed to fulfill any additional *mitzvos* that Hashem would command to them. In principle, *Rashi* concurs with *Ramban*'s interpretation of the plain meaning of the words: "We will do" means that the Israelites agreed to keep the laws they had received thus far (the Seven Noahide Laws, etc.), and "we will hear" expressed their willingness to fulfill any commandments they might receive in the future.

However, the Sages seem to interpret the Israelites' response differently. We learn, "R' Simai said: 'When Israel *preceded* [the reception of the Torah] by saying, "We will do and we will hear," 600,000 ministering angels came and bound two crowns upon each and every Israelite — one [crown] representing "we will do," and the other, "we will hear" ' " (*Shabbos* 88). In another Talmudic passage we learn, "When the Israelites *preceded* [the reception of the Torah] by saying, 'We will do and we will hear,' a heavenly voice proclaimed to them, 'Who revealed to My children this secret that is practiced only by the ministering angels? As the verse says, "Bless HASHEM, O His angels, mighty creatures who do His bidding, who hear His voice" ' (*Psalms* 103:20) — first they *do*, and only afterwards they *hear!*"

Hence it is evident that the Sages, unlike *Rashi* and *Ramban*, understood that *both* "we will do" and "we will obey" conveyed the Israelites' willingness to accept any *mitzvos* that Hashem would command to them in the future.

Still, the logic behind the Israelites' declaration requires some explanation. How can a person state that he is willing to *do* something before he has even *heard* what he is expected to do? The *Maharsha* offers the following explanation:

Angelic beings do not have an independent existence; since they are purely spiritual entities, their only purpose is to fulfill the will of the Almighty. Thus, in a manner of speaking, their willingness to carry out His will logically precedes the particular task which they will be assigned; because their entire existence is based on serving Hashem, they are willing to *do* His bidding even before hearing the details of their mission.

Human beings, on the other hand, are composed of both spiritual and physical elements. Because the corporeal facet of man gives him a sense of self, he does not feel *compelled* to serve His Creator, but rather has "free choice" to do so. As a consequence of Adam's sin, the primordial serpent injected him with a spiritual venom called the evil inclination (*yetzer hara*), which actively persuades him not to fulfill Hashem's will. At Mount Sinai, however, the Jewish people were purged of their evil inclination, and they ascended to the level of angelic beings. They attained the exalted spiritual level of Adam prior to his sin, which made them realize that the Torah was the basis of their entire existence.

That is why they were able to say, "We will do and we will hear"; that is why 600,000 ministering angels bound two crowns upon their heads.

We, too, must strive to strengthen our resolve to fulfill all the *mitzvos* that present themselves to us, and to emulate the attitude of our forefathers who stood at Mount Sinai and declared, "Everything that HASHEM has said, we will do and we will hear!"

The Sanctuary

When learning the *parashios* which discuss the construction of the Tabernacle, we must keep in mind *Rashi's* approach to the chronological order of events: The Israelites first committed the sin of the Golden Calf, and only afterwards were they commanded to construct the Tabernacle.

Sforno explains the logic behind this sequence. Before the sin of the Golden Calf, the Israelites were on such an exalted spiritual level that they were capable of approaching Hashem at all times, regardless of their location. The Divine Presence constantly resided in their midst, and because of their pure state, there was no need for it to be confined in one particular place. In the wake of the sin of the Golden Calf, however, this idyllic situation drastically changed. The Israelites' spiritual standing plummeted to the point where the Divine Presence could no longer roam freely among them. From then on, it would have to constrict itself and dwell within the confines of the Tabernacle, a collapsible edifice that the Israelites would carry along with them throughout their sojourns in the desert.

Rashi also comments about the Israelites' diminished spiritual state following the sin of the Golden Calf. The verse says, "When Moses descended from Mount Sinai — with the two Tablets of the Testimony in the hand of Moses as he descended from the mountain — Moses did not know that the skin of his face had become radiant when He had spoken to him. Aaron and all the Children of Israel saw Moses, and behold! — the skin of his face had become radiant; *and they feared to approach him*" (*Exodus* 34:29-30). In reference to these verses *Rashi* wrote, "Come and see how great is the power of sin. Until they extended their hand in sin [by worshiping the Golden

Calf], what does [the Torah] say? 'The appearance of the glory of HASHEM was like a consuming fire on the mountaintop *before the eyes* of the Children of Israel' (ibid., 24:17), yet they neither feared nor trembled. But from the time when they made the Golden Calf, they shivered and trembled even before the rays of glory of Moses!"

Other commentators disagree with *Rashi's* opinion concerning the chronological sequence of these events. According to them, Hashem commanded Moses to build the Sanctuary during Moses' first 40 days on Mount Sinai.

In reference to the verses, "They shall make a Sanctuary for me — so that I may dwell among them — *like everything that I show you,* the form of the Tabernacle and the form of all its vessels; and so shall you do" (ibid., 25:8,9), the Sages said, "A fiery Ark, Menorah and Table descended from heaven. Moses observed, and he was commanded to duplicate them" (*Menachos* 29). Further, we learn that when Moses encountered difficulties in constructing these artifacts, Gabriel the angel appeared and clarified the matter to him.

When we ponder these miracles, as well as all the myriad miracles Hashem performed on behalf of the Israelites throughout their 40-year sojourn, it is difficult to understand the verse, "Speak to the Children of Israel and let them take for Me a portion, from every man whose heart motivates him you shall take My portion" (ibid., v. 2). On the one hand, Hashem provided approximately 3,000,000 Israelite men, women and children with their every need — food descended from heaven, water flowed from the Well of Miriam, God's clouds of glory surrounded the Israelite camp from all sides — yet, on the other hand, He requested of the people to contribute the materials required to construct the Tabernacle. Why did He request the people's assistance? Why couldn't the artifacts of the Tabernacle miraculously descend from heaven ready made? Or at least, why didn't Hashem provide the raw materials in the same manner He provided the Israelites' other needs?

Indeed, we learn that as far back as the days of Jacob, it was understood that the Jewish people would be expected to supply the raw materials for the Tabernacle, as *Rashi* says: "How did they have acacia-wood staves in the desert? [The answer is that] the patriarch Jacob foresaw that Israel would eventually build a Tabernacle in the desert, and so, he brought trees to Egypt and planted them, and commanded his sons to take them with them when they would leave Egypt."

Let us ponder upon this for a moment. After an interminable period of mourning over Joseph's assumed death, Jacob suddenly learns that Joseph is alive and well in Egypt, and has asked his father and brothers to bring their entire household to that land. Finally, after deliberating the matter, Jacob gives his consent. Preparations for the journey begin in earnest, and Jacob anticipates the moment when he will finally see his long-lost son with his own eyes, saying "How great! My son Joseph still lives! I shall go and see him before I die" (*Genesis* 45:28). "But wait!" we can imagine Jacob having said, "We must take along acacia saplings, for our descendants will need wood with which to build the Tabernacle in the desert!" And then, in Egypt, Jacob commands his offspring to take the acacia trees along with them when they leave Egypt. What long-term preparations! Perhaps the point is best summed up in *Avos DeRabbi Nassan:* "R' Tarfon says: Great is work, for the Holy One, Blessed is He, did not rest His Divine Presence upon the Israelites until they did work."

The answer to why Hashem required the Israelites to actively participate in building the Tabernacle is as follows: The verse says, "They shall make a Sanctuary for Me so that I may dwell among them." Note that the verse does not say, "so that I may dwell *within it,*" but, "so that I may dwell *among them.*" This means that in addition to being the earthly abode of the Divine Presence, the existence of the Tabernacle also caused the Divine Presence to reside within each and every Jew. Now, it is a well-known maxim that "everything is in the hands of Heaven except for the fear of Heaven." Surely then, it would not have been appropriate for the Israelites to receive the sudden influx of spirituality that came in the wake of the Tabernacle's completion without any effort on their part. As the Sages said, "[If someone says,] 'I have not toiled, yet I have attained,' do not believe him." In order to merit the exalted level of Torah and fear of God that the Israelites attained in the desert following the completion of the Tabernacle, it was necessary that they exert themselves in constructing it. Indeed, it was even necessary that *their ancestors'* generations toiled to this end — hence, Jacob's acacia saplings, and hence, the oral tradition handed down through the years instructing them to take the wood when they leave Egypt. The Israelites' self-sacrifice in cutting down the trees and taking them along as they left Egypt — despite the fact that they did not even have enough time to prepare food for themselves — earned them the merit to have the Divine Presence "dwell among them."

It would seem that each Jew merited Divine revelation in direct ratio to the degree that he participated in the construction of the Tabernacle, whether by donating the required materials, or by taking an active part in the work. This concept is implicit in the *Nefesh HaChaim*'s interpretation of the Sages' statement, "Know what is above you" — everything that occurs in the upper realms of existence is a direct consequence of each individual's deeds. Thus, it is reasonable to assume that those Jews who exerted themselves more towards building the Tabernacle merited a greater degree of Divine revelation.

The Torah itself alludes to this idea by listing the materials used to build the Tabernacle in a curious order: "Take from yourselves a portion for HASHEM, everyone whose heart motivates him shall bring it, as the gift for HASHEM: gold, silver, copper; turquoise, purple, and scarlet wool; linen, goat hair; red-dyed ram skins, tachash skins, acacia wood; oil for illumination, spices for the anointment oil and aromatic incense; *shoham* stones and stones for the settings, for the *Ephod* and the Breastplate" (*Exodus* 35:5-9). Why were the most valuable materials — the "*shoham* stones and stones for the settings" — listed last? The *Ohr HaChaim* offers two possible answers. The first is that, according to the Sages, the precious stones came floating miraculously upon a cloud, whereas the rest of the materials were generously contributed by the Israelites. Thus, although the stones were of greater *monetary* value, the other materials were of greater *spiritual* value. The second answer is that the tribal princes, who contributed the precious stones, waited until the people had brought all the other materials before they presented their gift. Although their intentions were pure, they were still held accountable for their reticence, since the most essential component of the Tabernacle was the Jewish people's enthusiasm in constructing it. Hence, even though the prince's contribution was more valuable than the other materials, it was mentioned last because it contained the smallest measure of religious fervor.

Sforno infers from the following verses four reasons why the Tabernacle built by the Jewish people in the desert was never destroyed or captured by an enemy: "These are the reckonings of the Tabernacle, the Tabernacle of Testimony, which were reckoned at Moses' bidding. The labor of the Levites was under the authority of Issamar, son of Aaron the *Kohen*. Bezalel, son of Uri son of Hur, of the tribe of Judah, did everything that HASHEM commanded Moses" (ibid., 38:21-22). First, because it was "the Tabernacle of Testimony" — i.e., it contained the Tablets of Testimony. Second, because it was "reckoned at Moses' bidding." Third, because it was created through "the labor of the Levites ... under the authority of Issamar." And fourth, because it was constructed by the greatest *tzaddikim* of the generation, including Bezalel. As a result of these distinguishing qualities, the Divine Presence resided upon the Tabernacle, and the enemies of Israel were never able to destroy it.

In contrast, the First Temple built under King Solomon's authority was constructed by gentile workers from Tyre. Although the Divine Presence *did* reside upon it, in time it fell into disrepair, and eventually it was destroyed and pillaged by Israel's enemy.

The Second Temple, which did not contain the Tablets of Testimony or any of the other distinguishing qualities of the Tabernacle, fared even worse. The Divine Presence never resided upon it, and it, too, was destroyed by a foreign nation.

In light of these differences, we see that the relative strength of the physical materials used to build Hashem's Sanctuary do not determine its impregnability. The only factors are its spiritual makeup. It is for this reason that the seemingly flimsy Tabernacle, built from animal hide and wood, proved to be stronger than the First Temple's massive stone structure. It is religious zeal that makes a sanctuary eternal, not the quality and strength of the materials used to construct it.

The reason why such extensive preparations were necessary in order to construct the Tabernacle is discussed by *Ramban* in *Parashas Terumah*. *Ramban* explains that the ultimate purpose of the Tabernacle was to serve as a resting place for God's glory which was revealed to the Israelites at Mount Sinai. Although the cloud of Divine glory that resided upon the Tabernacle was less *perceivable* than the one which appeared at Mount Sinai, it contained the same intensity of Divine revelation. This congruence between the two incidents of Divine revelation is evident from the similarity of the verses that describe these events: In reference to the reception of the Torah at Mount Sinai the verse says, "The glory of HASHEM rested upon Mount Sinai, and the cloud covered it for a six-day period . . ." (ibid., 24:16), and regarding the cloud of glory that resided upon the Sanctuary the verses say, "The cloud covered the Tent of Meeting, and the glory of HASHEM filled the Tabernacle. Moses could not enter the Tent of Meeting, for the cloud rested upon it, and the glory of HASHEM filled the Tabernacle" (ibid., 40:34-35). Thus, Hashem's cloud of glory constantly resided among the Israelites, but in concealment. While at Mount Sinai it had resided in brilliant resplendence atop the mountain, in plain view for all to see, in the Tabernacle it resided upon the Ark, within the bounds of the Tent of Meeting.

After having established this parallel between the revelation at Mount Sinai and the cloud of glory that resided upon the Tabernacle, other corresponding aspects emerge: Just as the Israelites merited the Divine revelation at Mount Sinai because they declared, "We will do and we will hear," so too, they merited the cloud of glory that resided upon the Tabernacle by enthusiastically participating in its construction. As the verse says, "They shall make an Ark . . ." (ibid., 25:10) — the verse does not say, "You [Moses] shall make an Ark," but "They [all of Israel] shall make an Ark." In reference to this verse, Ramban says, "It would seem that the verse alludes to the fact that all of Israel participated in the building of the Ark. For it was an extremely holy vessel, and [by participating in its construction,] all the Israelites would merit to Torah. As the Midrash says, 'Why in regards to all the other vessels does the verse say, "You shall make . . .," while in reference to the Ark the verse says, "They shall make an Ark"? R' Yehudah the son of R' Shalom said: "The Holy One, Blessed is He, said, 'Let them all come forward and engage in constructing the Ark, so that they may merit to Torah!' " ' And in what way did they all 'engage in constructing the Ark'? Each Jew donated a golden vessel towards the construction of the Ark, or helped Bezalel in some small way."

Ramban's interpretation of this verse implies that participating in the construction of the Ark was a separate commandment on its own, which could not be fulfilled by engaging in the construction of the other holy vessels. Why? Because the Ark represents Torah study — just as Torah study is greater than all the commandments and is in a category all its own, so too, participating in the construction of the Ark was a greater commandment than engaging in the construction of the other holy vessels. This concept is also evident from the Midrashic interpretation of the verse, "Speak to the Children of Israel and let them *take for Me* a portion ..." (ibid., v. 2) — the verse may also be read, "*purchase Me* for a portion." Taken in this way, the verse conveys that Hashem in effect said, "I have been sold along with the Torah. To separate Myself from it, I cannot. Thus, wherever you may go, construct one house for Me where I may reside, as the verse says, 'They shall make a Sanctuary for Me, so that I may dwell among them ...' (ibid., v. 8)."

From this we glean a new awareness of the symbiosis between Torah and the Almighty — they are truly One, as the *Midrash* says, "To separate Myself from it, I cannot." The Sages alluded to the Divine aspect of Torah by recounting that when Yonasan son of Uziel (one of Hillel's disciples) would sit down to study Torah, birds circling above him would be instantly singed and consumed by a heavenly fire (*Sukkah* 28). *Tosafos* explains as follows: "For [he learned Torah] with the same joy as when it was given at Mount Sinai, where the Torah was transmitted amidst [heavenly] fire. The same theme is evident in the incident involving R' Eliezer and R' Yehoshua, when they were sitting down and having a meal [while discussing Torah], and a heavenly fire surrounded them."

Clearly, the Tabernacle constructed by the Israelites in the desert was no ordinary structure. For example, the verses say, "An Altar of earth shall you make for Me ... And when you make for Me an Altar of stones, do not build them hewn, for you will have raised your sword over it and desecrated it" (*Exodus* 20:21-22). Now, what difference could it possibly make to inanimate stone whether "you ... raised your sword over it"? *Rashi* explains that the stones may not be cut with iron tools, for iron, as the raw material of the sword, shortens life, while the Altar, by offering people the opportunity of repentance and atonement, lengthens it. Similarly, *Ramban* notes that the Hebrew word for sword [*cherev*] shares a common root with the word "destruction" [*churban*], for swords bring destruction to the world. Therefore, such an implement has no place in the Tabernacle. It is for this reason that the pegs of the Tabernacle were made of copper even though steel would have achieved better results. Hence, we see that the essence of the Temple was life, and its degree of sanctity was such that even a mundane act such as lifting a sword over the Altar was considered an act of utter desecration. Since death was the Altar's very antithesis, it would have been a contradiction in terms to hew its stones with a sword, the symbol of death.

The ineffable sanctity of the Sanctuary may also be inferred from King David's revelation to Solomon, his son: "David said to Solomon, 'My son, I wanted to build a House for the Name of HASHEM, my God. But the word of HASHEM came to me, saying, "You have shed much blood and fought great battles; you shall not build a House for My Name, for you have shed much blood on the earth in My sight. But you will have a son who will be a man of tranquility . . . Solomon will be his name . . ." ' " (I Chronicles 22:7-9). Radak explains that since HASHEM's Temple symbolized eternal life, it would not have been appropriate that it be constructed under the auspices of King David, who had shed so much blood during his lifetime. Now, let us remember who King David was, how close he was to Hashem, how he adhered to Him and trusted Him in the face of mortal danger. And yet, because he slayed so many of the enemies of the Jewish people in warfare — even though this was a commandment — he was found unsuitable to build the Temple. How profound was the sanctity of the Altar, how subtle its sacredness!

The Omission of Moshe's Name

Many commentators note that Moses' name does not appear even
once in this entire *parashah*. The *Baal HaTurim* explains that
this was due to Moses' prayer, "And now, if You would but forgive
their sin! And if not, *erase me now from Your book that You have
written*" (*Exodus* 32:32). Moses' request was fulfilled in this *parashah*,
from which his name was "erased." For even though Hashem *did*
forgive the Israelites, and therefore Moses' request to have his name
erased was no longer applicable, the words of saintly men are always
fulfilled regardless of the circumstances.

Alternatively, there is another explanation why Moses' name does
not appear even once in the *parashah*. Let us remember that the
majority of the *parashah* discusses the priestly appointment of Aaron
and his sons and the type of clothes they would wear while serving
in the Tabernacle. Let us also remember that Korah boisterously
accused Moses of showing favoritism towards Aaron, his brother.
Korah's contention was that Moses appointed Aaron as High Priest
(*Kohen Gadol*) of his own accord, that Hashem had not commanded
him to do so.

Thus, Hashem omitted all mention of Moses' name in this
parashah — which deals almost exclusively with priestly matters —
in order to prove that Moses had no ulterior motives in appointing
Aaron as High Priest. This negated Korah's accusation against Moses
of being impartial towards his brother. It also lent support to Moses'
counterclaim against Korah, "Therefore, you and your entire assembly that are joining together are against HASHEM! And as for Aaron,
what is he that you protest against him?" (*Numbers* 16:11) — *Rashi*
paraphrases this to mean, "Your complaints are directed against
Hashem, for when I appointed Aaron as High Priest, I merely carried
out His will. Therefore, it is not for us to argue about this matter."

The Prelude to Wisdom

T he Sages tell us (*Berachos* 55a), "HASHEM puts wisdom only into those who have wise hearts, as it says (*Exodus* 31:6), 'Into the heart of all those wise of heart I have placed wisdom.' " What is this "wisdom of the heart" which is considered a prerequisite for receiving wisdom? *Nefesh HaChaim* explains that in order for a person to truly incorporate the wisdom of the Torah, he must first have a basis in pureness of thought and fear of Hashem. As the *Mishnah* tells us (*Avos* 3:17), "If there is no fear (of Hashem) there can be no wisdom." Also in *Yoma* 72b we learn, "Woe to students of the Torah who involve themselves with Torah study but do not have the fear of sin. Of them it is said (*Proverbs* 17:16), 'For what purpose is money in the hand of a fool to attain wisdom, if he hasn't the heart for it?' " Again in *Avos* 3:9 we learn, "Whoever gives his fear of sin precedence over his wisdom, his wisdom may be retained permanently (but not the reverse)." The fear of Hashem is thus the basis upon which the acquisition and retention of knowledge is founded, and without which it is impossible to attain, as it says, "The beginning of wisdom is the fear of HASHEM" (*Psalms* 111:10).

This, then, is the key to Torah knowledge; one must first prepare a foundation of fear of Heaven. But this is no easy task; it must be acquired through great effort and toil, as King Solomon said (*Proverbs* 2:4-5), "If you seek it like silver and search for it like gems, then you will understand the fear of HASHEM." This is what we are obligated to do in order to acquire Torah wisdom, and this, in fact, is the essence of what the "forty-eight ways through which Torah is acquired" (enumerated in *Avos* 6:5) are all about.

The Sin of the Golden Calf

This *parashah* is extremely difficult to understand. Two questions must be answered in order to gain insight into its mysteries: What exactly was the Israelites' sin, and what prompted them to commit it?

Let us begin by analyzing the form of the punishment incurred by those who actively participated in this sin. The verse tells us, "Moses stood at the gateway of the camp and said, 'Whoever is for HASHEM, join me!' And all the Levites gathered around him. He said to them, 'So said HASHEM the God of Israel, "Every man, put his sword on his thigh and pass back and forth from gate to gate in the camp. Let every man kill his brother, every man his fellow, and every man his relative." ' The Levites did as Moses said, and about three thousand men of the people fell that day" (*Exodus* 32:26-28).

Regarding Moses' statement, "So said HASHEM the God of Israel, 'Every man, put his sword . . .,' " *Rashi* says, "Where did Hashem say this? In an earlier verse, 'One who brings offerings to the gods shall be destroyed — only to HASHEM alone!' " (ibid., 22:19).

Ramban, however, points out that the Israelites who participated in this sin were punished with unprecedented harshness, since it is a general Torah principle that capital punishment may only be prescribed against a sinner if he was explicitly warned against performing the transgression. Thus, *Ramban* concludes, the Israelites' punishment was an exception to the rule for the purpose of sanctifying God's Name.

In *Sanhedrin* 63 the Sages say, "Whoever combines the Name of Heaven with something else shall be uprooted from the world, as the verse says, 'One who brings offering to the gods shall be destroyed — only to HASHEM alone!' " (ibid.) *Ramban* explains this verse as follows: "To the gods" means to the angelic beings that dwell in the upper realms — people mistakenly thought that it would be more appropriate to direct one's requests to the King's servants, and not directly to the King. The end of the verse, however, warns that offerings be brought "only to HASHEM alone," and not to intermediaries, even though they reside in the heavenly realms. Those who violate this prohibition "shall be destroyed" — executed by the *Beis Din*, a Torah court.

Thus, we see that the Jews who participated in the sin of the Golden Calf incurred the death penalty for having "brought offerings to the gods," or as the Sages put it, "combining the Name of Heaven with something else." At face value, then, it seems that the Israelites performed a form of idolatry.

However, it is difficult to understand how they could have done such a thing so soon after the revelation at Mount Sinai. At the foot of the mountain, they saw the glory of Hashem with their entire being, with every fiber of their body. It was totally clear to them that "HASHEM is God, there is none other." How, then, could they have stooped so low as to exchange their faith in the Master of the Universe for belief in a golden statue?

In answer to this question, the Sages say it was indeed beneath Israel to do such a thing. Under normal circumstances, a people who witnessed the miracles at Sinai would never have committed such an ill-advised act. As proof they cite the verse, "Who can assure that his heart should remain theirs, to fear Me and observe all My commandments all the days ..." (*Deuteronomy* 5:26) — implicitly, Hashem testified that the Jewish people had reached a spiritual plateau. Nevertheless, it was decreed in Heaven that they stumble in this sin in order to provide future *baalei teshuvah* with a claim of vindication.

Thus, the Sages reaffirm our original assessment — the sin of the Golden Calf defies human understanding. Indeed, it was decreed by Hashem for reasons which we cannot fully grasp. In His great wisdom He saw the necessity of providing future sinners the possibility to repent for their sins, and to this end, He decreed that Israel commit the sin of the Golden Calf.

However, this explanation is difficult in its own right. For if the Israelites did not play a part in this sin, why was it ascribed to them? If they were forced into performing this transgression, why were they punished so harshly? Indeed, in reference to the verse, "My angel shall go before you, and on the day *that I make My account, I shall bring their sin to account against them*" (*Exodus* 32:34), *Rashi* says, "Mercifully, God consented not to punish the entire nation at that time, but He declared that whenever they would sin in the future, *they would suffer some of the punishment that they should have received in retribution for the sin of the Golden Calf.*" This implies that Israel will *forever* be held accountable for its role in the sin of the Golden Calf. But according to the Sages' opinion that Hashem compelled them to sin, why were they judged so harshly?

The answer must be that even though it had been decreed in Heaven that the Israelites commit this sin, *they were not forced to do so.* Their free will had only been severely challenged, but not taken away altogether. Therefore, had they shown more resolve against the impulses of their evil inclination, they could have restrained themselves from committing the sin. It was for this lack of determination, and for their willingness to play along with the whims of their evil inclination, that they were punished so severely. But you might ask, "Had they overcome the temptation to sin, what would have become of future *baalei teshuvah*? What about their plea of vindication? What about the Heavenly decree?" The answer is that a different generation would be compelled to sin.

The Sanctity of Shabbos

We learn in the *parashah*, "HASHEM said to Moses, saying, 'You shall speak to the Children of Israel, saying, "However, you must observe My Sabbaths, for it is a sign between Me and you for your generations, to know that I am HASHEM, Who makes you holy"'" (*Exodus* 31:12-13). *Rashi* explains that although the commandment to observe the Sabbath was part of the Ten Commandments (ibid., 20:8), it is repeated here to caution the nation that the construction of the Tabernacle does not override the Sabbath prohibitions.

The ramifications of *Rashi's* understanding of the verse are truly astounding — even though the construction of the Tabernacle would provide a resting place for the Divine Presence in this world, from where the splendor of God's glory would radiate outward and fill the world with knowledge of Hashem, the laws of the Sabbath still take precedence over it! What importance the Torah attributes to the observance of Shabbos!

This concept merely reinforces that which every Jew instinctively feels deep inside — that Shabbos is not merely an abstract idea, but rather a palpable entity of great spiritual intensity. In fact, the Talmud likens Shabbos to a physical object that has been given to us as a gift:

"R' Chama son of R' Chanina said: 'One who gives a gift to his fellow is not required to inform him, as the verse says, "Moses did not know that the skin of his face had become radiant when He had spoken to him"'" (ibid., 34:29).

"A difficulty is raised: [But the verse says,] '[However, you must observe My Sabbaths] . . . to *know* that I am HASHEM, Who makes you holy.' Hashem in effect said to Moses, 'I have a precious gift in My treasure house — it is called "Shabbos." I would like to give it to Israel, so please inform them.' [This implies that one who gives a gift *should* inform the recipient, just as Hashem informed the Jewish people that He gave them the Shabbos.]

"R' Yochanan said in the name of R' Shimon son of Yochai: 'HASHEM gave all the commandments [to the Israelites] in public with the exception of Shabbos, which He gave to them in private, as the verse says, *"Between Me and the Children of Israel* it is a sign forever that in a six-day period HASHEM made heaven and earth, and on the seventh day He rested and was refreshed" ' (ibid., 31:17).

"[A difficulty is asked,] 'If so, gentiles should not incur punishment for violations related to the laws of Shabbos!'

"[Gentiles] *were* informed of Shabbos, but they were not informed of 'the additional soul' [the *neshamah yiseirah* with which Jews are endowed on Shabbos]" (*Beitzah* 16).

Nevertheless, the question must be asked: Why, indeed, does the Torah ascribe more importance to Shabbos than to the construction of the Tabernacle?

The answer is that the spiritual entity called Shabbos is itself an "abode" for the Divine Providence. Thus, since it was created before the Tabernacle it is fitting that it take precedence over it. But what do we mean when we say that Shabbos is "an abode for the Divine Presence"?

The explanation lies in *Sforno's* commentary, where he expounds upon why the commandment to construct the Tabernacle came after the sin of the Golden Calf. *Sforno* explains that prior to the sin of the Golden Calf, the Jewish people were capable of adhering to the Divine Presence wherever they chose, as the verse says, *"In every place* where I permit My Name to be mentioned, I shall come to you and bless you" (*Exodus* 20:21). In other words, the Israelites remained "a kingdom of ministers and a holy nation" (ibid., 19:6) regardless of their location. Following the sin of the Golden Calf, however, the Israelites lost this supreme level of spirituality — this "additional soul" — and it became necessary for them to build a confined structure within which the Divine Presence would reveal itself to them.

Shabbos shares similar qualities with the unlimited spiritual relationship the Israelites had with Hashem prior to the sin of the Golden Calf. Shabbos is a conduit of spiritual force that enables a person to adhere to the Divine Presence regardless of his location. The holiness (*kedushah*) of Shabbos is not confined to a particular location, but is accessible to all Jews, wherever they may be. This "additional soul" aspect of Shabbos is evident from the verse, "God blessed the seventh day *and sanctified it*, because on it He abstained from all His work which God created to make" (*Genesis* 2:3). Also, the verse says, "Remember the Sabbath day to *sanctify it*" (*Exodus* 20:8), in regard to which *Ibn Ezra* said, "For Hashem sanctified this day in its appointed time to receive 'an additional soul' of wisdom that surpasses that of all other nations."

In this sense, Shabbos is an "abode for the Divine Presence" which takes precedence over the construction of the Sanctuary.

We, today, have lost much of our spiritual sensitivity, and for this reason, Shabbos is not as much of a palpable entity as it once was. The Talmud makes mention of the "tangible sensation" called Shabbos on numerous occasions. For example, the Sages said, "Rebbi once prepared a meal in honor of Antoninus on Shabbos. He brought cold food before him, and he enjoyed it. Then, on a weekday, he served him warm food, but [Antoninus] said, 'I enjoyed the other food [you served me on Shabbos] more! Perhaps it is missing a spice?' [Rebbi] replied, '[You are correct!] It is missing [the spice called] Shabbos!' "

Similarly, the *Mishnah* says, "A person who is suspected of not tithing his food [on weekdays] is not suspected [of this transgression] on Shabbos, for the awe of Shabbos is upon him." Imagine how tangible Shabbos must have been to that generation that even individuals who lied all week long spoke only the truth on Shabbos! Indeed, the *Zohar* says, "Whoever lies on Shabbos, it is as though he had lied against the entire Torah."

The Sages say that even *inanimate* objects feel the sanctity of Shabbos. We learn that the impassable Sambation River, which spewed forth rocks in all directions during the week, would become placidly serene on Shabbos.

The *Mashgiach* of *Lomza* used to say that if a person wants to gauge his standing in the World to Come, all he has to do is assess the extent to which he feels the sanctity of Shabbos, which is considered "a resemblance of the World to Come." In proportion to what he feels on Shabbos in this world, that is what he will feel in the World to Come.

How far we have yet to go!

ויקרא
Vayikra

Derech Eretz

The *Midrash* tells us, "Proper behavior (*derech eretz*) takes precedence over Torah. For we find that *derech eretz* preceded the Torah by 26 generations. It says [concerning the Tree of Life in the Garden of Eden], '... to guard the way to the Tree of Life' (*Genesis* 3:24). 'The way' refers to *derech eretz*; it is mentioned before the 'Tree of Life,' which refers to the Torah. For Adam (who preceded Moses by 26 generations) was commanded to observe the rules of *derech eretz*."

We find also that Hashem Himself acted with *derech eretz* towards Adam even after his sin. As the Sages tell us, "A person should never enter his friend's house suddenly (i.e., without announcing himself). People should learn from the actions of Hashem, Who stood at the entrance to the Garden of Eden and called out, 'Adam!' as it says (ibid. v. 9), 'HASHEM, God, called out to Adam, "Where are you?"' "

Angels also follow the rules of *derech eretz*. When the three angels came to visit Abraham (ibid., Ch. 18) and he offered them food and drink, they pretended to eat, even though angels do not eat or drink. The *Midrash* concludes from their behavior, "A person should never deviate from the customs of the place where he is found, because of *derech eretz*."

Similarly we find in the *Midrash* on *Parashas Vayikra* (*Vayikra Rabbah* 1:15), " 'He called to Moses, and HASHEM spoke to him ...' We may learn a lesson from Moses, who was the master of wisdom, the father of all prophets, who took Israel out of Egypt with wonders and miracles ..., yet did not enter the innermost part of the Tent of Meeting without having been called there first. From here we see that if a *talmid chacham* (Torah scholar) does not have sense, he is worse than a *neveilah* (carcass of an animal)." Apparently, if Moses *had* entered the Tent of Meeting without having been summoned, he would have been considered "one who lacks sense." The *Midrash* teaches us a great lesson in the centrality and importance of *derech eretz* in life by equating a lack of *derech eretz* with a lack of common sense! A similar idea is found in *Avos DeRabbi Nassan*, where we learn that "there is no wisdom [as basic] as the wisdom of *derech eretz*." We are also taught that if a student walks along his Rabbi's right side, he is called an ignoramus for his presumptuousness (*Chullin* 91a). *Rashi* explains that this is because he shows ignorance of the skills of *derech eretz*. Similarly, the Talmud (*Berachos* 61a) asserts that Manoah was an unlearned person because he walked behind his wife (*Judges* 13:11). *Rashi* explains that it was the knowledge of *derech eretz* that Manoah lacked.

There are many other places where the Sages derive principles of *derech eretz* from verses in the Torah. The dots over the word אֵלָיו (*Genesis* 18:9) intimate that the angels who visited Abraham asked about Sarah's well-being, teaching us that it is proper for a guest to inquire after the welfare of his host's spouse. The High Priest's (*Kohen Gadol's*) robe had bells along its border so that "its sound be heard when he enters the Sanctuary" (*Exodus* 28:35), teaching us that a person should not enter a king's palace without first notifying him of his presence (*Rabbeinu Bachya* ad loc.). When Joseph's mistress grabbed hold of his coat in an attempt to seduce him, he ran away, leaving the coat in her hand. He did not wrest the coat from her hand before escaping, although this would have prevented her from making her subsequent false accusation, because this would have been disrespectful behavior toward his mistress (*Ramban*).

The significance and centrality of *derech eretz* is illustrated by the fact that at the very creation of mankind, Hashem taught a lesson in *derech eretz*: He describes his action with a plural form ("Let *us* make man . . ." — *Genesis* 1:26), in order to teach us that one should always seek counsel from others, even from those who are one's inferiors, before embarking upon any course of action (*Midrash*). Even though the unconventional wording of this verse supplies heretics with "proof" that the Torah acknowledges more than one Divine being, God did not refrain from speaking in this manner in order to teach this important lesson (*Rashi* ad loc.).

We find that the Sages even caution us to act with *derech eretz* while performing *mitzvos*. For example, according to *Aruch* and *Rosh*, the reason we cover our eyes while reciting the first verse of the *Shema* is that we move our eyes in all four directions at this time, symbolizing our recognition of Hashem's mastery over the entire world. Since such eye movements would seem bizarre to others, it is proper to cover one's eyes and thereby prevent embarrassment. From this we learn that even when involved in an act of sanctifying God's Name, we must be careful not to neglect the rules of proper conduct!

A similar thought is expressed by *Ramban* in his commentary to *Exodus* 12:22 to explain why the Jews did not leave Egypt until the morning of Nissan 15, although Pharaoh had liberated them in the middle of the previous night. It was because it is generally not seemly for a person to leave or enter a city at night. And so, *Ramban* continues, was the case with Abraham (*Genesis* 19:27), Jacob (ibid. 28:18), Moses (*Exodus* 34:4), Joshua (*Joshua* 3:1) and Samuel (*I Samuel* 15:12); they also waited until morning to embark upon their various sacred missions. If our great Patriarchs and prophets of old, who were involved in carrying out the will of Hashem, acted according to the dictates of *derech eretz*, *Ramban* concludes, how much more must we!

Korbanos

The basic idea underlying the offering of those sacrifices which are brought for atonement is that the person involved should confess his sin and repent. Even an *olah*-offering, which atones only for relatively minor offenses, is disqualified if it is brought without contrition (*Zevachim* 7b), on the grounds that "the offering of a wicked person is an abomination" (*Proverbs* 21:27).

In fact, *Rambam* (*Hilchos Teshuvah* 1:1) derives the entire *mitzvah* of *teshuvah* from the verse, "they shall confess their sin" (*Numbers* 5:7), which is said in reference to sin-offerings. Furthermore, as

Rambam explains (*Hilchos Teshuvah* 1:3), if a person brings a sacrifice without showing true remorse and contrition, the sacrifice does not effect any atonement for him.

Sin-offerings are brought to atone for sins committed unintentionally. This shows how far the *mitzvah* of *teshuvah* goes: Even when a sin was committed in complete ignorance of any wrongdoing, it requires atonement through sacrifice. Although *Ramban* (*Leviticus* 1:4) points out that there is no sacrificial atonement ordained for one who unwittingly commits sins which carry the punishment of death by Heavenly means, or for sins which are punishable by lashes (*makkos*), he does not mean that atonement is unnecessary. Rather, he means that the required penitence is not achieved by bringing offerings, but through other means.

Sforno (ibid., v. 2) explains the wording of the verse, "When a man brings from among you a sacrifice," as follows: "You must bring your sacrifice *from you* (i.e., from your very souls), with confession and contrition, in accordance with the theme of the verses, 'We will offer up bulls through [the words of] our lips' (*Hosea* 14:3), and 'A broken spirit is an offering unto God' (*Psalms* 51:19). For Hashem does not desire fools who bring sacrifices without first feeling contrition for their act."

Similarly, when the Torah describes the bringing of a meal-offering, which is usually the offering of a poor man, it says (*Leviticus* 2:1), "When a soul offers a meal-offering to HASHEM . . ." *Rashi* comments: "This is the only voluntary offering for which the expression 'a soul offers' is used. The Holy One, Blessed is He, in essence said, '[Since he is a poor man,] I consider it as if he had brought his very soul to Me.' " This is the fundamental idea and the primary goal behind the bringing of any offering — that a person should "offer up his soul" and become close to Hashem through his sacrifice.

The Distinction of Israel

W e are taught in *Shulchan Aruch* (*Rama*, *Yoreh De'ah* 81) that a nursing woman should refrain from eating forbidden foods, for the taste of those foods would then be passed on, through her milk, to the nursing baby. *Taz* (ad loc.) adds that this is true even if the woman, because of extenuating circumstances, is permitted to eat a forbidden food; she should then refrain from nursing the child after eating such a food. From this *halachah* we learn that it is the physical nature of forbidden foods — even when they, for some halachic reason, cease to be "forbidden" — to adversely affect the soul of those who ingest them.

Similarly, *Mesillas Yesharim* (Ch. 11) expounds upon the negative repercussions of eating non-kosher foods. They fill a person's heart with impurity, causing the sanctity of Hashem to distance itself from that individual. Therefore, a person should regard forbidden foods as though they were physically dangerous poisonous foods which can cause severe physical damage even if they are eaten accidentally.

Perhaps it is for this reason that the Torah juxtaposes the section dealing with forbidden foods (at the end of *Shemini*) to that dealing with postpartum mothers (at the beginning of *Tazria*) — to show that it is especially important for a new mother, who is nursing her baby, to take great care to avoid eating non-kosher foods.

At the end of the section describing all the forbidden foods, the Torah concludes (*Leviticus* 11:45): "I am HASHEM, Who has *brought you up* from the Land of Egypt ..." *Rashi* comments, "It is considered an *elevation* of status for the Jewish people to have been given these laws of avoiding contamination by eating these foods like the other nations."

Also, in *Shabbos* 145b the Sages tell us, "The bodies of idol worshipers are putrid because they partake of disgusting and creeping animals" — this, despite the fact that these animals are absolutely permissible for them to eat. The foods that the Torah forbids Jews to eat apparently have a real deleterious physical effect on the body.

Elsewhere (*Pesachim* 118a) the Sages say, "When Hashem told Adam, '[the ground] shall sprout thorns and thistles for you' (*Genesis* 3:18), Adam began to shed tears. He said, 'Master of the Universe! Shall I and my donkey eat from the same trough?!' When Hashem responded, '. . . you will eat bread' (ibid., v. 19), Adam was mollified." The *Maharsha* (ad loc.) explains that the reason Adam was so upset was that he thought that if he would share the same diet as a donkey, he would begin to develop the same characteristics and (lack of) intellectual capabilities of donkeys, because a person's diet has extremely far-reaching effects upon the development of his character and intellect.

Excessive Familiarity

The Torah warns Aaron, and all successive High Priests: "Do not enter the Sanctuary at all times, for in a cloud will I appear upon the Ark-cover" (*Leviticus* 16:2). This translation follows *Rashi's* interpretation of the verse — Hashem is telling the *Kohanim*, "Since My presence is generally revealed there, take care not to enter that place too frequently ('at all times')." At first, we might think it strange that the presence of Hashem in a given place should be a reason why one should *not* frequent that place. After all, shouldn't a person always strive to expose himself to as much sanctity as possible, as often as possible? As King David said, "I have set HASHEM before me always" (*Psalms* 16:8). The answer, however, is that if a person develops too much of a familiarity with a particular phenomenon, even if that phenomenon is unmistakably a miraculous one, he will begin to lose his sense of appreciation towards that event. Furthermore, by being constantly exposed to supernatural occurrences, he will also lose his feeling of appreciation for the thousands of miraculous events that everyday life is comprised of. For every breath a person takes is made possible only by the intervention of the intricate laws of nature which were ordained by Hashem, Who "renews the work of Creation constantly, every day" (*Siddur*).

Similarly, we find that the Sages tell us (*Yoma* 76a) that Hashem rained down the manna upon the Jews in the desert every single day, so that they would realize to what extent they were dependent upon the grace of HASHEM for their sustenance. Apparently, if the manna had fallen only once a week, Hashem perceived that the people would stop appreciating His kindness towards them — this, despite the incontrovertibly miraculous nature of the manna.

When the Children of Israel arrived at Mount Sinai to receive the Torah on the first day of Sivan, the Torah says that *"on this day* they came to the Wilderness of Sinai" (*Exodus* 19:1). *Rashi* points out that the expression "on this day" is meant to urge each and every Jew to strive, as he studies the Torah, to feel as if the Torah had been given anew on that day. Even though the Torah itself is the very word of HASHEM, and its study involves a continuous relationship with Him, there is a danger that through constant exposure to the experience of Torah study day after day one is in danger of losing sight of its sanctity. This can only be prevented if one makes a conscious effort at recalling the day when the Torah was given at Sinai.

Love Your Neighbor

Rambam (*Hilchos De'os* 6:3) states: "There is a commandment that every person must love every other member of the people of Israel like himself, as it says (*Leviticus* 19:18), 'You shall love your fellow as yourself.' Therefore he should speak favorably of him and spare his money just as he would spare his own money, and just as he himself desires respect." In the following *halachah* Rambam says: "Loving a proselyte, who has entered under the wings of the *Shechinah* (the immanent presence of Hashem), is a fulfillment of two positive precepts — one because he is like any other fellow Jew whom one is obligated to love, and one extra *mitzvah* because he is a proselyte, of whom the Torah says (*Deuteronomy* 10:19), 'You shall love the proselyte.' [God] commanded us to show love for the proselyte just as He commanded us to show love for Him, as it says (ibid., 11:1), 'You shall love HASHEM your God.' Hashem Himself loves proselytes, as it says (ibid., 10:18), 'He loves the proselyte.' "

It is interesting to note the difference between *Rambam's* descriptions of the two *mitzvos*. When discussing the *mitzvah* to love all of one's fellow Jews, he does not mention the comparison to the *mitzvah* to love God; he does so only when speaking of the *mitzvah* to love proselytes. Why? Because since a convert independently chooses to enter into the Covenant of Hashem, he is entitled to a higher level of love from his new coreligionists — a level of love and respect that can be compared to that which is to be bestowed upon Hashem Himself. This is similar to the idea that the Sages express (*Berachos* 34b) in another context, "Even a completely righteous person cannot gain entry to the place of honor accorded to someone who [had sinned and] then repented." To emphasize the added importance of this *mitzvah* over the regular *mitzvah* of loving all fellow Jews, the *Rambam* ends off his presentation of the *mitzvah* by pointing out that Hashem Himself loves proselytes — and we are commanded (see *Sotah* 14a) to emulate the ways of Hashem's lovingkindness.

A similar theme is expressed by R' Chaim Volozhiner in his *Ruach Chaim* on *Pirkei Avos*. In *Avos* 4:1 the *Mishnah* reads: "Who is truly honored? One who honors others, as it says (*I Samuel* 2:30), 'I (HASHEM) honor those who honor Me.' " The question arises: How can this verse be brought as proof for the assertion of the *Mishnah*? The *Mishnah* speaks of honoring other *people*, while the verse speaks of giving honor to *Hashem*!

R' Chaim explains that one should honor his fellow human beings simply because they are the handiwork of Hashem. Abraham our father showed great honor for his "guests," whom he assumed to be idolatrous Arabs. This was certainly not due to any particular trait that he respected in his visitors, but because he gave esteem to any human being by virtue of his being a creature of Hashem. When one adopts this attitude toward his fellow human beings, he is actually showing, in an indirect way, respect for Hashem, Who created humanity. Thus, the verse "I (HASHEM) honor those who honor Me" can be applied to this case.

The Talmud (Yerushalmi, *Nedarim* 9:4) explains the Torah's prohibition of "You shall not take revenge nor bear a grudge against the members of your people" (*Leviticus* 19:18) with the following illustration: If someone was cutting meat with a knife and his hand slipped and cut his other hand, would the man then take the knife and stab the offending hand as punishment?! Certainly not. So too, all of Israel is like one individual, and it is unthinkable that one component of this being seek revenge against a different component.

The *Midrash* (*Vayikra Rabbah* 27:5), in explaining the verse, "God always seeks the pursued" (*Ecclesiastes* 3:15), comments that this is true even if it is a wicked man who is being pursued by a righteous man. Although it is a *mitzvah* to hate wicked people who do not follow the will of Hashem (*Pesachim* 113b), this is apparently only in order to show honor to Hashem. When a wicked person is being pursued, however, Hashem sets aside His own honor in order to take the side of the persecuted party.

We find a similar line of thought in the Talmud (*Berachos* 28b). Rabban Gamliel wanted to institute a nineteenth blessing ("*VeLa-Malshinim*") into the *Shemoneh Esrei* to denounce the heretics and sectarians who had begun to infiltrate the Jewish community, and Shmuel HaKatan was chosen to compose the prayer. I once heard in the name of a *gadol* that the reason it was specifically Shmuel HaKatan who was deemed worthy of this project was because of his aphorism by which he was known to all: "Do not rejoice at the downfall of your enemy" (*Avos* 4:19). As Rabbeinu Yonah comments (ad loc.), this axiom is true even if the enemy who has suffered defeat is a wicked person; one should not rejoice over his downfall unless one's intention in rejoicing is purely and honestly for the sake of honoring Hashem. It was only Shmuel HaKatan, who personally embodied this concept, who was able to compose a prayer against heretics without personal bias or hatred, but solely with the honor of Heaven in mind.

One of the corollaries of loving one's neighbor is the requirement to reprimand him when he acts improperly (*Leviticus* 19:17). One cannot be said to truly love a person if one does not try to persuade him to avoid a course of action which is harmful or unseemly. The punishment for refraining from admonishing someone — when the appropriate circumstances for reproof are present — is severe. In *Tanna DeVei Eliyahu* we learn: "Who was responsible for the deaths of the 42,000 people who died in the civil war at the time of Yiftah (*Judges* 12:6)? It was Phineas, for he could have spoken out against their behavior and brought them to reform their ways, but he did not. Likewise, any person who has the capability to deliver reproach to wrongdoers but refrains from doing so is held responsible for the Jewish blood that is spilled in his day, as it says (*Ezekiel* 33:7-8), 'I have set you up as a watchman for the House of Israel ... If I say of a wicked man, "You shall surely die, wicked man," and you neglect to warn him ... I shall demand his blood from your hand.' This is because all Jews are responsible for one another. Similarly, who was responsible for the thousands of deaths at *Givas Binyamin*? It was the *Sanhedrin*, for they should have circulated throughout all the cities of Israel and taught the Jews proper behavior in order that Hashem's Name be glorified and sanctified. But they did not; instead each of them went to his own vineyard (i.e., minded his own business) and said, 'With me, all is well.' " The extent and gravity of one's responsibility to admonish one's fellow Jews when the opportunity presents itself is truly remarkable!

Similarly, the Sages teach us that when Yiftah took his famous vow (that the first thing that he would encounter coming out of the door of his house upon his return unharmed from battle would be offered up to Hashem as a sacrifice), and wanted to carry it out on his daughter, Phineas the *Kohen* should have informed the misled warrior that the vow had no halachic validity in this case. By not doing so, they tell us, Phineas bore responsibility for the girl's tragic fate.

Rambam describes the *mitzvah* of *tochachah* (giving reproof) as follows (*Hilchos De'os* 6:7): "One who reprimands his friend should do so calmly and with gentle words, explaining to him that he is speaking to him for his own benefit, so that he may merit a greater reward in the World to Come." The *mitzvah* of giving reproof is thus an extension of the *mitzvah* to love one's fellow, for it is a result of a genuine concern for his spiritual well-being. If one is obligated to help out his fellow Jew in monetary matters, it is certainly no less of an obligation to help him obtain spiritual perfection!

The *Midrash* (*Bereishis Rabbah* 54:3) tells us, "Love between two people which is not accompanied by occasional admonishment (or 'constructive criticism') is not love. Admonition leads to love, as it says (*Proverbs* 9:8), 'Give reproof to a wise man and he will love you for it.' "

Similarly, King Solomon tells us, "He who spares the rod hates his son" (ibid., 13:24). There are numerous references to the greatest of men being punished for not admonishing their children when their behavior warranted it (see e.g., *I Samuel* 3:13).

The approach of Aaron the *Kohen* to the *mitzvah* of giving reproof is described by the Sages (*Avos* 1:12): "He loved peace, and aggressively pursued it . . . bringing people closer to the Torah." This is further expanded upon in *Avos DeRabbi Nassan*: "He would never say to any man or woman, 'You have sinned!' or 'You have acted improperly!' Rather, when he would meet a wicked man in the street he would extend a greeting to him." In this way he fulfilled the *mitzvah* of giving reproof, for he was able to draw these people close to the Torah in this friendly manner, through showing them love and respect.

There is a general rule that one should try hard to see the positive aspects of one's fellow Jew (ibid., 1:6). The seriousness of this requirement may be better appreciated if we consider that great men were punished because they did not fulfill it. The prophet Isaiah was punished (*Yevamos* 49b) for speaking ill of Israel, saying, "I dwell in the midst of a people with impure lips" (*Isaiah* 6:5). Elijah was taken to task for saying, "I have acted extremely zealously for HASHEM . . . for the Children of Israel have forsaken Your covenant" (*I Kings* 19:10); he was forced to relinquish his position as Hashem's prophet to Elisha. This requirement should not, however, be viewed as conflicting with the *mitzvah* of rebuking an offender in a constructive way.

Kiddush Hashem

There is a *mitzvah* of *kiddush Hashem* (to sanctify the Name of HASHEM), as it says (*Leviticus* 22:32), "I shall be sanctified among the Children of Israel." In reference to this *mitzvah*, *Rosh* says in *Orchos Chaim*, "When you say (in the *Shema*), 'You shall love HASHEM your God with all your heart and with all your soul and with all your might,' you should have in mind that you are prepared to sacrifice your body and your money for the sanctification of Hashem's Name, for in this way you will fulfill the verse (*Psalms* 44:23), 'We have been killed for Your sake every day.' "

Concerning this verse ("We have been killed for Your sake every day"), we find in *Sifrei*, "R' Shimon ben Menasia says: Is it possible for a person to be killed every day?! Rather, the meaning is that Hashem *considers* it as if the righteous person had been killed for Him every day." The explanation of this comment of *Sifrei* is most probably along the lines of *Rosh's* statement — that if a person is *willing* to give up his life for Hashem's Name, He considers this as tantamount to actually doing so.

The *Sefer Chareidim*, in his description of the positive *mitzvah*, "I shall be sanctified among the Children of Israel," considers the mere willingness to make the supreme sacrifice for Hashem as the fulfillment of this *mitzvah*.

The antithesis of *kiddush Hashem* is, of course, *chillul Hashem* (causing a desecration of Hashem's Name). The severity of this prohibition may be seen from *Yoma* 86a, where the Talmud tells us that even the worst sins may be atoned for through repentance, the day of Yom Kippur and/or physical suffering — with the exception of the sin of *chillul Hashem*, which cannot be atoned for except through death.

It is in this vein that the *Chafetz Chaim* explains the statement of the Talmud (*Yevamos* 62b) that all 24,000 of Rabbi Akiva's disciples perished between Pesach and Shavuos of one year for the sin of not showing sufficient respect for one another. The *Chafetz Chaim* explains that because Rabbi Akiva's students were such outstanding Torah scholars, by not showing mutual respect they brought about a tremendous *chillul Hashem*. It was only through death that this sin could be atoned for, as the Sages in *Yoma* (quoted above) pointed out.

We may see how far reaching the concept of *chillul Hashem* is by noting a comment in the Talmud (ibid., 79). The Sages comment on the demand of the Givonim to hand over seven of Saul's sons for execution in revenge for Saul's sin against them, and David's compliance with this cruel wish (*II Samuel 21:1*): "But does the Torah not say, 'Sons shall not be put to death on account of their fathers' (*Deuteronomy 24:16*)? R' Yochanan answered: It is better that one *mitzvah* (lit., "letter") of the Torah be disregarded so that Hashem's Name not be desecrated in the eyes of the nations. For people who would hear about this execution would ask, 'Why are these people, the sons of a king, being put to death?' And they would be told, 'It is because they dared to harm some people who were (defenseless) resident strangers in their land.' They will then exclaim, 'There is no other nation like Israel!' " The power of *chillul Hashem* is so intense that it can even bring about the abrogation of the Torah's laws itself, and lead to the deaths of innocent people!

In *Devarim* 4:6 we are told that we must keep the *mitzvos* of Hashem because "this is your wisdom and understanding in the eyes of the nations, who will hear all these decrees and say, 'Surely this great nation is a wise and understanding nation.' " This rationale for the keeping of the Torah — that it will provide us with a favorable reputation among the nations — is quite surprising and requires explanation. The *Sforno* (ad loc.) explains that the reason Jews should strive to make a favorable impression on the nations is that since Hashem is near to us and His Name is associated with us and we are considered His chosen people, it is important for *His* sake that the nations not regard the Jews as foolish or unintelligent.

במדבר
Bamidbar

The Law of the Nazir

In his comment to *Numbers* 6:2, *Rashi* quotes the Talmud's explanation as to why the Torah juxtaposes the laws of the *nazir* to those of the *sotah*. It is to teach us that anyone who witnesses the degradation of the *sotah* should accept upon himself to refrain from drinking wine as a *nazir*, because indulging in wine can lead to promiscuous behavior. Despite the fact that taking the *nazirite* vow is considered (according to one opinion) to be a reprehensible act, one who actually witnesses the ill effects of excessive wine is encouraged to do so. A person sins only because he is overtaken by a spirit of irrationality (*Sotah* 3a). This is especially so in the case of the sin of adultery — "One who commits adultery with a woman lacks sense" (*Proverbs* 6:23). Generally man's actions seem to be guided by common sense and logic, but in this case it is clear that this person has been overcome by irrational forces, such as passion, obsession, etc. When someone witnesses the outcome of such illogical behavior, he has no choice but to take the drastic step of taking the *nazirite* vow, although this is frowned upon under normal circumstances. Similarly, in *Nedarim* 8a the Talmud tells us that it is considered virtuous to take an oath to perform a *mitzvah* in order to motivate oneself to act expeditiously, although oaths should generally be avoided. Sometimes, in one's battle against his *yetzer hara*, one is advised to take certain drastic steps which might be discouraged in usual situations. In fact the *Chinuch* (§434) writes in the name of *Ramban* that such oaths are what the Torah means by its *mitzvah* of "Cleave to Him" (*Deuteronomy* 10:20). Indeed, in *Nedarim* 9b our Sages imply that the whole institution of *nazirism* in general is, in its ideal form, a way to combat the *yetzer hara*.

There is a disagreement in the Talmud (*Taanis* 11a) as to whether a *nazir* is considered holy, or alternatively, a sinner, for needlessly denying himself a permitted pleasure for no reason. This argument requires some explanation; there is no other act in the Torah concerning which there is a discussion as to whether it is commendable or condemnable. *Tosafos* (*Bava Kamma* 91b) asserts that both the positive and negative aspects of *nazirism* are true. He compares this to the Talmud (*Berachos* 31b) that permits fasting on Shabbos (the commentators, based on *Shabbos* 11a, explain that this is dealing with a case of someone who had a very disturbing dream and wishes to annul whatever bad omen the dream may indicate), but requires that the person carry out a second fast during the week to atone for the sin of abrogating the joy of Shabbos. Here, too, we find the paradoxical situation of a *mitzvah* which has a very high level of importance, but which in fact involves a minor sin in the course of its fulfillment. The explanation of this phenomenon is as follows. If a person would perfect his appreciation of the feeling of the sanctity and serenity of Shabbos, he would not let himself become so disturbed by his bad dream. When a person has not reached this epitome of sensitivity to Shabbos, and *does* feel distress because of his dream, he is permitted to address this feeling of anguish by fasting — but he must atone for his lack of sensitivity to the sacred aura of Shabbos by fasting again on a weekday.

The same could be applied to the case of the *nazir*. A person who has achieved perfection in self-control should be able to withstand the temptations and trials of life simply by coming to an intellectual realization that sin is not worthwhile. An ideal person should not have to resort to external schemes to overcome his *yetzer hara*. But if a person witnesses the *sotah* and begins to feel that intellect alone does not protect man from sin, he must take a *nazirite* vow and thereby attain the higher level of sanctity that is attained by the *nazir*. Becoming a *nazir* is indeed an act of holiness and is meritorious in and of itself; but it is considered to be a failure in one's strength of character that he could not attain the same spiritual heights without resorting to vows and self-restrictions. It is at one and the same time an attainment of sanctity and an indication of spiritual weakness.

But what exactly is the nature of the *nazir's* higher spiritual level? *Ibn Ezra*, in commenting on the unusual verb the Torah uses in describing the undertaking of a *nazirite* vow (*yafli*), explains that the *nazir* is doing something that is contrary to what the rest of the people in the world do. Most people follow their physical desires, while the *nazir* strives to distance himself from them and control them. On verse 6:7 in this *parashah* he notes that according to one opinion, the word "*nazir*" is related to the word "*nezer*," meaning "crown," as the Torah actually says in verse 7, "the crown (*nezer*) of his God is upon his head." He explains that people in general are enslaved to their passions, and only someone who frees himself from that "enslavement" can truly be considered a king — a master over his own character. According to *Ibn Ezra*, then, the greatness of the *nazir* is in the fact that he overpowers his physical desires and restricts himself even in matters that were not previously forbidden to him. This idea of the importance of exercising control over one's physical impulses is expressed by the Sages: "The righteous rule over their hearts, while in the case of the wicked, it is their hearts who rule over them."

When the *nazir* finishes fulfilling his vow for the specified period of time, the Torah calls for him to offer, among other sacrifices, a sin-offering. Why the *nazir* should be obligated to do this is not explained in the Torah, but *Ramban* suggests that it is to "atone" for the lapse in the level of sanctity that the *nazir* is about to undergo by renouncing his *naziritehood* and returning to normal life. It would have been better for him to permanently retain his previous spiritual heights. According to this interpretation, the laws of *nazir* teach us an important lesson about our spiritual lives in general. A regular person does not bring a sin-offering for being involved with day-to-day mundane matters; it is only the *nazir*, who had refrained somewhat, for a brief time, from the pleasures of life, and is now about to return to normal, who must do so. Each person is judged differently for the same act — people who have achieved a higher level of spirituality are held to a higher standard than others. As the Sages tell us, the verse (*Psalms* 29:4), "The sound of Hashem is through strength," homiletically teaches that Hashem responds to each individual according to his own personal strengths. Just as King Solomon commands us, "Give honor to Hashem from your wealth," which means "according to your monetary means," so too each person is required to serve Hashem according to the spiritual resources at his disposal. The more a person is capable of giving to Hashem, both monetarily and spiritually, the more he is *expected* to give.

The story is told in the Talmud (*Bava Basra* 10b, *Pesachim* 50a) of someone who had undergone an other-worldly experience — he had been deathly ill and actually had a glimpse of the World to Come before recovering his health. R' Yehoshua asked, "What did you see there?" He replied, "I saw an upside-down world — exalted people at the bottom and lowly people at the top." R' Yehoshua responded to him, "What you saw was the World of Truth!" *Mabit*, in his work *Beis Elokim*, explains that in the World to Come people are judged not according to their *achievements*, but according to their *potential* to achieve. Thus, a person who achieves a lofty status in this world, in the eyes of men, may find himself in a lower position in the World of Truth than people of lesser stature who utilized their full potential. This idea mirrors the lesson of the *nazir* — that a higher level of spirituality entails not so much *distinction* as *obligation* and responsibility.

In a similar vein, the *Alshich* notes the wording of the verse, "afterwards the *nazir* may drink wine." Although the Torah is referring to a person who has fulfilled the required time-period of *naziritehood*, brought all the requisite sacrifices, and performed all the necessary rituals, it still refers to him as "the *nazir*." This, he explains, is to show that even after a *nazir* has completed his vow, he must continue to act with a higher degree of purity than an average person. Although "he may then drink wine," he should continue to restrict his enjoyment of worldly pleasures and retain some trace of his previous spiritual elevation.

Perhaps this concept can shed some light on a difficult Talmudic passage. In *Sanhedrin* 6b we are told, "Anyone who praises Judah is tantamount to being a blasphemer, for it says, 'He who blesses the one who seeks unjust monetary gain (*botze'a*) blasphemes Hashem,' and Judah is the one who said (*Genesis* 37:26), 'What monetary gain (*betza*) is there if we kill our brother? ... (Let us sell him to the Ishmaelites instead.)' " Judah was the only brother who had enough pity on Joseph to save him from death and instead sell him into slavery, yet it is Judah who, of all the brothers, is denounced, to the point that we are forbidden to praise him! The explanation of this difficulty lies in what was discussed above. Judah's brothers, for whatever reason, had decided that Joseph had done something for which he deserved to die. Judah realized that this punishment was actually too harsh for Joseph, and he rose above his brothers by suggesting that Joseph's punishment be mitigated. But once he rose to that level of understanding, he was held accountable for not doing more to save Joseph. He was judged according to his level of understanding, and they according to theirs.

Just as a person's reward for *mitzvos* is commensurate to the amount of effort he exerts (לְפוּם צַעֲרָא אַגְרָא — "The reward corresponds to the toil" — *Avos* 5:26), so is he held culpable for failing to apply himself according to his full potential.

The Spies

Rashi explains that the story of the spies (*Numbers* 13) is juxtaposed to the story of Miriam (ibid., Ch. 12) (although the two events did not happen together chronologically — *Sifsei Chachamim*) in order to show a comparison between the two episodes. Miriam was punished for speaking slanderously of Moses, yet the spies did not learn a lesson from her misfortune and they committed the same sin.

In *Deuteronomy* 24:9 the Torah tells us, "Remember what HASHEM, your God, did to Miriam on the way." *Ramban* (ad loc.) comments that this verse should be counted as a regular commandment, just like the verse, "Remember the Sabbath day"; the Torah is commanding us to consider the bitter punishment for speaking *lashon hara* (slanderous speech) and to thereby refrain from committing that sin. "It would be unthinkable," *Ramban* concludes, "that the sin of *lashon hara*, which is tantamount to the shedding of blood (*Arachin* 15b), should not be mentioned as a specific prohibition anywhere in the Torah!"

Rambam (end of *Hilchos Tumas Tzaraas*) also cites this verse, along with the verse "Beware of the affliction of *tzaraas*" (*Deuteronomy* 24:8), and comments: "The Torah bids us to consider what happened to the prophetess Miriam who spoke against her younger brother, whom she had helped to raise as a child, and for whom she had risked her life when he was an infant. She did not intend any malice against him, for her only mistake was that she deemed him equal to all other prophets. He was not even upset by what she said, as the verse says, 'The man Moses is exceedingly humble ...' (*Numbers* 12:3). Nevertheless she was stricken with the dreaded *tzaraas*. How much more should ordinary, simple people take care not to speak against others!"

Being that the episode of Miriam is given as the paradigm of the sin of *lashon hara*, we must examine this case and try to understand exactly what sin was involved in Miriam's deed. *Rashi* explains that Miriam and Aaron spoke out against Moses' separation from his wife Tzipporah. Moses himself did not react to their statements — out of his tremendous modesty (ibid.) — but HASHEM did come to his defense. He explained that Moses was not like all other prophets, and that his exalted status of being in constant direct communication with HASHEM required that he separate from his wife. "So why," concludes HASHEM, "did you not fear to speak out against My servant Moses?" (ibid., v. 8). It would seem from this description of Miriam and Aaron's sin that their only mistake was not realizing that Moses was qualitatively different from all other prophets. They believed that Moses had deluded himself into thinking that he was in a constant spiritual state such as he had experienced on Mount Sinai, when he did not eat or drink for 40 days (*Exodus* 34:28), and that these delusions of grandeur had prompted him to refrain from marital relations. It is for this reason that Hashem made a point of noting that "the man Moses is exceedingly humble" — this unequivocally disproved their opinion about Moses. Far from suffering delusions of grandeur, he was the humblest man in the world!

After explaining to them about Moses' exalted status and reprimanding them for speaking against him, Hashem added, "How did you not fear to speak out against *My servant* Moses?" As *Rashi* explains, the implicit reproach here is that Miriam and Aaron should have realized that if Hashem had designated Moses to be His chosen prophet ("My servant"), this should have been ample evidence of Moses' exaltedness. Unless, of course — Hashem continued — you do not have faith in My judgment of character; but that would be an even more serious offense! (*Rashi*).

The entire offense of Miraim and Aaron was, then, a failure to appreciate Moses' high spiritual status. Since this episode of Miriam forms the very basis of the Torah's prohibition of speaking *lashon hara*, it can be said that the sin of *lashon hara* is rooted in this same problem — the failure to recognize the importance and true worth of one's fellow man. If we would make more of an effort to judge our fellow's actions favorably and to appreciate him according to his real value, we would never think or speak disparagingly of him. Similarly, King Solomon says (*Proverbs* 10:18), "He who speaks slander is a fool." This is because the root cause of speaking ill of someone is a lack of perception and comprehension of the individual's true worth.

Rashi, as quoted above, asserts that the sin of the spies was of the same sort as that of Miriam's. But where is there an element of *lashon hara* in the words of the spies? Were they not instructed to "see the land — how is it; and the people who dwell in it — are they strong or weak" (*Numbers* 13:18)? What, then, was wrong with their report that "However, the people . . . are powerful . . ." (ibid., v. 28)? Where is the *lashon hara*? *Ramban* explains that the sin of the spies was in the word "*However*," which implied that the might of the land's inhabitants would present an insurmountable obstacle to conquering the land. This sin was exacerbated further by their subsequent comment that "We cannot ascend to that people!" Be that as it may, the Talmud (*Arachin* 15a) clearly states that the spies transgressed the principle of *lashon hara* against the Land of Israel when they said, "It is a land that devours its inhabitants." This point requires further clarification.

The answer is that the root cause of the sin of the spies was exactly analogous to the sin of *lashon hara* as described above. They failed to perceive the true greatness of the Land of Israel when they formulated their opinion of it. When they saw "a land that devours its inhabitants," which *Rashi* explains to mean that they encountered burials and mourners wherever they went, they should have realized that this situation was brought about intentionally by Hashem in order to divert attention from them. Similarly, when they said "[the land] is too strong for us" — which, as *Rashi* explains, can also be translated as "[the land] is too strong for *Him* — they were guilty to an even greater degree of underestimating the true powers and capabilities of the Almighty.

Ran, in his *Drashos*, points out that throughout all the various trials and tribulations with which the wandering Israelites were faced in their 40 years in the desert, they never once uttered the unthinkable words, "Let us appoint a leader and return to Egypt," except in the case of the spies (*Numbers* 14:4). It was for this reason — for their utter rejection of the gift of *Eretz Yisrael* — that the punishment meted out to the people was that they would not see the promised land which they had spurned. This is in accordance with the idea developed above — the main sin of the spies was their lack of appreciation of the greatness and awesome sanctity of *Eretz Yisrael*. This caused them to formulate and express a totally distorted idea about the true character of the land.

It is possible that the spies were misled by the fact that they were given such specific instructions as to what they were to find out about the land — "How is the land in which they dwell — is it good or bad? What are the cities in which they dwell — are they open or fortified? How is the land — is it fertile or lean; are there trees in it or not, etc.?" Perhaps they were under the impression that they were to make an assessment of the feasibility of conquering the land *through natural means*, without Divine intervention. Nevertheless, their mistake was in not realizing that Hashem's leadership of the nation so far had surpassed all natural obstacles, and that it would continue to do so.

The *Alter* of Slobodka used to illustrate the idea of not under-appreciating the greatness of *Eretz Yisrael* by quoting the *Gemara* which describes how R' Ammi and R' Assi would be careful to move into the shade when it became unpleasantly hot, and move into the sun when it became cool, all in order to avoid developing the slightest feeling of dissatisfaction with even the weather of *Eretz Yisrael* (*Kesubos* 112a-b).

At any rate, we have seen that the root cause of *lashon hara* is the tendency to underestimate the true worth of our fellow human beings. As the verse says in *Psalms* 101:5, "I shall destroy the one who slanders his friend in secret; I cannot bear the man with haughty eyes and arrogant heart." The slanderer is referred to as "one with haughty eyes," for it is his inability to perceive the merits of his fellows that causes him to speak in this way. Similarly, in *Arachin* (15b) we are told, "What is the remedy for someone who speaks *lashon hara*? If he is a scholar (*talmid chacham*), let him engage in Torah study [for this will gain him humility — "*Ruach Chaim*"], and if he is an ignorant person let him adopt a more humble attitude." Similarly, the purification process of a *metzora* requires a branch of the lowly hyssop plant and a cloth colored with the *shani* worm. As *Rashi* points out (*Leviticus* 14:4), this teaches that the penitence for *lashon hara*, the sin which brings about *tzaraas* in the first place, is for man to humble himself.

Korah's Rebellion

*R*ashi explains that the main motivation behind Korah's disastrous rebellion against Moses was his jealousy over the fact that Elitzafan was chosen over him to be the leader of the Levites. Even when Moses told him and his men to bring incense pans before the Tabernacle (*Mishkan*) so that it could be shown that "the man whom HASHEM will choose — he is the holy one" (*Numbers* 16:7), implying that only one man would survive the trial (*Rashi*), Korah was not dissuaded, but continued on his stubborn path of resistance. He assured himself that if there would be one survivor, it would be he.

Throughout the story of Korah and his insurrection, it can be seen how incredibly strong the forces of greed and quest for power can be in blinding a person from seeing where his own best interests lie. The Talmud (*Sanhedrin* 109b) quotes the objection raised by On ben Peleth's wife to his participation in Korah's revolt: "If Moses wins, you will be subservient to him, and if Korah wins, you will be subservient to *him*! So why get involved where you stand to gain nothing?" Yet, despite this cogent line of reasoning, 250 men joined forces with Korah, all driven by the irrational hope that somehow they would achieve a more respected position.

Ibn Ezra explains that the main point of the rebellion was to protest the fact that the right to serve HASHEM in the Tabernacle (and later in the Temple) had been taken away from the firstborn sons of the Israelites, and was instead given to the Levites — or, more specifically, to Aaron and his sons, with the rest of the Levites ministering to them. The people believed that Moses conceived this change of status in order to give more honor to his brother. Thus, they demanded that the old order be reinstated. In light of this explanation, the argument of On's wife certainly seems to be a strong one for Korah and his family as well — why should they care if the privilege of performing the service of HASHEM would revert to the firstborn rather than the Levites! Again we see how the thirst for power and honor can prevent a person from thinking clearly.

Rashi quotes from the *Midrash* that Korah, in his attempt to discredit Moses and his ability to transmit the Torah to Israel, brought his 250 men before Moses wearing cloaks made of pure *techeiles*. He asked Moses, "Do these cloaks need the *techeiles* thread (described in *Numbers* 15:37-41) attached to them?" When Moses answered in the affirmative, they ridiculed him. "If one string of *techeiles* is enough to fulfill the *mitzvah* for a regular garment," they argued, "how can you say that a garment made completely out of *techeiles* is not enough in itself?!" I believe that this argument of Korah can be viewed as a symbol of the entire theme of the rebellion. Korah's point was (ibid., v. 3) "the entire assembly is holy, and HASHEM is among them, so why do you exalt yourselves over the congregation of HASHEM?" Since everyone is holy — the argument went — there is no need for a leader. But this is a grave mistake. Even people who are on a high spiritual plane are in need of someone to guide them, for everyone, including great people, are not always capable of overcoming their own character flaws, and it is very difficult for anyone to see his own faults, even when they are obvious to others.

The *mitzvah* of *techeiles* is intended to help man overcome the temptations of life, for the color of *techeiles* is supposed to remind us of the color of Heaven and the Heavenly Throne. This should serve as a reminder that we must submit ourselves to the will of Heaven at all times. Even when a garment is completely made of *techeiles*, it is important to have this *techeiles* string as a reminder of one's duty to submit to the will of HASHEM.

The power of Korah's jealousy was even strong enough to pull the rest of the congregation into his controversy with Moses. Surely the people believed in Moses' right to his position as leader — as the verse says, "they believed in HASHEM and in His servant Moses" (*Exodus* 14:31). Not long before, they witnessed Miriam's punishment for uttering the words "has HASHEM only spoken with Moses; has He not also spoken with us?" Yet Korah, in his enthusiasm and zeal for his misguided cause, managed to stir a large part of the congregation to rebel.

The extent of Korah's blindness is further illustrated by the *Yalkut Shimoni*, which states that Korah proclaimed that "Moses was no prophet, Aaron was no *Kohen* and the Torah was not Divine." Once a man — even one as wise as Korah — is swept up into controversy, there is no limit to the depths to which he will sink and to the amount of untruths he will embrace.

We find a similar concept in the case of Haman. After reviewing for his family and friends all his wondrous achievements and honors in life, he laments, "But all this is worth nothing to me whenever I see the Jew Mordechai sitting at the king's gate!" Haman's thirst for absolute, undisturbed power depressed him to the point where he could not live with himself. This ultimately drove him to attempt genocide against Mordechai's entire race.

As a further example, the Talmud (*Sanhedrin* 102a) tells us that the evil Yerovam — who permanently splintered the people of Israel into two nations, and who set up an idolatrous cult, outlawing any participation in the service of Hashem in Jerusalem — was offered a chance to repent by Hashem Himself: "Repent, and you and I and [David] the son of Yishai will walk together in Paradise!" Yerovam responded, "Who will be in front?" When Hashem answered, "The son of Yishai," Yerovam unequivocally rejected the offer. Once again we see how envy can cause a person to lose his reason and act against his own best interest.

Doing for Others

The laws of the the red cow (*parah adumah*) are among the most mysterious in the entire Torah. It is to this section that King Solomon was referring when he said (*Ecclesiastes* 7:23), "I had said, 'I am wise,' but this matter remains distant from me" (*Yoma* 14a). The whole *parah adumah* procedure is performed in order to release someone from a state of ritual impurity, yet everyone who is actually involved in performing the ritual becomes impure. Although the explanation of how this process works is a mystery beyond human understanding, all the words of the Torah are intended to impart some lesson to us. Hence, let us try to see what we can learn from the laws of the *parah adumah*.

There is a principle in *halachah* that "Every person of Israel is responsible for the other." There is another rule that states that one person cannot perform a *mitzvah* (such as *shofar*, *megillah*, *berachos*, etc.) and have another person fulfill his obligation by listening to him, unless the first person is himself obligated to do that *mitzvah*. For example, a minor or a non-Jew cannot blow the *shofar* for an adult Jew. However, because of the first principle — that of "mutual responsibility" (*arvus*) — *halachah* allows a person to perform a *mitzvah* on behalf of someone else even if the first person has already performed the *mitzvah*. For example, an adult Jew who has already heard the *shofar* on Rosh Hashanah may blow it for someone who has not. The principle of *arvus* dictates that as long as there is a fellow Jew somewhere in the world who has not yet fulfilled his obligation to perform the *mitzvah*, every other Jew — even someone who has already performed that *mitzvah* — is still considered to be in a state of "obligation" for that *mitzvah*.

The principle of *arvus* also decrees that every Jew is held responsible for the wrongdoing of any other Jew, as long as it was in his power to dissuade the transgressor. It is of the utmost importance for every Jew to try to prevent other Jews from sinning. If the Torah commands us to help out a fellow Jew from stumbling in the physical sense (*Exodus* 23:55), how much more must we prevent him from stumbling spiritually, where the effects can be so much more serious.

The section of the *parah adumah* teaches us a further application of the principle of *arvus*. The *Kohanim* are obligated to prepare the *parah adumah* so that people may become purified and be permitted to enter the Temple and eat sacred food. However, the *Kohanim* themselves become deprived of these very same privileges in the process. Although there is a rule that "Your own life (and well-being) takes precedence over that of your fellow man" (*Bava Metzia* 62a), here the Torah teaches us that the *Kohanim* cannot absolve themselves of their obligation on the grounds that they do not wish to become impure for the sake of others. Instead, they must assist their fellow Jew to undergo purification even though it comes at a cost to themselves.

This lesson is a very practical one in our daily lives. We must strive to deal with people who do not act according to the Torah and try to persuade them to change their ways. A person cannot exempt himself from this facet of *arvus* with the argument that contact with sinful people may have detrimental effects on his own spiritual purity. Instead, he is obligated to take this minor risk in order to provide his fellow Jew the opportunity to make a major improvement in his spiritual status.

The Sin of Mei Merivah

It was the sin of the Waters of *Merivah* that determined that Moses and Aaron would not be permitted to enter *Eretz Yisrael* because they "did not believe in [HASHEM] to sanctify Him" (*Numbers* 20: 12), and because they "transgressed against [HASHEM] among the

Children of Israel" (*Deuteronomy* 32:51). It was indeed a grievous sin that Moses and Aaron committed. Thus, all of Moses' supplications before Hashem did not allay His wrath and annul the decree. However, we are never clearly told what it was that these two great men did to deserve such harsh punishment. The only thing that is clear from the events of the Waters of *Merivah* is that it exemplified the principle that "Hashem is exacting with the righteous to a hairbreadth." Whatever oversight Moses and Aaron committed was only deemed a sin because of their tremendous spiritual stature. Perhaps that is why this section is juxtaposed to the section dealing with the *parah adumah* — both are laden with deep, mysterious undertones that are impossible for us to fully grasp.

Many different theories have been proposed by the commentators to explain what exactly the sin of the Waters of *Merivah* was. Perhaps the best-known explanation is that of *Rashi*, that Moses was supposed to *speak* to the rock rather than to hit it. Had the rock yielded its waters simply by being spoken to, the people would have been taught an invaluable lesson in obedience to Hashem: If a rock, which has no intelligence and does not have any needs for survival, follows the command of Hashem, how much more must we human beings do so. *Ramban* objects to this interpretation because the miracle of getting water to flow from a rock by hitting it does not seem any less miraculous than eliciting water by speaking to it. Perhaps this objection could be answered by suggesting that once a physical act was done to the rock, there was an excuse for the cynical people in the congregation to attribute Moses' feat to some physical, logical phenomenon, or to some form of deception. Had Moses only spoken to the rock, the miraculous nature of the event would have been undeniable.

Ramban also quotes *Rambam's* interpretation of the episode at *Merivah*. According to *Rambam*, Moses sinned by becoming angry at the congregation. We do not find that Hashem Himself was angry with the people for requesting water, yet the fact that Moses *did* show anger towards them would no doubt give them the impression that Hashem felt likewise. Moses in effect transmitted a message to the people that he had not been authorized to communicate.

Ramban asks several questions on this interpretation, such as: Where do we see that Moses became angry with the people? If it is because he said, "Listen now, you rebels," this is no worse than what he had said on another occasion, "from the day you left the land of Egypt . . . you have been rebels against HASHEM" (ibid., 9:7), which is merely a statement of rebuke and not an expression of anger. *Ritva* answers this objection by pointing out that the verse in *Deuteronomy* is a recapitulation of past historical events, and thus cannot be understood as an expression of spontaneous rage, while the verse in our portion does seem to indicate an outburst of anger. The fact is that a *Midrash* quotes Moses as saying, "It is true that *I* became enraged, but what is Aaron's sin [that he should be punished along with me]?" This clearly supports *Rambam*'s interpretation that Moses' sin was becoming angry at the congregation.

The explanation that *Ramban* prefers is that of *Rabbeinu Chananel*, that Moses and Aaron's sin involved the wording of their announcement, "Can *we* bring forth water for you from this rock?" Elsewhere, whenever Hashem was about to perform a miracle, Moses always made it clear that the coming event was of Divine nature. For example, Moses said, "When . . . HASHEM gives you meat to eat" (*Exodus* 16:8). Also here he should have said, "Can *Hashem* bring forth water . . .?" The wording they did use left open the possibility for people to attribute the flowing of the water from the rock as a natural act performed by Moses' hand, through his own wisdom. This is especially so, *Rabbeinu Chananel* explains, because the first time Moses drew water out of a rock (ibid., Ch. 17) Hashem's presence was there for all to see (ibid., v. 6), while here there was no such demonstration of Hashem's presence during the performance of the miracle. This explanation may be compared to the *Midrash* (quoted by *Rashi*) that says that the angels who went to destroy Sodom were punished for saying, "*We* are destroying this place" (*Genesis* 19:13), instead of "*Hashem* is destroying this place."

This interpretation of *Rabbeinu Chananel* explains why Moses was punished so severely for this particular sin. For these events came soon after Korah's rebellion, which was based, as we discussed elsewhere, upon the mistaken belief that Moses acted on his own when he disqualified the firstborn from serving in the Tabernacle and substituted them with the Levites, his own tribe, and also when he appointed his own brother Aaron as *Kohen Gadol*. It was thus especially important at this time that Moses make it perfectly clear to all the people that his actions were not arbitrary or motivated by self-interest, but were based on Divine directives. We must keep in mind that the incident of the spies had only recently occurred, and it was there that the congregation had suggested (*Numbers* 13:31) that perhaps "the people is too strong for Him" (according to the interpretation mentioned in *Rashi* there). Hashem reacted by exclaiming (ibid., 14:11), "How long will they not have faith in Me, despite all the wonders that I have performed in their midst?" This also helps to explain why Moses' words were judged so severely at this particular time, for they left room for the people to think that Hashem was not involved in their salvation.

We explained elsewhere why the actions of Nadav and Abihu were considered so sinful. After all, the law requires that fire be brought from an ordinary source even though there was a miraculous fire upon the altar at all times (*Yoma* 21b), so what was wrong with what they did? The explanation we offered was that at that particular time — the time of the inauguration of the Tabernacle, when the Divine Presence was about to be rejoined with the Congregation of Israel after it had departed during the episode of the Golden Calf — it was necessary to have a display of Divine grace by having supernatural fire descend from heaven. Bringing fire from an ordinary source, in this particular situation, prevented this show of grace from taking place. Thus, it was completely inappropriate, and was considered an "alien fire" (*Leviticus* 10:1). Similarly, when Elijah offered his sacrifice at Mount Carmel, in his confrontation with the Baal worshipers, he commanded that no fire be brought to the sacrifice. At that time of Divine concealment, Elijah wanted to show that despite all that the people had come to believe, Hashem was the true God, and He insisted that the sacrifice be ignited through miraculous means.

The Sages tell us that it is our duty to always recognize the fact that everything that befalls us is by the grace of Hashem. "Whoever benefits from the pleasures of this world without having praised HASHEM beforehand is guilty of theft from Hashem" (*Berachos* 35b). This is all the more true when one beholds a miraculous occurrence — one is obligated to recognize that the hand of Hashem was involved and to publicize the event to others. This was Moses' shortcoming in the episode of the Waters of *Merivah* — he underestimated the need to emphasize that it was Hashem Who played the central role in causing the water to flow from the rock.

We find that Samuel was taken to task for a similar lack of sensitivity. When Saul unwittingly asked him for directions how to find "the seer" he replied, "I am the seer" (*I Samuel* 9:19). Later, the Sages tell us, he was reprimanded for this apparently self-centered comment by mistakenly identifying David's brother Eliav as the man whom Hashem had sent to anoint as king of Israel (ibid., 16:6).

Later in this *parashah* we find an incident that bears a similar theme. The people were punished with an attack of poisonous snakes for their insubordination towards Moses and Aaron. As a remedy for those who had been bitten, Moses was commanded to fashion an image of a snake and to hoist it upon a pole (*Numbers* 21:8). As our Sages (*Rosh Hashanah* 29a) point out, there was nothing magical about this remedy; rather, when the people would gaze at the snake image that had been created by Hashem's command, they would remind themselves that it was His hand that had stricken them. They would thus humble themselves before Him, and be forgiven and healed by Him. Here, too, the idea was that the people had to be constantly reminded that Hashem was directing their daily affairs without the agency of any outside forces.

True Zealousness

In the previous *parashah* we read how Phineas, in his zeal for the honor of Hashem, killed the Simeonite prince who had brazenly brought his Midianite paramour into the camp. In this *parashah* we are told that his reward for this heroic act was an expression of gratitude from Hashem, and the gift of *kehunah* for him and all his descendants for all time (*Rashi*). However, the Sages tell us (*Sanhedrin* 82b) that the angels wanted to reject his prayers to Hashem to end the plague that had begun to afflict Israel as a result of their licentiousness with the Midianite women. It was not until Hashem allayed the angels' objections by pointing out that Phineas was a "zealot son of a zealot (i.e., Levi — see *Genesis* 34:25), and a placater son of a placater (i.e., Aaron — see *Numbers* 17:12)" that they let him proceed. Afterwards, the people of the congregation murmured to each other, "Did you see this Phineas, whose mother was descended from [Jethro, who] was an idolatrous priest. He had the audacity to slay one of the leaders of the tribes of Israel?!" It is for this reason, the Talmud continues, that the Torah takes the trouble at this time to recount Phineas' genealogy, emphasizing that he was the grandson of Aaron. It is difficult to understand why the angels wanted to reject Phineas' plea to Hashem. After all, he had just performed an act of supreme zealousness, at no small personal risk to himself, fulfilling the Torah's ruling (*Sanhedrin* 81b) that "zealous people may summarily execute" the perpetrator of this sin. He even merited to have six miracles performed on his behalf during the course of his brave act (ibid., 82b), which certainly indicates that Hashem approved of his actions.

The explanation of this *Gemara* is as follows. Since Phineas *did* have the taint of idol worship in his ancestry, the people — as well as

Parashas Pinchas / 199

the angels — suspected that he may have inherited some negative traits from that ancestry. Perhaps when he killed the Simeonite prince and the Midianite princess, his intentions had not been solely for the sake of Heaven, but there had been an element of hatred or personal vengeance involved. However, Hashem appeased the angels by telling them that Phineas was a "zealot, son of a zealot" — that is, the zealousness which he exhibited had nothing to do with the negative aspects of his ancestry, but stemmed from the righteous zealousness exhibited by his ancestor, Levi. The people's criticism of Phineas' actions was thus also alleviated when Hashem stressed his paternal lineage, which conveyed that the emotions which drove Phineas to act were virtuous and sacred passions, and were in no way related to the disreputable side of his ancestry.

At any rate, we learn from this incident that if an act of violence is performed in the name of religious zeal, but it is motivated — even partially — by insincere or personal motives, it is invalidated and judged as a common act of violence. If there had been even a slight element of base motivation in Phineas' actions, he would have been held liable for murder.

The Talmud (*Yoma* 86) tells us that it is important for people to expose hypocrites who give the impression of being righteous, but who are in fact secret sinners. As *Rashi* explains, this is in order to prevent innocent, unsuspecting people from using this person as a model whose actions should be emulated. *Rabbeinu Yonah*, in *Shaarei Teshuvah* (3:219), points out that the *mitzvah* to expose hypocrites is not meant to be practiced by just any person. If the "exposer" is himself guilty of this sin, then his intentions would undoubtedly not be motivated by noble and righteous indignation, but by a desire to spoil that person's reputation for personal reasons. This reflects the same idea mentioned above.

We find a similar concept involved concerning Jehu, the king of Israel. In *Hosea* 1:4, Hashem says, "I shall punish the House of Jehu for the blood he spilled in Jezreel." The reference is to the house of Jehu's predecessors — the House of Ahab, whom Jehu exterminated. Why was Jehu condemned? Yehu acted by explicit orders of a prophet of Hashem, who had commanded him, "Strike down the House of your master Ahab" (*II Kings* 9:7). The answer is that since Yehu himself imitated the practices of his predecessors and "did not keep the Torah of HASHEM, God of Israel . . .; he did not turn away from the sins of Jeroboam" (ibid., 10:31), his assassination of Ahab's household, although ordained by Hashem, became in retrospect an act of cold-blooded murder, for it became evident that his deeds had not been for the sake of Heaven. In fact, *Smak* quotes *Riva* as saying that if a person carries out the rule of *rodef*, by which he may kill in order to prevent someone from performing an act of murder or adulterous rape, that person must be sure that he never allow his behavior to be tainted with the slightest trace of murder or sexual immorality. If he would suffer a lapse in these respects it would cast a shadow over the sincerity of his motivation for killing the *rodef*, for the summary execution of a *rodef* may only be carried out by someone guided by the purest of motives.

Similarly, the Sages (*Nazir* 23) interpret a verse in *Judges* (5:24) as meaning that Yael, by seducing Sisera to have relations with her, although this constituted adultery, committed a "sin" that was as great an act as the performance of a *mitzvah*. But, the Talmud objects, did she not derive pleasure from her actions? (The Talmud then explains that she actually *did not* derive any pleasure.) Apparently, if there had been even the slightest admixture of personal benefit involved in Yael's heroic deeds, her action would have been considered an ordinary sin of adultery. It was only because she was able to eliminate any trace of personal interest in her conduct that her course of action was deemed praiseworthy.

This idea may be used to explain a saying of the Sages. In *Yoma* 22b we learn, "R' Yochanan said . . ., 'Any Torah scholar (*talmid chacham*) who does not act with vengeance and bear hatred *like a snake* is no Torah scholar at all.' " We understand that it is important for a religious leader to take a firm stand and to act with great passion against evildoers, but why the comparison "like a snake"? The answer is that other animals may inflict injury on a person, but this is generally in order to be able to consume them as prey. The snake, however, inflicts injuries on its victim without deriving any personal benefit from its destructive act. A Torah scholar must be like a snake when he reprimands or punishes his constituents — acting without any trace of personal interest, but only for the sake of Heaven.

In *Pesachim* 113b the Sages interpret the verse (*Exodus* 23:4), "If you encounter an ox of your *enemy* or his donkey . . .," as referring to a fellow Jew who has committed an immoral act, whom one is permitted to hate. (It is ordinarily forbidden to harbor hatred to a fellow Jew — *Leviticus* 19:17.) *Tosafos* (ad loc.) quotes another *Gemara* which seems to contradict this interpretation: In *Bava Metzia* 32b the Talmud says that the reason the Torah commands us to deal kindly with the lost animals of our enemies is to teach us to curb our feelings of ill will for others. If, as the *Gemara* in *Pesachim* asserts, the "enemy" of the verse is someone whom we are *supposed* to hate, why would the Torah want us to restrain these feelings of hatred? The answer that *Tosafos* gives is that although hatred between two people may have begun with healthy intentions — for the sake of Heaven — it is very common for these righteous intentions to give way to base, personal hatred, beyond what is called for by Torah law. It is these extraneous, non-virtuous feelings of hatred that the Torah wants us to contain. Again, we see that even when the Torah permits harsh actions — or even harsh feelings — these may only be carried out with complete sincerity.

Perhaps this is the reason why the "bitter waters" of the *sotah* (*Numbers* 5:11ff) only work if the husband himself has not sinned (*Sotah* 28a). The waters are only used in a case where the husband has "acted zealously" (*Numbers* 5:14) towards his wife. If his "zealousness" is tainted by a less-than-perfect record in the same area as that sin of which he suspects his wife, this is not "zealousness" at all, but hypocrisy.

We have learned that the rule that "zealous people may summarily execute a man who has relations with a non-Jewish woman" must only be performed by someone who is not motivated by personal feelings, but only by the desire to honor the name of Hashem. This is why this punishment has a limitation imposed in terms of who may carry out the penalty — "zealous people" alone may execute this particular criminal. Since it is a punishment which is based on zealousness for Hashem's name, an ordinary person may not execute judgment in this case, but only someone who has the rare capability of overcoming his personal feelings and acting solely for Hashem's sake. This also explains why this is the only *halachah* in the Torah which "although it is the accepted *halachah*, it should not be taught [publicly]." Since it is so uncommon to find someone who possesses the requisite strength of character to implement this *halachah*, publicizing it would only lead to misinterpretation on the part of the common people.

Perhaps we can now understand why Moses did not wish to carry out the execution of Zimri himself. As *Rashi* relates, Zimri confronted Moses with a personal insult: "If you say this woman is prohibited to me because she is not Jewish, then who permitted you to marry your wife Tzipporah (who was also a Midianite)?" After being subject to such a vicious personal affront, Moses felt that he would not be able to perform the execution without allowing his personal hatred for Zimri to enter his mind and corrupt the pure spirit of zealousness for Hashem's sake.

The Importance of Gratitude

In *Numbers* 31:2 our teacher Moses is told, "Avenge the vengeance of the Children of Israel from the Midianites; afterward you will be gathered unto your people." As *Rashi*, quoting *Sifrei*, points out, HASHEM implies that Moses' death would immediately follow upon the heels of the battle against the Midianites. Nevertheless, *Rashi* notes, the very next verse goes on to tell how Moses expeditiously began to implement Hashem's commandment by organizing an army from all the tribes of Israel. Even though Moses knew that this act would be his last, he did not hesitate to carry it out, so great was his zeal to enthusiastically fulfill the word of Hashem. Moses' burning desire was to be granted the right to enter the Land of Israel — for, as the Sages tell us (based on *Deuteronomy* 3:23), Moses prayed 515 times for Hashem to rescind the decree that forbade him to cross the Jordan. Nevertheless, despite the fact that Moses realized that his petition had been rejected, he wholeheartedly undertook to fulfill, without delay, the task that Hashem had assigned him.

In *Numbers* 31:6 the Torah tells us that Moses sent off the force he had assembled, along with Phineas to lead them, to wage war against Midian. According to a Midrashic interpretation in the *Daas Zekeinim*, Hashem asked Moses, "I told *you* to take vengeance from the Midianites, and you send Phineas as your agent?!" Moses answered that since he himself had grown up in Midian he did not think it proper for him to betray them by personally leading Israel in battle against them. As the saying goes, "If you drank from a well, don't throw dirt into it afterwards." Moses' response is truly remarkable. We noted above how enthusiastic Moshe was in his desire to carry out Hashem's commandment precisely and promptly. Yet, despite his own devotion in fulfilling Hashem's word, his appreciation of the role that the Midianite people had played in his own upbringing prompted him, out of a profound sense of propriety, to have Hashem's wish carried out through the agency of another man. This does not mean that Moses did not follow Hashem's command faithfully; rather, he understood that when HASHEM told him, "Avenge the vengeance of the Children of Israel . . ." He must have meant for him to do so through someone else, as Hashem — Moses reasoned — would certainly not have wanted him to act contrary to the rules of appropriate conduct.

דברים
Devarim

With All Your Heart

The Torah bids us to "love HASHEM with all your heart" (*Deuteronomy* 6:5). The word לְבָבְךָ ("your heart") is spelled with a double ב, which, the *Gemara* explains, is to intimate that we must serve HASHEM with both halves of our heart — with our good inclination (*yetzer hatov*) and with our bad inclination (*yetzer hara*). But how does one serve Hashem with his negative dispositions? R' Yisrael Salanter used to explain that we should use our noble character traits when dealing with our own lives, and our baser, more menial instincts when dealing with our fellow men. For instance, the desire for honor is considered a negative trait ("the pursuit for honor . . . can cause someone to be driven from the world" — *Avos* 4:21) — when it is a question of one's own self-respect. However, when dealing with others, a person must strive to give them the utmost respect and honor, even while he eschews these vain pursuits for himself ("One must always show honor for other people — ibid. 4:1).

In *Kesubos* 67b the *Gemara* tells us that Hillel — who was the very epitome of the trait of modesty, as related in *Shabbos* 31a — once ministered before a rich man who had become impoverished. He ran before him three miles, in order to supply him with the level of comfort and honor he was accustomed to. When it came to his own lifestyle, Hillel would never have stood for such homage being showered upon him, but when it came to bestowing it upon others, he was careful to carry the concept of showing respect to one's fellow man to the farthest extreme.

Similarly, in respect to the trait of *bitachon* (faith in Hashem), when it comes to himself, a person must be careful to realize that everything he achieves comes from Hashem, and that any human being who helps bring about whatever prosperity he finds is only acting as His agent. We know that Joseph was punished for putting his faith in Pharaoh's Chamberlain of the Cupbearers (*Sar HaMashkim*), asking him to mention him and his plight to Pharaoh (*Genesis* 40:23 and *Rashi* ad loc.). However, when another person puts his faith *in us* to act in his benefit, we must consider it as if this man's fate truly lies completely in our own hands, in order to ensure that we can fulfill his wishes with the utmost efficiency.

A person must thus be very careful when deciding how to use the many facets of his character — restraining them at times and fostering them at others. A human being was created from both the "upper, sublime realms" (his soul) and the "lower, physical realms" (his body). For his own spiritual development he must perfect the sublime aspect of human existence, striving to emulate the sanctity of HASHEM Himself — "You shall be holy, for I, HASHEM, am holy" (*Leviticus* 11:44). But when it comes to relating to one's fellow man, a person must use his baser, physical instincts in order to determine what the other person's material needs and desires might be. It is said of Moses, who is described as "the man of God" (*Deuteronomy* 33:1), that he was "a man from half of his body downwards, and godlike from half of his body upwards." This means that for himself, he was completely involved in an ethereal world, far removed from any contact with the physical realm; yet when it came to understanding and appreciating the necessities of the people whom he led, his feet were firmly planted upon the ground.

Being on Guard for Mitzvos

The Torah tells us (*Deuteronomy* 12:23), "Only be strong not to eat the blood." *Rashi* (ad loc.) remarks, quoting from *Sifrei*, "R' Shimon ben Azzai said: 'Here the Torah teaches us how vigilant we must be in strengthening ourselves in the performance of *mitzvos*. If the eating of blood — which is easy to avoid because people by nature do not have a desire for it — requires a warning to "be strong," how much more so when it comes to other *mitzvos*!'"

Similarly, in a later verse (v. 25), "You shall not eat [blood], in order that it be well with you and your children after you," *Rashi* quotes the Sages: "We can learn from this the reward for *mitzvos* in general. If for [refraining from] blood — which people naturally abhor — one brings merit upon himself and upon his children after him, how much greater must the reward be for refraining from theft or sexual prohibitions, which people naturally desire!"

Concerning the first quote, we may ask that if it is indeed human nature to abhor the eating of blood, why does the Torah need to exhort us to refrain from this practice? The answer lies in *Sforno's* comment on the continuation of v. 25: "... [in order that it be well with you ...] *when you do what is right in the eyes of HASHEM.*" *Sforno* explains that the reward spoken of in the verse is not for refraining from the drinking of blood per se, but for avoiding blood *because it is right in the eyes of Hashem*. If a person abstains from blood because he is naturally revolted by it, there is no reward in store for him. *Rashi* expresses a similar thought in his commentary at the end of *Parashas Kedoshim*: "A person should not have the attitude that 'I despise pig's meat; I have no desire to wear clothes of wool and linen (*shaatnez*).' Rather, he should think, 'I do have a desire for these things, but my Father in Heaven has forbidden them to me.'" Even if a person would have in any case refrained from doing a certain action which is forbidden by the Torah, he should think that his abstention is in reality for the sake of Heaven, in order to submit himself to God's will.

This, then, is the reason why the Torah has to provide words of caution and exhortation in respect to the prohibition of eating blood. This prohibition is in fact one of the most difficult ones to observe in the proper spirit of "acting for the sake of Heaven." The more one is naturally predisposed to avoid a given action, the harder it is to do that act "for the sake of Heaven." Hence, it is quite appropriate that the Torah write these words of exhortation in this particular instance. There is a saying that "it is easier to fast for the sake of Heaven than it is to eat for the sake of Heaven"!

According to this explanation, however, there is a difficulty in the words of *Sifrei*. If it is so appropriate that a repulsive act such as eating blood be explicitly prohibited, then how can *Sifrei* continue to say, "If the eating of blood — which is easy to avoid because people by nature do not have a desire for it — requires a warning to be strong in our keeping of it, how much more so when it comes to other *mitzvos*"? The words of the Torah do not apply "much more so" in other cases, but "less so"!

The explanation is as follows. The Talmud (*Kiddushin* 31a) tells us that "someone who fulfills a *mitzvah* because he is commanded to do so is greater than one who fulfills it without being obligated to do so." This is because when someone is obligated to do something, his *yetzer hara* automatically develops a resistance to doing that act, but when he has nothing at stake in doing something, the *yetzer hara* has no interest. Thus, when a person does an act under an obligation to do so, he is on a higher level than someone who performs the act on a volunteer basis. The former has to overcome a battle with his *yetzer hara*, while the latter does not. When an action is officially prohibited, even one which is innately repugnant, the *yetzer hara* manages to provide a desire to engage in that action.

This, then is the meaning of the *a fortiori* argument (*kal vachomer*) of *Sifrei*: If a *mitzvah* such as refraining from the drinking of blood — which has a very low amount of opposition from the *yetzer hara* (that "resistance to fulfilling obligations" described in the previous paragraph) — requires words of reinforcement and exhortation, how much more so do other sins, which have a much larger degree of opposition from the *yetzer hara* (natural human desire, in addition to the "resistance" described above).

Perhaps we can now shed new meaning on the dictum of the Sages, "The greater the man, the greater his temptations" (*Sukkah* 52a). The more challenges a person is faced with — the greater his *yetzer hara* — the higher level of reward he earns. A person who is on a high spiritual level is likely to have an easier time defeating the *yetzer hara* than an ordinary person. In order to ensure that great people *do* face constant challenges — through which they may rise to even higher spiritual heights — Hashem sees to it that they are supplied with a more formidable *yetzer hara*.

When the Jews were about to leave Egypt, Hashem told Moses, "Please speak to the people: Let each man request of his fellow . . . silver vessels and gold vessels [to despoil the Egyptians]" (*Exodus* 11:2). *Rashi* addresses the use of the word "Please," explaining that Hashem was anxious, as it were, that the people enable the fulfillment of His promise to Abraham (*Genesis* 15:14), "and afterwards [your descendants] will go out with much property." This comment may be better understood in light of the thoughts developed above. Although it is natural for a person to desire wealth and to despoil his master who has wrongfully enslaved and exploited him for many years, since there was an element of "commandment" involved — for Hashem had His own reasons for wanting the people to plunder the Egyptians — the *yetzer hara* not to obey came into play, and the expression of appeal ("Please") became necessary.

R' Yisrael Salanter, in his *Ohr Yisrael*, remarks how amazing it is that people are startled by the slightest unexpected noise, even by the rustling of a leaf, yet they do not fear being punished for their sins. This is true even of people who believe with complete faith and conviction that such punishment indeed exists. And why? Because the *yetzer hara* has been given the ability to cloud man's mind and induce him to act in an irrational manner. Otherwise, there would be no temptation, and hence, no spiritual growth.

The Roots of Heresy

In defining the origins of heresy, the Sages said, "[It is written,] 'You shall not have within you [בְּךָ] a foreign god' (*Psalms* 81:10). What 'foreign god' resides within man's body? The evil inclination (*yetzer hara*)" (*Shabbos* 105). It is this negative stimulus that constantly tests man and spurs him to oppose his Creator and commit sin. An exterior personification of this powerful force is the false prophet mentioned in *Parashas Re'eh*. The Torah openly admits that at times his false pronouncement will actually be fulfilled in order to test the people's faith in God. As the verses say, "If there should stand up in your midst a prophet, or a dreamer of a dream, and he will produce to you a sign or a wonder, *and the sign or the wonder comes about*, of which he spoke to you, saying, 'Let us follow gods of others that you did not know and we shall worship them!' — do not hearken to the words of that prophet ... *for* HASHEM, *your God, is testing you to know whether you love* HASHEM, *your God*, with all your heart and with all your soul" (*Deuteronomy* 13:2-4). Despite the prophet's apparent authenticity, however, we are warned against believing him.

The same can be said of the evil inclination within us. It will give us what appears to be sound advice, convincing us with infallible logic that its propositions are the only ethical option open to us, that any other course of action would be morally unforgivable. Before we know it, though, sin is suddenly looming before our eyes.

This idea is illustrated in the verse, "My Sabbaths shall you observe and My Sanctuary shall you revere — I am HASHEM" (*Leviticus* 19:30). In reference to this verse the Sages said: "[Our verse teaches that] just as the 'observance' mentioned in regard to the Sabbath warns us not to revere the Sabbath, but rather the One Who commanded us to observe the Sabbath, so too, we should not revere the Sanctuary, but rather the One Who warned us to observe the laws of the Sanctuary" (*Yevamos* 6). We see from here that the evil inclination has the ability to turn the epitome of sanctity — the very place where the Divine Presence dwells — into an instrument of moral corruption, for otherwise, why would the Torah warn us against "revering the Sanctuary"? For the same reason the Sages said, "A person should not pray while standing behind his Torah teacher, for he causes the Divine Presence to withdraw from the midst of Israel" (*Berachos* 27). *Tosafos* explains, "Because it looks as though he is bowing down to his teacher." What a formidable adversary we must confront every single day of our lives! There is indeed but a hairsbreadth between *Gehinnom* and *Gan Eden!*

There is another potentially powerful source of heresy residing within the human psyche — the trait of arrogance. As the Sages said, "Whoever has within him [the trait] of arrogance, it is as though he worships idol" (*Sotah* 4). This is also the intention of the verse, "Every haughty person is an abomination to God" (*Proverbs* 16:5), in regard to which the Sages said, "Whoever is arrogant, it is as though he dislodges the legs of the Divine Presence."

Why did the Sages speak so caustically about the trait of arrogance? Because only a person who feels totally self-sufficient exhibits this trait. Such a person deludes himself into believing that his livelihood is dependent on nothing other than the toil of his own hands, that if he has prospered, it is due solely to his intelligence and proficiency. In addition to inflating his ego, this ideology leaves no room for Divine Providence. The Sages thus liken a person who adopts this attitude to one who "dislodges the legs of the Divine Presence" — arrogance implicitly denies the existence of Hashem. And what does such a person believe in? In an idol — namely, himself!

On the other hand, when a person realizes that everything he owns, including his very existence, is a gift of God — that a person's degree of prosperity is not a function of how hard he has toiled or what level of proficiency he has attained, but is rather the fulfillment of a Heavenly decree — how can he possibly feel arrogant? A person with this outlook on life sees the Hand of God at all times, and thereby lays a firm foundation for the "legs of the Divine Presence" to stand upon.

In addition, this way of thinking keeps a person well away from sin, as the Sages said, "Ponder upon three things, and you shall not come to sin: An eye observes, an ear listens, and all your deeds are recorded in a ledger."

The Sages' statement implies that the act of committing an intentional transgression manifests a weakness in faith. This principle applies to all types of people, even to the very righteous. For even a person who sincerely believes in Hashem's omnipresence can be momentarily blinded by the malicious tactics of the evil inclination. If he lets down his guard for even one moment, if he allows his evil inclination to persuade him to believe that his righteousness is a result of his untiring efforts to reach ever higher spiritual levels, then he, too, has inadvertently "dislodged the legs of the Divine Presence." His faith in Hashem's absolute control over the world is weakened, and in the wake of this vacillation comes sin.

The Talmud recounts that when R' Yochanan ben Zakkai lay on his deathbed, his disciples asked him to bless them. He said, "May the fear of Heaven be upon you to the same extent as is the fear of flesh and blood." Disappointed, the disciples asked, "Is that all?" He answered, "If only! Know that when a person commits a transgression, he thinks, 'I hope no person will see me!' " (Berachos 28). R' Yochanan was obviously referring to all kinds of people, including righteous individuals such as his disciples. Apparently, even truly God-fearing people are liable to be momentarily blinded by the evil inclination even though they sincerely believe that Hashem perceives their every deed. What a formidable adversary is the evil inclination! How careful we must be not to fall prey to its malicious tricks!

The Purpose of Commandments

The Talmud tells us, " 'The speech of HASHEM is purified' (Psalms 18:31) — Rav explained, 'The commandments were given to us in order for man to become purified through them. Does it matter to Hashem if someone slaughters an animal from the front of its neck or the back of its neck? Does it matter to Him if someone eats impure animals or pure animals? Certainly, then, the commandments were only given in order for man to become purified through them.' "

Ramban (commentary to *Deuteronomy* 22:6) explains at length the meaning of this Talmudic statement: "Hashem derives no benefit from man's fulfillment of the commandments, just as He has no need for the light kindled in the Menorah of the Temple, or for the meat of the sacrifices offered upon the Altar. Even when it comes to those commandments which were ordained to recall miracles that happened to the Jewish people, upon their Exodus from Egypt or elsewhere, we should not think that they are for Hashem's benefit. Rather, they are for our own edification, for through them we may arrive at an understanding of the truth, and through them we may merit the protection of Hashem. The reason we are instructed to slaughter animals from the front of the neck rather than the back of the neck is to teach the importance of feeling mercy for the animal even while engaged in its slaughter (for slitting the animal's throat is more humane than chopping its head off from the rear) . . ."

In fact, the formula we use while reciting a blessing on the performance of a commandment reflects this perspective: ". . . Who has sanctified us with His commandments, commanding us to . . ." The commandments are purely instruments through which the Jewish people may attain an elevated level of holiness, nothing more and nothing less.

Property of Others

The Torah commands that "There shall not be for the *Kohanim*, the Levites ... a portion and an inheritance with Israel" (*Deuteronomy* 18:1). *Sifrei* explains that the "portion" they may not partake of along with the rest of the people refers to the spoils of war. *Sefer HaChinuch* (§505) offers a reason for this prohibition: "Since these are the ministers before Hashem, it is not fitting for them to make use of articles that have been seized from another person in war ... for only things which have been procured through peaceful and honorable means may enter into the House of Hashem, and not articles in which lie the anguish of another man or woman." This commandment, then, teaches us to what extent we should be careful to avoid using something that became available to us through another person's suffering. This is what is required of us if we want to achieve the Torah's ideal level of sensitivity to others — even if the suffering of the other person was completely justified according to the laws of the Torah, such as the spoils of war captured in the course of the conquest of the Land of Israel. It is not enough to refrain from rejoicing at one's enemies' downfall (*Proverbs* 24:17), but one must also refrain from deriving any benefit from their possessions.

When Jacob was about to confront his hostile brother Esau, he was "afraid, and greatly distressed" (*Genesis* 32:8) — "afraid" that he might be killed by Esau, and "greatly distressed" that he might have to *kill* Esau (*Rashi* ad loc.). Even though he would have killed Esau in self-defense, Jacob was distressed by the thought that his own welfare would be brought about at the expense of another human being's life.

Similarly, in the prayer of R' Nechunia ben HaKaneh (*Berachos* 28b), which we recite before our daily study in the study hall (*beis medrash*), we say, "May I not make a mistake in some matter of *halachah*, whereupon my colleagues will rejoice in me" (translation according to *Rashi* ad loc.). We express concern not only for the possibility that we might err in our interpretation of Torah law, but also for the fact that such an error might cause another person to sin by ridiculing us for our mistake. This prayer shows that even when we ourselves suffer, we must be concerned with the ill effects that our actions may have on others. From this we see to what extent it is necessary to be sensitive to not becoming the vehicle through which another person is led to improper conduct!

The Rebellious Son

The Torah describes the punishment for the "wayward and rebellious son" (*Deuteronomy* 21:18-21). After being duly admonished and warned, if he continues in his "gluttonous and drunken" ways he is to be put to death. The Talmud (*Sanhedrin* 72a) explains the reasons for this harsh punishment as follows: "It is better for him to die while he has some merit than to die as a [complete] sinner. R' Yosi HaGlili explained: Is it because this boy ate a *tartimar* of meat and drank half of a *log* of wine that the Torah demands that he be stoned?! Rather, the Torah understands the psyche of the rebellious son: He eventually depletes his parents' money supply and then, seeking to continue the pleasures that he has become accustomed to, resorts to armed robbery."

There is an opinion in the Talmud (ibid., 71a) that, due to all the numerous minutiae and loopholes in the law of the rebellious son, it is all but impossible to ever implement it. Why, then, ask our Sages, does the Torah bother to record this law altogether? So that we may study it and derive moral lessons from it.

Just what is the teaching that we can learn from this section? It is an all-important lesson throughout man's life. In *Avos* 4:2 we are taught: "Ben Azzai said: Always run to do even a minor *mitzvah*, and flee from sin, for one *mitzvah* leads to another, and one sin leads to another; the reward for a *mitzvah* is another *mitzvah*, and the reward for a sin is another sin." The reward in store for a person in Heaven for doing a *mitzvah* is certainly a great one; even for fulfilling a minor *mitzvah* the Torah testifies that "it will be well for you, and you will have long lives" (*Deuteronomy* 22:7). Yet Ben Azzai found an even better incentive to fulfill *mitzvos*: one *mitzvah* leads to another, etc! [The source for Ben Azzai's aphorism, according to the *Midrash*, is derived from the beginning of our *parashah* — if one indulges his *yetzer hara* by marrying a non-Jewish war captive (ibid., 21:10-14), it will eventually lead to an unsound family situation (ibid., vs. 15-17), which will in turn give rise to a case of a rebellious son (vs. 18-21).]

So many times a person sins, thinking, "I will sin just once, and afterwards I will mend my ways." This frame of mind is very harmful, for it prevents the person from even realizing that he is doing anything wrong. He thus loses a battle to his *yetzer hara* without even putting up a fight.

The first two of the Thirteen Attributes of Divine Mercy are "HASHEM, HASHEM" (*Exodus* 34:6). The Sages explain this as follows: "I am Hashem (the Divine Name connoting mercy) before a man sins, and I am still Hashem after he sins." We see from this that were it not for God's mercy, it would be impossible for a sinner to regain his former level of spiritually. Such is the power of sin — it pulls a person further and further down the ladder of spirituality. The rebellious son begins with a problem of lack of self-control, but this weakness of character indicates that he has become a slave to his *yetzer hara*. If continued unchecked, he will become a serious menace to society.

There is another lesson to be learned from the rebellious son. As the *Mesillas Yesharim* points out in his introduction: "The foundation of righteousness is for a person to realize that there is an essential goal in life, and to realize that one's entire life in this world is just a preparation for entry into the World to Come." The sin of the rebellious son, explains *Ibn Ezra*, is that "he does not engage in any worthwhile occupation, but only indulges his physical appetites; he is thus considered an *apikoros*." From this we may learn that a person who does not recognize the essential reason for living in this world, but instead devotes himself to attaining earthly pleasures, is regarded as an *apikoros*. If he does not recognize his responsibility to himself, how can he possibly know his responsibility to God?

The Benefits of Fearing Hashem

K ing Solomon said, "The fear of HASHEM adds days [to one's life]" (Proverbs 10:27). It is a known fact that worry and anxiety tend to diminish a person's lifetime, but in the case of the fear of Heaven, the opposite is true — in this regard, fear and apprehension miraculously lengthen one's days. In a similar vein the verse goes on to say, "... and the years [i.e. lifetime] of the wicked are shortened." Although one would think that pampering oneself with the pleasures and delights of the world would enhance one's physical constitution, and hence promote a larger life span, the wicked experience the very opposite — their lives are shortened. This is part of the miraculous manner in which Hashem rules over the people of the world. Every single individual in fact encounters miracles on a daily basis, without which he would not be able to survive, yet he tends to overlook them.

The Sages tell us that when one is about to measure the amount of a particular year's harvest, he should say a prayer: "May it be Hashem's will that there be found a blessing in this produce." After the produce has been measured, however, it is forbidden to utter this prayer, as it would constitute a "prayer in vain," a prayer which can no longer be fulfilled. This is because Hashem constantly performs hidden miracles for us throughout life, and it is thus appropriate to pray that he miraculously bless our crops. Once the crop has already been measured, however, to pray for a blessing (that is, for increased production) would be to ask for a revealed, noticeable miracle, for which we may not pray.

ימים טובים
Festivals

Fear of Judgment

The *Chafetz Chaim* quotes the *Vilna Gaon* as having said: "A person who commits a sin will be held responsible in the World to Come not only for the sinful act, but also for having wasted the time that was spent on the sin. Instead, he could have used that time for doing *mitzvos*, especially learning Torah, where every single word constitutes a separate *mitzvah*!"

In *Chagigah* 5a we learn: "R' Yochanan used to cry when he reached the following verse: 'I will draw near to you for judgment . . . against the adulterers and those who swear falsely, as well as those who withhold the pay of workers . . . and mistreat strangers . . .' (*Malachi* 3:5). He would say, 'If a servant's master counts all of his infractions against him — the minor ones as well as the severe ones — does he have any hope at all?' " It is indeed a sobering thought to realize that even the most seemingly insignificant misdeeds are held against a person on the Day of Judgment.

The Torah (*Deuteronomy* 10:17) tells us that Hashem "does not show favor and does not accept a bribe." What sort of "bribe" is the Torah referring to? *Ramban* explains that even a very righteous person who sins cannot expect Hashem to overlook his wrongdoing, or to merely "subtract" the sin from his list of abundant good deeds. Rather, Hashem will hold even him liable for every last misdeed that he has committed. As *Sforno* puts it, "A commandment cannot extinguish a sin."

In *Taanis* 21a, Nachum of Gamzo recounts for his students how it came to be that he became crippled and debilitated by disease. One day he was traveling to his father-in-law's house with three donkeys laden with various foods. A poor man, on the verge of collapse, approached him and asked him for some food. Nachum replied, "Wait a moment while I unload the donkeys." As he began to unload the donkeys, however, the poor man collapsed and died from hunger. Nachum thereupon fell upon the man's body and wept, and would not be consoled until he beseeched Hashem to take away his vision, for his eyes did not sufficiently pity the poor man, and to have his hand and feet fall off, for they did not act swiftly enough on behalf of the poor man. When his students exclaimed, "Woe to us that we have to see you in this condition!" he replied, "Woe to *me* if you would not see me in this condition!" Nachum was thus telling his students that as a result of this "evil" of not unpacking the food fast enough for the poor man — which was not even a "sin" of action but of *in*action — he would have been condemned to a much worse fate in the World to Come had he not accepted upon himself these horrendous afflictions. As the Days of Awe approach, we must contemplate the far-reaching consequences of our slightest errors, each person according to his level!

In a similar vein, in *Yevamos* 105b we are told how a student of Rebbi named Abadan once spoke disparagingly to another student, R' Yishmael ben R' Yosi, who was heavyset and had some difficulty getting to his seat for Rebbi's lecture. The *Gemara* says that at that time Abadan became smitten with *tzaraas*, and two of his sons drowned. R' Nachman bar Yitzchak thereupon exclaimed, "Praised is Hashem Who humbled Abadan in this world [thus absolving him from being punished in the World to Come]." This story also gives us cause to ponder the harsh punishment that is incurred for even the slightest misdeed, for Abadan's disparaging comment to R' Yishmael ben R' Yosi stemmed from righteous indignation — the students who were already seated were inconvenienced by R' Yishmael stepping over them, as the *Gemara* explains. Nevertheless, being stricken with *tzaraas* and suffering such terrible tragedies were considered acts of "kindness" in comparison to what should have been Abadan's lot in the World to Come!

It is especially important for people in the Torah world to contemplate these ideas, in view of what *Rambam* (*Hilchos Talmud Torah* 3:13) notes: "Anyone who is capable of engaging in Torah study but neglects to do so (out of laziness — *Lechem Mishneh*), or if someone has studied elementary Torah studies and suffices himself with that, going on to indulge in the frivolities of the pleasures of the world — such a person has transgressed the Torah's admonition (*Numbers* 15:31), 'He has scorned the word of HASHEM [. . . that soul shall be completely cut off].' " It is thus advisable for people who are capable of learning Torah to contemplate the seriousness of neglecting Torah study (*bitul Torah*), and the severe repercussions their sin will have upon their existence in the World to Come.

The Power of Repentance

In the *Ne'ilah* prayer we say, "You have given us this Day of Atonement, for an ending, a vindication and forgiveness for all our sins, in order that we may restrain our hands from wrongdoing." What is meant by the word "ending"? What, in fact, is the purpose of having one day of the year set aside for forgiveness and atonement altogether?

The ability to repent and thereby, as it were, "erase" the evil that has been committed through a sin, is a great gift from Hashem and it is one of the major manifestations of His attribute of mercy. As the Midrash says in *Bereishis* (see *Rashi* to 1:1), Hashem originally intended to create the world based on a system of strict justice, but then He saw that it would not endure, so He created the world with the Attribute of Mercy. It seems from the expression quoted above from *Ne'ilah* that one of the elements of Hashem's merciful institution of the concept of repentance (*teshuvah*) is the existence of a day when all sins "come to an end" (provided a person repents also). Often, the heavy burden of sin can cause a person to think, "I have sunk to such a low spiritual level; what hope do I have? How can I improve myself spiritually?" Or, "I have already committed this sin so many times. Whom am I fooling by trying to correct myself in this regard?" Such thoughts make a person despair of ever improving, and lead him to continue in the path that he himself realizes is wrong. In recognition of this phenomenon, we find several examples where our Sages instituted special decrees in order to make it easier for a sinner to rehabilitate himself (see, e.g., *Gittin* 55a). Similarly, the *Mishnah* in *Avos* (2:13) cautions us, "Do not be wicked in your own eyes." It is true that the *Gemara* in *Niddah* (30b) says, "Even if everyone in the world tells you that you are a righteous man, in your own eyes you should regard yourself as a wicked person," for recognizing one's shortcomings is the first step towards repentance, without which self-improvement is impossible. Nevertheless, it is important not to allow oneself to sway to the other extreme and completely despair over one's shortcomings. We find that Acher, when asked by R' Meir why he did not repent for his sins, replied, "I have already heard from behind the curtain of Heaven that 'everyone in the world may be forgiven through repentance — except for Acher!' " If a person gives up hope of ever rehabilitating himself, he becomes a lost case.

In order to counteract this tendency to feel despair over one's situation, Hashem, in His great mercy, designated a particular day of the year for repentance. This day, if it is used properly, provides one with the opportunity to throw off the yoke of past sins and begin life anew, with a fresh start. This is the meaning of the prayer that calls Yom Kippur "an ending in order that we may restrain our hand from wrongdoing." It is a time for repenting, and thus bringing an end to the feeling of guilt and shame we feel for our past deeds. This feeling of being unencumbered enables us to go on, improve ourselves, and refrain from further sin.

This is perhaps also the reason why the Sages say that a bride and groom are forgiven all their past sins on the day of their wedding. It is in order to enable them to confront their new lives with a clear conscience, which gives them the necessary peace of mind to grow and improve spiritually.

The *Chinuch* (§185) states: "In His great mercy Hashem designated one day of the year for the atonement of sins. Had He not done so, people's sins would continue to accumulate year after year, eventually reaching a point where they would be too numerous to bear, and the world would become deserving of annihilation ... It was at the beginning of Creation that Hashem designated this day." This last statement is puzzling, because we know that Yom Kippur only became a day of atonement for sins when Moses, after praying for Israel's forgiveness for the sin of the Golden Calf, was told by Hashem on the tenth of Tishrei that He would forgive the people. How, then, can the *Chinuch* say that Yom Kippur was designed at the very beginning of time? The answer is that it was not this particular day of the tenth of Tishrei that had been designated at the beginning of Creation, but rather the general concept of repentance; as mentioned above, it was incorporated by Hashem into the very fabric of Creation. Repentance provides, as we have said, the opportunity to erase a backlog of sin, to enable people to make a fresh start. However, the actual designation of the day of Yom Kippur as that day of reprieve did not take place until the sin of the Golden Calf.

The Torah refers to sacrifices as "a covenant" (*Leviticus* 2:13). *Daas Zekeinim* explains that this is to teach us that the sacrifices are not for God's benefit, but are designed rather for the good of mankind. "When a person sins and offers a sacrifice and his sin is atoned for, the knowledge that he has been cleansed from his sin will dissuade him from becoming tainted with sin again. If he would not be able to achieve atonement, he would just repeat the same sins. It is comparable to a man who is wearing soiled clothing — he does not bother to prevent them from becoming increasingly dirty. When a person wears a perfectly clean garment, however, he takes great care to keep it perfectly clean." This reflects the essential concept of Yom Kippur, as we discussed above.

Confession and Atonement

In *Yoma* 86b we learn: "If someone confessed a particular sin on one Yom Kippur he should not confess it again on a subsequent Yom Kippur — unless he has committed that sin again in the interim — for if he does so, the following verse may be applied to him: 'As a dog who returns to his vomit, so is a fool who repeats his folly' (*Proverbs* 26:11). But R' Eliezer ben Yaakov says that, on the contrary, it is praiseworthy to do so, as it says, 'my sin is opposite me forever' " (*Psalms* 51:5).

Several points require further clarification regarding this statement. Firstly, why does the *Tanna* have to mention that if a sin was committed again it should be confessed again? It is obvious that any sin committed requires atonement, and the fact that a sin had been committed in a previous year as well should not be a reason for one not to confess it this year! Apparently the *Gemara* means to tell us something else. As *Rambam* explains (*Hilchos Teshuvah* 2:2), part of the repentance (*teshuvah*) process involves a steadfast resolution never to commit the sin again. If someone repented for a sin one year and found that he again succumbed to that sin the following year, this second sin proves that there had been a lack of sincerity in his repentance process in the first place. When the *Gemara* says that if a sin was repeated during the foregoing year one should confess that sin, it means that he must confess the *original* sin once again, for his repentance process has been shown to be flawed, retroactively. This may be compared to a disease which receded for a while, but then returned to afflict the patient. The new attack just shows that the disease had never really completely healed in the first place.

Another question regarding the *baraisa* quoted above is: Why does the first opinion speak so critically of someone who confesses a sin that had been committed and atoned for in a previous year? The opinion of R' Eliezer ben Yaakov seems to make more sense; surely it is better to show a sense of shame for every wrong that has been committed — and the more remorse shown the better! Perhaps the answer is that once a person has succumbed to the temptation to commit a particular sin, it is easier for him to fall prey to the evil inclination and repeat this sin than for someone else with no previous record for that sin. Thus, once a person has repented for a sin, it is better for him to completely put it out of his mind and not provoke the evil inclination by thinking of the old sin. Even in the context of contrition and confession, thinking about a sinful act committed in the past might actually prompt a person to repeat that act.

Rabbeinu Yonah, in *Shaarei Teshuvah* 4:21, suggests other reasons to explain the first *Tanna's* objection to confessing a sin that had already been atoned for. He proposes that to do so would indicate a deficiency in one's belief in the efficacy of his previous repentance. Another possible reason he suggests is that by dwelling on past sins, one insinuates that he has no other, more recent sins to rectify, which is obviously an unhealthy attitude.

The Time of Our Gladness

The *Tur* asks why it is that we celebrate Sukkos in autumn, since it is a remembrance of the Exodus from Egypt, which took place in the spring. He explains that if the Torah would have commanded us to leave our houses and live in Sukkos during the spring, it would not be evident that our intention is to fulfill the commandment of commemorating the Exodus, for it is common for people to spend time in flimsy, airy huts in the warmer weather. It is specifically in autumn, when people begin to move back into their more sturdy, weatherproof homes, that it is most recognizable that one's intention is solely for the purpose of fulfilling the commandment.

Perhaps we may note another reason for the timing of the holiday of Sukkos in the month of Tishrei. The joy that we experience during the festive Sukkos holiday is the joy of feeling close to Hashem. In *Rambam's* words (*Hilchos Lulav* 8:15), the joy of Sukkos is "the joy that a person experiences in the performance of commandments and in the love of God Who commanded them" — the recognition of what a privilege it is to observe commandments, for this is the prime purpose of man's creation — "I created him for My glory" (*Isaiah* 43:7)." We recall the "clouds of glory" in which we basked in the desert, when all of our daily needs were met through the direct, supernatural intervention of Hashem. The Torah itself attests to the reason why Hashem chose to sustain us in the desert in this way — it was in order to teach us that "it is not by bread alone that man lives, but by all that comes out from the mouth of HASHEM that man lives" (*Deuteronomy* 8:3). This was the case until the Jews arrived at their final destination, the Land of Israel. There they began to live a life that was governed completely by the laws of nature — if they plowed and sowed and reaped they would have food, and if they did not, they would starve. It was at this point that the lesson of the manna was in danger of being forgotten. After toiling long hard days in the field, when a farmer finally gathers in the harvest, he is liable to think, "My strength and the might of my hand made me this prosperity" (ibid. v. 17). It is for this reason that specifically in Tishrei, during the harvest season, Hashem commanded us to leave our secure, comfortable homes and move into flimsy, temporary dwellings where we are exposed to the forces of nature and dependent on the grace of Hashem to protect us from them. This is to remind us, in the midst of harvesting the bounty of the year's crops, that we are indeed still dependent upon Hashem for our daily sustenance, no less than in the days of the manna.

To Rejoice in Torah

A t first glance, it would seem that the commandment to rejoice over the Torah comes up only once a year, on Simchas Torah. However, if we would ponder upon this issue a little longer, we would see that this is not at all the case. Rather, this commandment is applicable every single day of the year, twenty-four hours a day, as will be evident from the following exposition:

The Talmud (*Shabbos* 30) recounts that the Sages seriously considered hiding away the Book of *Ecclesiastes* because "its words contradict each other." One example of the many apparent inconsistencies found in this work are the verses, "Of merriment [I said], 'What good is it?' " (*Ecclesiastes* 2:2), and "I therefore praised merriment" (ibid., 8:15). Ostensibly, these two verses are irreconcilable. However, one of the Sages eventually resolved the apparent contradictions in *Ecclesiastes* and reinstated it as part of Scripture. The resolution to the contradiction stated above is as follows: The verse "Of merriment [I said], 'What good is it?' " refers to mundane pleasures, while the verse "I therefore praised merriment" refers to the joy of commandments, which is an essential component of Divine service, for "the Divine Presence only resides [upon one who feels] joy in fulfilling the commandments."

Similarly, *Tosafos* on *Sukkah* 50 says, "According to the Talmud Yerushalmi, [the joyful celebration held at nighttime throughout the Sukkos Festival was called *Simchas Beis Hasho'eivah*] because those who participated would 'draw' (*sho'avim*) Divine inspiration (*ruach haKodesh*) from the event. For the Divine Presence dwells amidst joy, as the verse says, 'As the musician played, God's spirit came upon him. . .' (*II Kings* 3:15). [The Talmud Yerushalmi] teaches that Jonah son of Amitai, who was among the pilgrims who came up to

Jerusalem, had the Divine Presence reside upon him during a *Simchas Beis Hasho'eivah*."

Sefer Chareidim reports that the *Arizal* disclosed to one of his closest disciples that he merited to have the gates of wisdom and Divine inspiration open before him because he always felt great joy when performing commandments.

This idea is firmly based on a Talmudic source: "R' Ila said to Ulla, 'When you go up there [to Jerusalem], ask after R' Bruna, my brother, and about his stature among his peers. For he is a great man, always joyous over commandments. Once, he recited [the blessing] of redemption ["Blessed are You ... Who redeemed Israel"] adjacent to the [silent] prayer, and a smile did not leave his face the entire day!' " (*Berachos* 9).

In Tractate *Sukkos*, we learn that only the greatest Sages and righteous individuals danced during the *Beis Hasho'eivah* celebration, while the rest of the people looked on. The Sages would sing, "Happy is our childhood, for it did not shame our old age," or "Happy is our old age, for it has atoned for our childhood." Both groups would sing, "Happy is he who has not sinned!" Clearly, then, the intensity of the Sages' joy was in direct ratio to the degree to which they observed the commandments — this was their true source of joy. And following the atonement of their sins on Yom Kippur, their joy knew no bounds.

The joy a person feels when performing commandments is also the reason why Scripture refers to the city of Jerusalem as "Joy of all the Earth" (*Lamentations* 2:15). The Sages explain that when a person commits a transgression, he is overcome with worry and remorse. In the past, however, a transgressor could come to Jerusalem to offer a sacrifice in the Temple and thereby atone for his sin. This act transformed his sense of worry and remorse into pure joy. Thus, Jerusalem was called, "Joy of all the Earth."

Similarly, the Sages said, "There were no occasions of greater joy to Israel than Yom Kippur and *Tu B'Av* ..." (*Bava Basra* 121). At first glance this statement is difficult to understand, since we do not normally associate Yom Kippur with joy. On the contrary, the verse says, "This shall remain for you an eternal decree: In the seventh month, on the tenth of the month, you shall *afflict* yourselves and you shall not do any work, neither the native nor the proselyte who dwells among you" (*Leviticus* 16:29). However, the following verse provides the answer: "For on this day he shall provide *atonement* for you to *cleanse you*; from all your sins before HASHEM shall you be cleansed." It is because of the spiritual cleansing that is possible on this day that makes Yom Kippur an occasion of unparalleled joy for Israel. And what is the significance of *Tu B'Av*? On this day, they would complete the commandment of felling trees to provide wood for the Altar. Again, we see that completing a commandment is a source of great joy.

In *Shaar HaSimchah*, the *Orchos Tzadikim* says that an individual who performs a commandment with joy earns 1,000 times more reward than someone who does the same commandments merely out of a sense of obligation. The same idea is expressed by *Rabbi Ovadiah Bartenura* in his commentary on the *mishnah* in the fourth chapter of *Pirkei Avos*: " 'The reward for a *mitzvah* is a *mitzvah*' means that the joy a person feels when doing a commandment is itself considered a commandment!"

From all the sources quoted above, it is evident that feeling joy over the performance of commandments is obligatory. There is, however, one major commentator who seems to disagree with this tenet: *Rambam*.

In *Hilchos Lulav*, *Rambam* seems to suggest that performing commandments with joy is not an outright obligation, but merely a higher level of Divine service. However, *Rambam* clarifies his opinion by citing the verses, "All these curses will come upon you and pursue you and overtake you until you are destroyed, because you will not have hearkened to the voice of HASHEM, your God, to observe His commandments and decrees that He commanded you. They will be a sign and a wonder, in you and in your offspring, forever, *because you did not serve HASHEM, your God, amid gladness and goodness of heart*, when everything was abundant" (*Deuteronomy* 28:45-47). *Rambam* explains that although one who performs a commandment without joy is technically regarded to have *fulfilled* his obligation, he has also incurred the wrath of Hashem, as is evident from the verse in *Deuteronomy*.

Thus, we see that even *Rambam* agrees that performing commandments with joy is an obligation incumbent upon everyone. The only point of contention between him and the other commentators is whether a lack of joy is an inherent component of observance of commandments, or whether it is a separate obligation. All agree, however, that it is unquestionably an obligation.

Simchas Torah marks the end of the period of spiritual renewal which we call "the High Holidays." The cleansing and uplifting effects of experiencing Heavenly judgment on Rosh Hashanah and Yom Kippur are behind us, and the ripples of spiritual joy have reached their crescendo. What awaits us now? We reassume our regular routines, hopefully with a heightened awareness of ourselves, and with a greater determination to fulfill our spiritual potential.

The *Gaon* of Petersburg, however, warns us that formidable obstacles have been placed in our way. To illustrate the point, he quotes the words of the *Rosh* (*Yom HaKippurim*, Ch. 24): "The Satan advocates on behalf of Israel on Yom Kippur, for they resemble angelic beings." What comes over the Satan at this time? the *Gaon* of Petersburg asks. Why is he suddenly so congenial towards the Jewish people?

The answer is that the Satan is no fool — he is willing to make a small investment in order to reap bountiful profits in due time. In other words, it is in his best interests to praise the exalted spiritual level of the Jewish people on Yom Kippur to no end, for then, when the awe elicited by the High Holy Days wears off and they reassume their regular routine, he will point his finger at them and call out to the Heavenly Court, "Look at the Jewish people now! This is the nation that resembled angelic beings on Yom Kippur! See how far they have fallen!"

It is advisable to ponder upon this idea in the days following *Simchas Torah*. We must keep our guard up in the aftermath of this period of spiritual elevation, for otherwise, all our achievements can and will be used against us in the Heavenly Court of law. We must focus our energy on Torah study and take advantage of every single moment. For who can imagine the awesome reward earned by a single moment of Torah study? As the *Shnos Eliyahu* points out in his commentary on tractate *Pe'ah*, "With every single word [of Torah], one fulfills a positive commandment. And the [reward earned by] fulfilling *this* positive commandment is equivalent to [the collective reward] of *all* Torah commandments."

In a similar vein, *Rabbeinu Gershom* explains the reason why the Sages considered *Tu B'Av* one of the two most joyful days of the year (the other was Yom Kippur; see explanation above). The reason given by the Sages is that on this day the people stopped cutting down trees to supply the Temple with wood for the Altar. "But how does this answer why this was a joyous occasion?" *Rabbeinu Gershom* asks. In answer, he explains that during the woodcutting season, the people were not free to study Torah. Now that the Temple had a sufficient supply of wood, however, they were finally able to lay down their axes and return to their studies. Since the end of the woodcutting season was officially on *Tu B'Av*, the people gave expression to their joy over having the opportunity to resume Torah study by commemorating the occasion with joyous celebration.

Let us reflect upon *Rabbeinu Gershom*'s explanation for a moment. If the reason why the people celebrated *Tu B'Av* is because now they would finally be able to resume their Torah studies, it would seem that they were very perturbed about not being able to do so beforehand. But what is it that they were doing when they were not learning Torah? Were they working for a living, occupying themselves with mundane tasks? No, they were *cutting wood for Hashem's Altar in the Holy Temple!* What a merit! In view of the discussion above, we can safely assume that they performed this commandment with enthusiasm and joy. And as far as not having the opportunity to study Torah, it is a well-known rule that "he who is occupied with a commandment is exempt from others." Yet, we see that the people felt a lack all the same. Why? Because they realized the true value of Torah study, and the awesome eternal reward earned with every single word.

The Sages convey the value of Torah study as follows: "[The verse says,] 'For Mordechai the Jew was viceroy to King Ahasuerus, and a great man among the Jews, and popular with the multitude of his brethren' (*Esther* 10:3). [The *Megillah* states that Mordechai was popular *with the multitude of his brethren*, implying that he was] not [popular] with *all* of his brethren. [This] teaches that some members of the *Sanhedrin* parted from him. [Similarly,] R' Yosef said: 'The study of Torah is greater than saving lives, for initially, Mordechai is reckoned [by Scripture] after four [sages], but in the end, [after the Purim story had taken place, Mordechai is reckoned] after five [sages, indicating that his importance among the Sages had declined]' " (*Megillah* 16).

In explanation of the Sages' statement, the *Turei Zahav* (*Yoreh De'ah* 251:6) wrote: "A person who is not put into a situation in which he must interrupt his Torah study in order to save lives has more merit than one who is."

The *Meiri* (*Berachos* 3) uses the example of King David to illustrate the importance of Torah study: "A person must always be very careful to occupy himself with Torah study. For who was greater than King David, who occupied himself with numerous issues every single day? And yet, he would make sure to rise early to study Torah by placing a harp by his pillow which would begin playing on its own at midnight. He would rise from his bed and occupy himself with Torah study until dawn, when he would have to begin taking care of the other issues that came before him."

Hence, we see that a student of Torah (*ben Torah*) must seize every opportunity, every spare moment, to learn Torah. His mind should not stop from thinking in Torah at all times, for continuous Torah study protects one from contemplating sinful or flighty thoughts. As the *Shulchan Aruch* (*Even Ha'ezer* Ch. 25) writes, "One should turn his thoughts to words of Torah; one should broaden his intellect with wisdom, for sinful thoughts can only gain a foothold in a heart that is devoid of wisdom."

If, heaven forbid, a person should squander opportunities to study Torah, he will be judged most severely. In reference to such an individual the Sages said, "R' Nehorai taught: [The verse says,] 'A person who shall act high-handedly, whether native or proselyte, he blasphemed HASHEM! — that person shall be cut off from among his people, *for he scorned the word of HASHEM* and broke His commandment; that person will surely be cut off, his sin is upon him" (*Numbers* 15:30-31). Who does this refer to? To a person who is capable of occupying himself with Torah, but refrains from doing so" (*Sanhedrin* 99). R' Chaim of Volozhin said about this, "Therefore, a person — even one who learns Torah — must assess himself and determine whether he, too, is guilty of having 'scorned the word of HASHEM.' For who knows how many hours he could have occupied himself with Torah, yet for some reason he did not?" Similarly, *Mishnah Berurah* (Ch. 155) writes, "When a person has the opportunity to learn Torah but willingly refrains from doing so, he closely resembles the individual about which the Sages said, 'he scorned the word of HASHEM,' for he does not feel the true value of time spent studying Torah."

In addition to incurring harsh Heavenly judgment, a person who fails to take advantage of opportunities to learn Torah will encounter great difficulties in his studies. As the Sages said, "If you neglect it, you shall have numerous interferences arrayed against you" (*Avos* 4:12). *Tiferes Yisrael* explains as follows: "You will be punished in kind with your sin — even if in the end you want to occupy yourself with Torah, they will splash the cup in your face, and you will not be given the merit to do so."

It is fitting to conclude this exposition about the importance of Torah study with the following statement of the Sages:

"R' Yehudah said in the name of Rav: What is the meaning of the verse, 'For what reason did the land perish, become parched like a desert, without passersby?' (*Jeremiah* 9:11). This question was asked of the Sages and the Prophets, but they did not have an explanation. In the end, the Holy One, Blessed is He, explained it: 'And HASHEM said, "*Because they forsook My Torah* that I put before them, and did not heed My voice nor follow it." ' R' Yehudah said in the name of Rav: Because they did not recite a blessing prior to Torah study" (*Nedarim* 81).

Ran explains in the name of *Rabbeinu Yonah* that if we would interpret the statement, "Because they forsook My Torah" literally, it would imply that the people abandoned Torah study altogether. However, this was not the case, for on the contrary, Jeremiah's generation studied Torah diligently. Thus, the Sages and Prophets could not explain why the land had been destroyed. Hashem answered by saying, "Because they forsook My Torah." This means that although the people *did* learn Torah, they did not "recite a blessing prior to Torah study" — in other words, deep in their hearts, they did not appreciate the true importance of Torah study, and they did not learn it purely for the sake of Heaven.

How great is our obligation to appreciate the true value of Torah study!

To Proclaim Miracles

The Talmud asks, "What is Chanukah?" (*Shabbos* 21). *Rashi* paraphrases the question as follows: "In commemoration of what miracle was [the festival] instituted?"

The Sages answered, "When the [Syrian-Greeks] entered the Sanctuary, they rendered all the oil impure. [Later, when the Hasmoneans drove away the gentiles,] they discovered one flask of pure oil bearing the seal of the High Priest (*Kohen Gadol*). It contained sufficient oil to light [the Menorah] for one day, but a miracle occurred and the Menorah remained lit for eight days. The following year, the Sages established these days as a festival (*Yom Tov*) for praise and thanksgiving." *Rashi* explains, "Work is not prohibited on these days — they were only designated for reciting the *Hallel* and saying *Al Hanissim*."

The immense spiritual importance of Chanukah is reflected in the *Shulchan Aruch*'s ruling that a poor person who lives off charity must light Chanukah candles, even if this requires that he borrow money or sell his clothes. This stringency is unprecedented in regard to rabbinically ordained commandments, and it is rarely applicable even to Torah-ordained commandments. Why, then, is so much importance attributed to lighting Chanukah candles?

The answer is that this commandment contains the element of פִּירְסוּמֵי נִיסָא, or "proclamation of the miracle." This is evident from the Talmud's statement, "What takes precedence? Chanukah candles or *Kiddush*? Chanukah candles takes precedence, for it proclaims the miracle" (ibid., 23). Still, you might wonder, "But why is proclaiming the miracle so important?"

The answer is that by proclaiming the miracles which took place on Chanukah, we reinforce the concept that the entire Creation, including the life force of every living thing, is a function of God's will. As the verse says, "I am HASHEM in the midst of the land" (*Exodus* 8:18). Miracles demonstrate that the "laws" of nature are not immutably etched in stone, but rather were set in motion by God. He initially created the entire cosmos *ex nihilo*, and it is He Who constantly renews its existence. When He sees fit, He intervenes and momentarily suspends the laws of nature, and their perpetuation is entirely dependent on His will. If God were to withhold the life force of the universe for even one moment, all matter would instantly vanish, and the universe would revert back to a state of utter disorder.

These fundamental principles of Jewish faith are given full expression when miraculous events take place. For example, when Hashem delayed the setting of the sun in order to enable Joshua to rout his enemies (see *Joshua* 10:12), God conclusively demonstrated that the cycle of the sun is not a "natural" law, but rather a miraculous phenomenon that He controls. Likewise, all the laws of nature were set in motion by Him.

With this understanding we can well understand why so much importance is ascribed to the festival of Chanukah. By kindling the Chanukah candles, we remind ourselves — as well as all those who see our flickering lights — of the astounding miracles which transpired in the days of the Hasmoneans. We thereby disseminate the concept that the universe has a Creator and Overseer Who sustains it with His will, and Who occasionally intervenes by suspending the laws of nature. Our candles confirm the Sages' statement: "Were it not that it had been decreed in Heaven, a man would not be able to bend his finger."

Ultimately, the purpose of praising God for the Chanukah miracles is to acknowledge in the depths of one's being that they were solely His doing; that all of nature itself is a series of astounding miracles for which we must praise Hashem with our every breath.

By studying the character of the threat posed by the Greeks and their Greco-Jewish compatriots, we may derive another important lesson regarding Jewish continuity and survival.

Let us remember that the Greeks did not wish to exterminate the Jews, but rather to strip them of their unique status as God's chosen people. The Greeks correctly surmised that the wellspring of Israel's distinctiveness was Torah and commandments. They knew that if they could impede the Jews from studying Torah and fulfilling Hashem's commandments, Israel's spiritual existence would gradually expire. Accordingly, the Greeks focused all their energies on severing the eternal link between Israel and the Almighty.

However, led by Mattisyahu the Hasmonean and his sons, the Torah scholars of that day took up arms and courageously fought to protect the authentic national character of the Jewish people — "a nation that will dwell in solitude, and not be reckoned among the nations" (Numbers 23:9). For in times of religious persecution, when other nations seek to undermine Israel's unique connection to God and Torah, every Jew is bound to give up his life in order to preserve even seemingly insignificant Jewish customs.

Through their selfless dedication to Hashem's Torah, the Hasmoneans merited colossal miracles. In the military arena, "the impure fell into the hands of the pure," while in the spiritual domain, Jewish identity overcame the onslaught of Greek culture.

The miracle of the oil proved that a small measure of light is capable of dispersing much darkness. Similarly, even the smallest measure of spiritual light — authentic Judaism — can drive away the thick impure darkness of spiritual impurity and ethical distortion. Indeed, like the flask of oil, the Jewish people's continuing existence in the darkness of exile is a miracle in its own right.

The Talmud says, "Rav Pappa asked Abaye [the following question:] 'In what way did the preceding [generations] differ that miracles occurred on their behalf? We [on the other hand] practice self-mortification and call out in a loud voice, but are not heard!' Abaye answered, 'The preceding generations selflessly dedicated themselves to sanctify God's Name, but we do not' " (Berachos 20). The Talmud then cites one example of the earlier generations' selfless dedication: R' Ada bar Ahava once saw a gentile woman — whom he thought to be Jewish — dressed immodestly. Without a moment's hesitation, he ripped the immodest garment from her.

From this incident we see that the preceding generations exhibited "selfless dedication" in protecting the entire cultural framework of Judaism, down to the clothing style of women, from the contaminating influence of the gentile world. For such seemingly insignificant acts, they merited the most awesome miracles. Clearly, then, any efforts on our part to stem the tide of assimilation and dissuade Jews from following gentile customs are tantamount to "sanctifying God's Name."

Likewise, the Hasmoneans, in refusing to allow for assimilation or even a slight distortion of authentic Jewish priorities and customs, merited miraculous Heavenly assistance in their struggle against the mighty Greek Empire.

The essential purpose of kindling Chanukah candles is that the person lighting them acknowledge that Hashem is the true source of salvation, and that he express sincere gratitude for the miracles God performed on behalf of the Jewish people in the days of the Hasmoneans. Nevertheless, the Sages also decreed that the candles be visible to the outside so that the miracle be proclaimed to others as well, thereby reinforcing the idea that Israel's collective existence is in itself a miracle.

Significantly, the Sages instituted the festival of Chanukah in commemoration of the miracle of the oil flask, and not in commemoration of the military victory over the Greek Army. They were concerned that with the passing of time, people would mistakenly attribute the miraculous victory to the Hasmoneans' battle tactics and military prowess, instead of to Divine intervention. In contrast, the miracle of the oil flask, where the human element did not come into play, could never be confused for anything other than what it was — an open miracle.

According to the Sages, man was created last of all the creatures for this same reason — to prevent him from ever claiming that he played a role in Creation. By creating man last, Hashem emphasized that it was He, and He alone, Who created the universe *ex nihilo*, matter from the void.

Similarly, the prophet Elijah prayed, "Answer me, HASHEM, answer me!" (*I Kings* 18:37). The Sages explain that Elijah beseeched Hashem, "Answer me, that fire should descend from the heavens, answer me, that they should not say that it is witchcraft." In other words, Elijah prayed that the people would recognize the miraculous nature of the extraordinary phenomenon they would soon witness, and not confuse it with an act of sorcery. From the fact that Elijah had to *pray* for this, it is evident that mankind has a tendency to mistake the miraculous for the mundane, the Hand of God for mere circumstance.

Hence, the Sages instituted the festival of Chanukah in commemoration of the miracle of the oil, and not of the military victories. And since the ultimate purpose of commemorating miracles is to recognize that "there is none other than Him," that He is the true God, the Sages decreed that *every Jew* must kindle Chanukah candles, including the most destitute members of the nation. For the lessons to be gleaned from Chanukah comprise the essential tenets of Jewish belief, which every Jew — without exception — must comprehend and internalize into the depths of his being.

The miracle of Chanukah teaches us yet another insight into the nature of Torah and commandments. We tend to take the service of God for granted, as though it were something that we can do whenever we feel the inclination. *Bach (Orach Chaim* 670), however, in answering the question of why the Sages did not decree that a festive meal be held on Chanukah as on Purim, shatters this myth.

Bach explains that Chanukah and Purim commemorate inherently different aspects of salvation. In the days of Ahasuerus, the Jews were held accountable for attending the king's feast. Since their sin was a *physical* one, a heavenly decree calling for their *physical* extermination was implemented. They rectified their transgression by fasting three consecutive days, thereby nullifying the *physical pleasure* they experienced by attending Ahasuerus' meal. In commemoration of their salvation from the threat of death, the Sages instituted the Purim meal, which gives direct pleasure to one's *physical* body.

In contrast, the threat against the Jews in the days of the Hasmoneans was brought about by their neglectful attitude towards observance of commandments. Because the Jews grew lax in Divine service it was decreed in Heaven that they should lose the opportunity to serve Hashem. This punishment came in the form of the Greeks, who prohibited the Jews from observing the commandments. To make their point the Greeks entered the Sanctuary and defiled the oil. Through this gesture the Greeks conveyed to the Jewish people that Divine service had ceased to be sacrosanct, and that the only viable set of beliefs to be followed were those delineated by Greek culture and philosophy. The Jews rectified their sin by renewing their commitment to Torah and the commandments. Their willingness to sacrifice their lives for the sake of Torah rectified their past neglect towards spiritual matters. As a consequence, Hashem brought about their miraculous salvation a short time later.

From this we learn an astounding principle: A person is presented with the opportunity to perform commandments *in direct proportion* to the degree of dedication with which he serves Hashem. The more a person becomes lax in his spiritual endeavors, the less commandments he will have the opportunity to perform. As the Sages said, "If you leave [the Torah] for one day, *it* will leave you for two."

Similarly, the *Mishnah* says, "If you should neglect the [study of] Torah, you will have many reasons to neglect it" (*Avos* 10:12). *Tiferes Yisrael* explains this to mean that if a person neglects Torah study out of indifference, he will later be prevented from studying Torah *even if he truly desires to do so*. Just as the Sages say that a heavy rainfall on Sukkos indicates that Hashem is displeased with Israel's Divine service — they use the analogy of a master splashing the proffered cup of wine in his servant's face (see *Sukkah* 25) — so too, a person who neglects Torah study will later have "the cup of wine" splashed in his face when he feels the desire to resume its study.

This explains why people experience difficulties in Torah study; Torah and the service of God require heartfelt commitment. They may not be treated as a hobby to be indulged in when one feels the urge. As the Sages say, "[If someone says,] 'I toiled and I found,' believe him. [But if someone says,] 'I did not toil and I found, do not believe him.' " Spiritual opportunities must be grabbed immediately, and not left to be pursued when we are in the right mood. The Sages liken a person who learns Torah to a suckling infant — as long as he continues suckling he will have no shortage of nourishment, but if he stops, his mother's breasts will cease producing milk. We must realize that the Torah texts (*sefarim*) are not just sitting there waiting for us — for every moment that we neglect Torah study, the lessons contained within them become more and more inaccessible to us, more and more difficult to comprehend. As the verse says, "If you search after [Torah] like silver, seek after it like buried treasure, *then you will understand fear of God.*" Only one who truly cherishes the search for Godliness, who applies himself with the alacrity that he would devote towards amassing material wealth, will be granted success in his spiritual endeavors.

God's Hidden Hand

The Sages instituted the holiday of Purim in commemoration of the miracles which transpired in the days of Mordechai and Esther, when the Jews were saved from utter destruction at the hands of the wicked Haman and King Ahasuerus. The day is graced with several commandments:

The reading of the *Megillah* recounts the natural and seemingly happenstance events which God, behind the scenes, wove together into a miraculous tapestry of salvation. *Hallel* is not recited on Purim because the *Megillah* reading itself serves as our vehicle to express gratitude and praise to God for the miraculous protection He granted us. In addition, the Sages decreed three other commandments: to give gifts to the poor, to send portions of food to fellow Jews, and to partake of a festive meal.

The Talmud describes the Purim saga as a reacceptance of the Torah by the Children of Israel. At Mount Sinai, the Jewish people were coerced into accepting the Torah, for Hashem suspended Mount Sinai over them and threatened to crush them (see *Shabbos* 88a). This cast a dark cloud over the entire affair, which resulted in the Jewish people harboring deep-rooted reservations concerning their commitment to Torah — the Sages referred to this latent resentment as, "a plea of vindication against the Torah."

Rabbeinu Tam translates the Sages' account of the Divine coercion which took place at Sinai into more human terms: The Jewish people's encounter with revealed Divinity completely overwhelmed their senses, rendering them incapable of seriously considering the question of whether to accept or reject the Torah. Quivering before the thundering mountain that was ablaze with supernal fire, dazed by the temporary suspension of natural laws, the people had no choice but to accept the Torah. This is what the Sages meant by saying that the Jewish people were "coerced" into accepting the Torah.

With the Israelites' misgivings towards the pact at Sinai, the relationship between them and Hashem rapidly deteriorated. This negative undercurrent ushered in the era of "hiding of the Divine countenance" (הַסְתָּרַת פָּנִים), which culminated in the days of Mordechai and Esther. As the Sages said, "Where [is there a hint] of Esther in the Torah? From the verse, 'But I will surely have concealed My face [וְאָנֹכִי הַסְתֵּר אַסְתִּיר פָּנַי] on that day...' " (Deuteronomy 31:18). This "Divine concealment" left a spiritual vacuum in which Israel's enemies flourished and gained power. Their greatest moment came when Haman persuaded King Ahasuerus to ratify a decree calling for the extermination of the Jewish people.

Now, Esther knew that the chasm that had developed between the Jews and Hashem was the source and wellspring of Haman's power. She knew that if the Jewish people would seek reconciliation by simply opening their hearts to Hashem and acknowledging that "there is none other than Him," Haman and his cronies would immediately wither and die. This is why she invited Haman to attend her wine feast.

Until that moment, the Jews had felt secure in the knowledge that the queen was one of their own. "Surely she will protect us from danger," they thought. Esther shattered this false sense of security by inviting Haman to her feast. By inviting the most rabid Jew-hater of all time, Esther gave the impression that she had betrayed her fellow Jews and was forming an alliance with the enemy. The Jews had no one left to rely upon.

With nowhere to turn, the Jews looked to Hashem for salvation. For the first time, they realized that relying on temporal methods of protection was absolutely futile. They had been deceiving themselves all this time, relying on illusory sources of salvation, instead of turning directly to the Almighty, the Master of the Universe.

In this manner, Esther served as a catalyst to bring about the redemption, and made it very clear to the Jews Who would bring about their salvation. With the onset of the redemption, the Jews exalted in the knowledge that Hashem accepted their prayers and intervened on their behalf. They recognized beyond a shadow of a doubt that He, and He alone, had performed these miracles and saved them from certain death. With profound love and joy, they reaccepted the yoke of Torah and commandments.

Where is this reacceptance of Torah alluded to in the Megillah? The Maharal of Prague says that the willingness of the Jews to accept upon themselves the additional commandments of Purim is itself an indication that they were eager to fulfill the Torah, and that as far as they were concerned, the more commandments, the better.

This concept is discussed in the Talmud. The Sages said, "What is the difference between past and present generations? Preceding generations brought in their produce through the house in order to make it necessary to separate tithes from it, while latter generations bring the produce in [through other means] in order to avoid having to separate tithes from it." It is evident from this that although it is not *prohibited* to find legal loopholes in order to avoid performing certain commandments, it is certainly more meritorious to desire commandments and look for ways to fulfill them.

The *Arizal* mentions another, more esoteric, aspect of this festival — namely, that Purim and Yom Kippurim are interrelated, for in Hebrew Purim is spelled פּוּרִים, while Yom Kippurim is spelled יוֹם כִּפֻּרִים, which literally means, "a day *like* Purim."

R' Yeruchom Levovitz of Mir explained this idea as follows: The essential obligation incumbent upon a person on Purim is to feel love and a sense of brotherhood towards every Jew. Commandments such as sending portions of food to friends (*mishloach manos*) and gifts to the poor (*matanos le'evyonim*) are simply means by which to awaken these feelings, but the ultimate goal is that one should feel closer to one's fellow Jews.

This concept is reflected in the commentary of *Bach*. According to *Bach*, a guest who is invited to partake of a Purim meal is considered to have fulfilled the obligation of *mishloach manos*. As proof, he cites a Talmudic passage which relates that Abaye bar Avin once invited R' Chananiah bar Avin to be his guest for the Purim meal. The next year, R' Chananiah bar Avin reciprocated the gesture and invited Abaye bar Avin to his house for Purim. The Talmud states that both sages fulfilled the commandment of *mishloach manos*. At first glance, this ruling is difficult to understand, for how can a *guest* fulfill this obligation? *Bach* explains that since the goal of this commandment is to awaken feelings of love and brotherhood, a guest can also fulfill it.

It is this same spirit of mutual love among Jews that we strive for on Yom Kippur. On this day, Jews try to forgive each other and rid themselves of all rancor and jealousy. Thus, Yom Kippur *is like Purim* — by fulfilling the commandments of Purim, we merit to attain the mindset that we strive for on Yom Kippur.

May we always merit to renew our commitment to Torah with a spirit of love for all Jews!

The Destruction of the Temple

The Talmud *Yerushalmi* (*Pe'ah* 1) says, "For any generation which does not witness the rebuilding of the Temple (*Beis HaMikdash*) in its days, it is as though it had been destroyed in its days." The meaning of this statement is that we should not relate to the Temple as something that has been missing since long before our grandparents were born; rather, we must develop a feeling of disaster and loss as if we had once beheld the Temple in its existence, and then witnessed its destruction.

There is a similar concept mentioned in respect to the commandment of retelling the story of the Exodus on Pesach night: "Everyone is obligated to regard himself as if he personally had been part of the Exodus from Egypt" (*Haggadah*). The reason we are obligated to imagine that we ourselves took part in the Exodus is because it is only with such a frame of mind that we can truly feel the full measure of gratitude to Hashem for having taken the Jews out of Egypt. Also, in regard to the Temple, the reason the Sages say that we must visualize the Destruction of the Temple (*Churban*) as if it had happened in our lifetime is because only in this manner can we truly appreciate its true worth — it was the abode for the Divine Presence in this world, a source of atonement and forgiveness for our sins, and the means by which Hashem's presence dwelt within each and every Jewish soul. Feeling the loss of the Temple means becoming aware that there is a lack of Divine revelation in the world today, and that we no longer enjoy the closeness of Hashem that was once our lot. As the Sages say, "Since the day the Temple was destroyed, an iron wall stands between Israel and their Father in Heaven" (*Berachos* 32b). The Sages also say, "Whoever mourns over Jerusalem will merit to see it in its joy" (*Taanis* 30b). This means that only if one develops the sensitivity described above, fully appreciating the loss of the Temple, can one truly rejoice when it will be rebuilt.

Another point we should ponder is that the delay in the rebuilding of the Temple indicates that the sins which led to its destruction have not yet been rectified. The Talmud tells us that although there were many grave sins being committed at the time of the destruction of the First Temple (see *Yoma* 9b), the real reason for its destruction was that "the people did not say the blessing over Torah study" (*Bava Metzia* 85b). Although this does not seem at first glance to be such a serious misdeed, *Ran* explains the Talmud to mean that the people did not show a true appreciation of the great worth of the Torah, and they thus neglected to express gratitude to Hashem for having given it to them. The blessing recited before Torah study is, "Blessed is Hashem . . . Who has chosen us from all the other nations and given us His Torah." By not reciting this expression of gratitude, the people revealed their lack of appreciation of Torah. This was the root cause of their negative attitude, which in turn led to all their other sins.

The fact that the central theme of the Blessing of the Torah (*Bircas HaTorah*) is the appreciation of the greatness of Torah may be proven from the Talmud. In *Berachos* (11b) we learn that if someone had already said the prayer *Ahavah Rabbah* before beginning his Torah study, he need not say the Blessing of the Torah, as this prayer may be regarded as a substitute. Yet when we examine the text of the *Ahavah Rabbah* prayer, we find no mention of the idea that "God commanded us to perform the commandment of Torah study"; rather, the text of *Ahavah Rabbah* is completely dedicated to the theme of how important Torah study is to us, and what a great gift Hashem gave to us: "You have shown us exceedingly great compassion . . . Have mercy on us and plant in our hearts wisdom and understanding to understand and examine the words of Your Torah . . ." If this prayer can serve as a substitute for the Blessing of the Torah, it is obvious that the Sages considered this theme (recognition of the value of Torah study) to be the essence of the Blessing of the Torah. We must thus try to rectify this sin, which was the root of all the other sins that caused the Destruction of the Temple — the lack of appreciation of how central Torah study is to our lives. Lack of appreciation is, after all, considered to be a very serious offense in the Torah, as is evident from numerous verses — e.g., the commandment not to despise Egyptians [despite their cruelty and attempted genocide of the Jewish people] because the Egyptians gave refuge to our ancestors (*Deuteronomy* 23:8).

It is interesting to note that the root of all future tragedies on *Tishah B'Av* (foremost among them being, of course, the Destruction of the Temple) is the sin of the Spies (*Numbers* 13-14), which, the Sages tell us, also happened on the ninth of Av. Hashem told the people, "You cried unjustifiably on this night; I will designate this night as a night of weeping for all time!" (*Taanis* 29a). The sin of the Spies, as we have explained elsewhere, was also based on a lack of appreciation — appreciation for the greatness of the Land of Israel, the land "where the eyes of HASHEM are focused, from the beginning of the year to the end of the year" (*Deuteronomy* 11:12), the holy land where the Temple would be built. In order to rectify the sin of the desert generation, and those sins which led to the Destruction of the Temple, we must strive to strengthen our awareness of just how much we lack today because of the Destruction, in terms of the loss of the Divine Presence among us.

Opportunities for Introspection

R*ambam* writes in *Hilchos Taanis* (1:1): "There is a positive commandment to cry out in prayer and blow the *shofar* whenever any type of disaster befalls the community ... If people do not cry out ... but think, 'This is due to natural circumstances; it is merely by chance' — this is a manifestation of cruelty, and it causes people to cling to their evil ways, so that the disaster will lead to further disaster. This is what the Torah means when it says (*Leviticus* 26:28), 'If you behave towards Me with the attitude of "chance," I will behave towards you with the wrath of chance.' "

It would seem at first glance that if a person attributes the adversities of life to chance rather than to Divine Providence, his only fault would be weakness of faith in Hashem. However, we see from this quote of *Rambam* that such a person has an additional flaw — namely, that he exhibits the trait of cruelty: cruelty towards himself, and cruelty towards his community, by not seeking to alleviate the plight which faces them. This is because even if a person's belief in Hashem is not complete, he should nevertheless *try* to pray to Him out of desperation, with the attitude that "It couldn't hurt." Since he does not even bother to do this, it shows that his weakness in faith is in fact coupled with a lack of consideration for his fellow man. We see this theme illustrated in the story of Jonah. When the ship began to toss and it appeared that it was about to sink (*Jonah* 1:4), the sailors reprimanded Jonah for sleeping instead of praying to God (ibid. v. 6). These men did not then know who Jonah's God was, nor did they believe in the God of Israel themselves, yet nevertheless they admonished Jonah for not trying to pray. It was not out of their strength of conviction that Jonah's prayer might work that they were so upset with him, but because they thought it inconsiderate and thoughtless of Jonah not to make the effort anyway. We find a similar idea concerning Pharaoh. After Pharaoh declared, "HASHEM is the righteous One, and I and my people are the wicked ones" (*Exodus* 9:27), he hardened his heart and refused to let the people go. Pharaoh's lack of cooperation was not due to his lack of faith in Hashem, for he had just accepted the mastery of Hashem with a full heart. His refusal to act on his faith was due purely to cruelty.

At any rate, we have learned from *Rambam's* words that the main point of a fast day is to jolt ourselves into the realization that we must improve our ways and repent before Hashem. As the prophet Jeremiah put it, "In vain I have stricken your children, for they have not learned from the rebuke" (*Jeremiah* 2:30). If suffering does not bring repentance, it is in vain.

In fact, we find that whenever there was hope that Israel might repent as a result of the prophets' rebuke, Hashem did not punish them. In *Megillah* 14a we learn, "The removal of Ahasuerus' ring [when it was put on Haman's finger] had more of an effect on Israel than the forty-eight prophets who prophesied to Israel." While forty-eight prophets failed to bring the people to repentance, in one single act Ahasuerus succeeded. Similarly in *Jeremiah* Ch. 25 we learn, "For twenty-three years, the word of HASHEM has been coming to me, and I have spoken to you, starting from early in the morning, but you have not listened ... Therefore, thus says HASHEM, Master of Legions: Because you have not heeded My words, behold I am sending for and instigating all the families of the North ... and Nebuchadnezzar king of Babylonia." Only when reproof through the prophets proved to be ineffective did Hashem resort to the other method of bringing about contrition and repentance among the people — through bringing calamity upon them.

The Talmud (*Berachos* 5a) tells us, "If a person sees that misfortune befalls him, he should search his ways [for misdeeds that he may be committing]." This is why our reaction to calamity and disaster must be one of introspection and repentance; this is the only reason Hashem brings suffering upon people in the first place. If we miss the cue that Hashem gives us, we will be guilty of indifference towards our fellow man's plight — "Do not stand idly by the blood of your fellow man" (*Leviticus* 19:16). In *Berachos* 12b we are taught, "If a person is in the position to pray for his friend and does not do so, he is called a sinner" for his lack of empathy.

The Talmud (*Megillah* 15b) tells us that the reason Esther invited Haman to the banquet that she made for the king (*Esther* 5:4) was in order to give the Jews of Shushan reason to think that she was not truly committed to her people's cause. The Jews thought that Esther, in her comfortable position of queen of the empire, decided to befriend Haman and save her own life at the expense of her countrymen. She did this in order that the Jews should not be lulled into a sense of complacency, adopting an attitude of "The queen is one of our own!" She wanted to ensure that the atmosphere of soul-searching and contrition that had begun would continue and grow, so that the Jews' prayers would intensify and be heard by Hashem. In this manner, they would be sure to recognize that the salvation that would come about would be the doing of Hashem. Once again we see the importance of recognizing that when disaster is near, it is because Hashem wishes to rebuke us, to prod us back to the proper path.

There is a fast known as *Taanis Chalom* (a fast for a dream). *Rambam* (*Hilchos Taanis* 1:12) describes this fast as follows: "If someone has a bad dream, he should fast the following day in order that he may repent and arouse himself to introspection concerning his way of life." The purpose of fasting in this case is perfectly clear — it is to motivate repentance and self-improvement, and thereby annul whatever evil decree the dream may have augured. This theme is also evident in *Rambam's* description of the four fast days that commemorate the Destruction (ibid., 5:1) : "There are certain days on which all of Israel fast because of the misfortunes that happened on those days, *in order to arouse people's hearts, to make them open to the ways of repentance, for by recalling these events we are likely to improve our ways . . .*"

The *Mishnah* itself (*Taanis* 15a) expresses this same thought: "It does not say concerning the men of Nineveh (*Jonah* 3:10) that 'God saw their sackcloth and their fasting,' but rather, 'God saw their *deeds*, that they had turned away from their evil ways.' "

Similarly, it is quite obvious that fasting on Yom Kippur is intended to move us to inspect — and mend — our ways.

Beis Yosef (*Orach Chaim* 550) mentions an opinion (although he himself disagrees with it) that *Asarah B'Teves* is more strict than the other three fast days that commemorate the Destruction, so that if it would occur on Shabbos (which, in actual fact, never happens) it would not be postponed as the other fasts are, but would require us to fast on Shabbos. This opinion requires clarification: Why should *Asarah B'Teves* be so much stricter than the other fast days, including *Tishah B'Av*, which are never allowed to interfere with the enjoyment of Shabbos? Perhaps the explanation lies in the fact that, as we discussed above, the Sages teach that we must try to develop a feeling that the Temple would be rebuilt in our own days if only we would rectify the sins which were responsible for the Destruction. We also mentioned earlier that the root sin which was the catalyst for all the major transgressions that led to the Destruction of the Temple was a lack of appreciation for the value of Torah study. This negative attitude precipitated a general decline in morality among the people, for which sin the Temple was destroyed. Since the Destruction came in gradual stages, and at each stage Hashem was sending a further message to the people that they needed to repent for their sins, it is the commemoration of the very first stage — the siege of Jerusalem on the tenth of Teves — that marks the most important occasion for introspection, when we should strive to rectify those sins which led to the Destruction of the Temple.